A Reading Skills Book

mosaic two

A Reading Skills Book

Third Edition

mosaic two

Brenda Wegmann

Miki Prijic Knezevic

Marilyn Bernstein

The McGraw-Hill Companies, Inc.

New York   St. Louis   San Francisco   Auckland   Bogotá   Caracas   Lisbon
London   Madrid   Mexico City   Milan   Montreal   New Delhi   San Juan
Singapore   Sydney   Tokyo   Toronto

This is an  book.

McGraw-Hill

A Division of The McGraw·Hill Companies

Mosaic Two
A Reading Skills Book
Third Edition

1 2 3 4 5 6 7 8 9 0 DOC DOC 9 0 9 8 7 6

ISBN 0-07-068998-9
ISBN 0-07-114515-X

This book was set in Times Roman by Clarinda.

The editors were Tim Stookesberry, Bill Preston, and Eden Temko; the designers were Lorna Lo, Suzanne Montazer, Francis Owens, and Elizabeth Williamson; the production supervisor was Phyllis Snyder; the project editor was Stacey Sawyer; the cover was designed by Francis Owens; the cover illustrator was Susan Pizzo; the photo researcher was Cindy Robinson, Seaside Publishing; illustrations were done by David Bohn, Axelle Fortier, Rick Hackney, Lori Heckelman, and Sally Richardson.

R. R. Donnelley & Sons Company, Crawfordsville, IN, was printer and binder.
Phoenix Color Corporation was cover separator and printer.

Library of Congress Catalog Card Number: 95-82407.

INTERNATIONAL EDITION

When ordering this title, use ISBN 0-007-114515-X

Photo credits: *Page 1* © Spencer Grant/Stock, Boston; *5* © N. R. Rowan/Stock, Boston; *11* © Jeff Isaac Greenberg/Photo Researchers, Inc.; *13* © Hugh Rogers/Monkmeyer Press Photo Service; *19* © David Wells/The Image Works; *27* © Poncet/Sygma; *29* © Rob Stapleton/AP Wide World Photos, Inc.; *31* © Guy Savage/Vandystadt/Photo Researchers, Inc.; *32* © NASA; *33* © Wide World Photos, Inc.; *47* © Leonard Lee Rue/Monkmeyer Press Photo Service; *51* © Wide World Photos, Inc.; *53* © Nina Howell Starr/Photo Researchers, Inc.; *57* © D. Kirkland/Sygma; *58* © David Austen/Stock, Boston; *59* © AP Photo; *63* © Miki Knezevic; *68* © Remy LeMorvan/Bettmann Archives; *71* © E. Crews/The Image Works; *83* © Stock, Boston; *104* © Hilda Bijur/Monkmeyer Press Photo Service; *105* © George Molton/Photo Researchers, Inc.; *109* © The Bettmann Archive; *112* © Dallas and John Heaton/Westlight; *113* © Will and Deni McIntyre/Photo Researchers, Inc.; *116* © Michael Weisbrot and Family/Stock, Boston; *122* © Michael Howell/Stock, Boston; *125* © Paul Conklin/Monkmeyer Press Photo Service; *126* © Dallas and John Heaton/Stock, Boston; *129* © AP/World Wide Photos; *133* © Michael Dwyer/Stock, Boston; *141* © Thierry Pratt/Sygma; *155* © Griffin/The Image Works; *163* © The Bettmann Archive; *164* © The Bettmann Archive; *172* © Steve Apps/*The Post-Crescent*; *175* ©

(continued on p. 343)

Contents

CHAPTER one

Language and Learning   *1*

CHAPTER two

Danger and Daring   *27*

CHAPTER three

Man and Woman   *53*

CHAPTER four

Mysteries Past and Present

CHAPTER five

Transitions

CHAPTER six

The Mind

CHAPTER seven

Working

CHAPTER eight

Breakthroughs 203

CHAPTER nine

Art and Entertainment 233

CHAPTER ten

Ethical Questions 263

Preface to the Third Edition
The Mosaic Two Program

The Mosaic Two Program consists of four texts and a variety of supplemental materials for high-intermediate to low-advanced students seeking to improve their English language skills. Each of the four texts in this program is carefully organized by chapter theme, vocabulary, grammar structures, and where possible, learning strategies and language functions. As a result, information introduced in a chapter of any one of the Mosaic Two texts corresponds to and reinforces material taught in the same chapter of the other three books, creating a truly integrated, four-skills approach.

The Mosaic Two program is highly flexible. The texts in this series may be used together or separately, depending on students' needs and course goals. The books in this program include:

- **A Content-Based Grammar.** Designed to teach grammar through content, this text introduces, practices, and applies grammatical structures through the development of high-interest chapter topics. This thematic approach motivates students because they are improving their mastery of grammatical structures and vocabulary while expanding their own knowledge.
- **A Content-Based Writing Book.** This text takes students step-by-step through the writing process—from formulating ideas through the revision stage. Writing assignments progress from paragraphs to essays, and students write about interesting, contemporary subjects from the sciences, social sciences, and humanities that are relevant to their current or future academic coursework.
- **A Listening/Speaking Skills Book.** This text teaches learning strategies and language functions, while maintaining a strong focus on both listening and speaking. Each chapter includes a realistic listening passage on an interesting topic related to the chapter theme. Short conversations also provide comprehension practice, while a variety of speaking activities reinforce use of language in context.
- **A Reading Skills Book.** The selections in this text help students develop their reading skills in a meaningful rather than a mechanical way, enabling them to successfully tackle other academic texts. The three readings per chapter come from a variety of authentic sources, such as textbooks, magazines, newspapers, interviews, and so on, and are accompanied by pre- and post-reading exercises, including skimming, scanning, making inferences, paraphrasing, and group problem solving.

Supplemental Materials

In addition to the four core texts outlined above, various supplemental materials are available to assist users of the third edition, including:

Instructor's Manual

Extensively revised for the new edition, this manual provides instructions and guidelines for using the four core texts separately or in various combinations to suit particular program needs. For each of the core texts, there is a separate section with answer keys, teaching tips, additional activities, and other suggestions. The testing materials have been greatly expanded in this edition.

Audio Program for *Mosaic Two: A Listening/Speaking Skills Book*

Completely re-recorded for the new edition, the audio program is designed to be used in conjunction with those exercises that are indicated with a cassette icon in the student text. Complete tapescripts are now included in the back of the student text.

Audio Program to Accompany *Mosaic Two: A Reading Skills Book*

This new optional audio program contains selected readings from the student text. These taped selections of poems, articles, stories, and speeches enable students to listen at their leisure to the natural oral discourse of native readers for intonation and modeling. Readings that are included in this program are indicated with a cassette icon in the student text.

Video/Video Guide

New to this edition, the video program for Mosaic Two contains authentic television segments that are coordinated with the twelve chapter themes in the four texts. A variety of pre- and post-viewing exercises and activities for this video are available in a separate Video Guide.

Mosaic Two: A Reading Skills Book, Third Edition

Rationale

The main purpose of *Mosaic Two: A Reading Skills Book,* Third Edition, is to polish and perfect the English skills of intermediate students and enable them to deal effectively with sophisticated reading materials of both a scientific and humanistic nature. In other words, it aims to bring readers from a basic level of comprehension of the English language to the higher competence necessary for tackling more difficult work, such as that of the college classroom. While the orientation is primarily academic, the book is also helpful for students who simply wish to read English with a deeper understanding.

In response to advice from reviewers, the third edition of the *Mosaic Two* reader focuses more directly and consistently than in previous editions on the development of the important academic skills of summarizing and paraphrasing. Cooperative learning through group and pair exercises also receives more emphasis. A visual summary of the skills presented throughout the text is provided at the end of this Preface.

The *Mosaic Two* reader differs from the *Mosaic One* reader in several ways. *Mosaic Two* emphasizes the advanced skills of interpretation, inference, critical analysis, evaluation, summarizing, paraphrasing, and application, although it also reviews basic comprehension skills such as skimming, scanning, and guessing meaning from context. It includes more work with charts, tables, and graphs; more discussion of style and tone; more technical and literary terminology; and longer, more varied, and more difficult selections. In general, *Mosaic Two* covers the reading skills for the high-intermediate to low-advanced levels as recommended by the guidelines of numerous universities throughout the country. The second half of *Mosaic Two* (Chapters Six to Twelve) contains special exercises that focus on the acquisition and practice of study skills, such as underlining, glossing, and study mapping.

Like *Mosaic One,* the *Mosaic Two* reader is designed to guide students in the development of a conscious, reflective attitude toward reading, to teach them to anticipate context, to evaluate difficulty and to decide on the level of understanding desired, to distinguish between different types of selections and different purposes for reading, and to avoid wasting time in a useless mechanical thoroughness. For this reason, timed readings are included in the second half of the book even though speed reading for its own sake is not generally encouraged at this level.

The reading selections were drawn from a variety of sources: scientific, literary, textbook, trade book, periodical. They were chosen to be relevant and interesting to a multicultural readership and to present in a challenging way representative customs, personalities, values, and ways of thinking of Americans and Canadians.

Chapter Organization

Every chapter begins with a brief introduction to the chapter theme. This can be used as a starting point to set the stage for later discussion and to give both teacher and students an idea of the class's knowledge and prejudices on the subject. The introduction is followed by three reading selections, each one preceded by one or two prereading exercises and followed by comprehension and skill-building exercises. These are usually accompanied by a "Talking It Over" section and occasionally by activities, such as group problem solving, discussions that require expressing reactions or applying what has been read to new situations, and composition or library research assignments. These latter features are optional and are included primarily to give the book greater flexibility. Also included are sections called "Stories Behind Words," which focus on particular aspects of vocabulary; and exercises on technical terms, slang, idioms, and differences among American, British, and Canadian English.

A quick glance through the book will show you that there is no set sequence of exercises repeated chapter after chapter. The types of exercises vary according to the difficulties particular to each selection and the skills being emphasized. This variety lessens the chance that the student will relapse into a mechanical approach of nonreflective reading. Previously presented skills are reinforced throughout, however, often by using different styles of exercises to review the same skill.

The principal aim of the prereading exercises is to condition students to stop and think before plunging into a reading. In the first chapters, the skill-building exercises that follow each selection focus on reviewing basic skills such as skimming, scanning, and vocabulary analysis. Later chapters emphasize more advanced skills while reviewing basic ones. These exercises at times practice and reinforce a skill that has been introduced in a prereading exercise. Optional readings also appear in the second half of the book along with comprehension quizzes that offer practice in reading for a set purpose and under a time constraint.

Teaching Suggestions

The prereading exercises may be used in different ways depending on the level of the students. At first, a teacher will probably do them orally with the class as a means of introducing each selection and ascertaining class level. These exercises, especially the ones using direct quotations from the selection, can act as a bridge, helping students over some of the difficult sections of the article. If, after a few weeks, the class seems to have little problem with the readings, however, these exercises can be assigned for homework and corrected quickly at the beginning of the class.

A good way of adding spontaneity to completion of the exercises following the selections is to occasionally reserve some challenging ones for group work, especially if there are no group activities included in the lesson. The class may be divided into small groups and given ten or fifteen minutes to do the exercise, with one of the group members reporting results to the class afterwards. In any event, it is a good idea at times to assign only some of the exercises to be done with the reading as homework. Then, if time permits, the others can be worked out in class, adding an element of the unexpected. When an exercise aimed at reviewing a skill is used in this way, one of the more extroverted students might be asked to play the role of teacher (perhaps after having been warned in advance). This is a sure way of gaining class attention, since everyone wants to see if the new "teacher" will make a mistake, and it also serves to challenge a confident, highly motivated student who might otherwise begin to lose interest.

Cooperative learning through pair and group work can be effective and beneficial for students, and numerous activities that lend themselves to this approach are included in this third edition. The "Talking It Over" section, which follows most reading selections, works well with pairs or groups. As an interactive exercise, it can provide a stimulating change of pace to classroom routine as well as the opportunity for students to develop much needed confidence and interpersonal skills.

For many groups, cooperative work should be introduced gradually. For example, during the second week toward the end of class, two or three particularly interesting questions may be singled out from the "Talking It Over" list and students asked to discuss these with a partner for five minutes and then to report on what they have learned about the other person's views. After doing this a couple of times, it is good to have a general class discussions about the advantages of this kind of learning and how important it is for the overall class objectives and evaluation. Tips on how to introduce, manage, and evaluate pair and group activities are in the Instructor's Manual.

Answers to certain puzzles and problem-solving exercises as well as to the "You Be the Judge" article can be found in the appendix.

New to the Third Edition

1. **Streamlined Design.** The two-color design and revised art program make this edition more appealing to today's students. It is also more user friendly because many directions have been shortened and clarified, exercises and activities have been numbered, and key information has been highlighted in shaded boxes and charts.

2. **New Chapter Theme: Breakthroughs.** The new edition features an entirely new theme for Chapter Eight: Breakthroughs. In addition, themes for other chapters have been broadened to include new content, and many new reading selections have been added throughout the text.

3. **Audio Cassette.** The new optional tape includes selected readings from the text. Selections are read by skilled native readers to provide samples of oral reading style for imitation and modeling. Readings included on the cassette are indicated with a cassette icon in the student text.

4. **What Do You Think?** This entirely new boxed feature appears in every chapter. This feature interests, amazes, amuses, or in some other way provokes a response and stimulates class discussion of popular culture that goes beyond the text.

5. **Focus on Testing.** This new boxed feature presents practical tips and strategies for maximizing a student's advantage in the vocabulary and reading sections of standardized exams for English, such as the TOEFL. Appearing in every chapter except the last one (which is devoted to open reading), Focus on Testing features are accompanied by an exercise designed to put the tips and strategies into immediate practice.

6. **Skills Chart.** A chart summarizing the reading, vocabulary, and test-taking skills for all twelve chapters follows the preface.

Acknowledgments

Our thanks to the following reviewers whose comments, both favorable and critical, were of great value in the development of the third edition of the Interactions/Mosaic series:

Jean Al-Sibai, University of North Carolina; Janet Alexander, Waterbury College; Roberta Alexander, San Diego City College; Julie Alpert, Santa Barbara City College; Anita Cook, Tidewater Community College; Anne Deal Beavers, Heald Business College; Larry Berking, Monroe Community College; Deborah Busch, Delaware County Community College; Patricia A. Card, Chaminade University of Honolulu; José A. Carmona, Hudson County Community College; Kathleen Carroll, Fontbonne College; Consuela Chase, Loyola University; Lee Chen,

California State University; Karen Cheng, University of Malaya; Gaye Childress, University of North Texas; Maria Conforti, University of Colorado; Earsie A. de Feliz, Arkansas State University; Elizabeth Devlin-Foltz, Montgomery County Adult Education; Colleen Dick, San Francisco Institute of English; Marta Dmytrenko-Ahrabian, Wayne State University; Margo Duffy, Northeast Wisconsin Technical; Magali Duignan, Augusta College; Janet Dyar, Meridian Community College; Anne Ediger, San Diego City College; D. Frangie, Wayne State University; Robert Geryk, Wayne State University; Jeanne Gibson, American Language Academy; Kathleen Walsh Greene, Rhode Island College; Myra Harada, San Diego Mesa College; Kristin Hathhorn, Eastern Washington University; Mary Herbert, University of California–Davis; Joyce Homick, Houston Community College; Catherine Hutcheson, Texas Christian University; Suzie Johnston, Tyler Junior College; Donna Kauffman, Radford University; Emmie Lim, Cypress College; Patricia Mascarenas, Monte Vista Community School; Mark Mattison, Donnelly College; Diane Peak, Choate Rosemary Hall; James Pedersen, Irvine Valley College; Linda Quillan, Arkansas State University; Marnie Ramker, University of Illinois; Joan Roberts, The Doane Stuart School; Doralee Robertson, Jacksonville University; Ellen Rosen, Fullerton College; Jean Sawyer, American Language Academy; Frances Schulze, College of San Mateo; Sherrie R. Sellers, Brigham Young University; Tess M. Shafer, Edmonds Community College; Heinz F. Tengler, Lado International College; Sara Tipton, Wayne State University; Karen R. Vallejo, Brigham Young University; Susan Williams, University of Central Florida; Mary Shepard Wong, El Camino College; Cindy Yoder, Eastern Mennnonite College; Cheryl L. Youtsey, Loyola University; Miriam Zahler, Wayne State University; Maria Zien, English Center, Miami; Yongmin Zhu, Los Medanos College; Norma Zorilla, Fresno Pacific College.

We also wish to thank McGraw-Hill for its inspirational support and the innovative coordination of this edition, which began so propitiously in the multi-hued city of San Francisco. We are especially indebted to our publishing team of Thalia Dorwick, Tim Stookesberry, and Bill Preston for their astute and creative direction, encouragement, and unflagging patience and flexibility. Finally, a very special thank you to Elyane Steeves and Ivo Knezevic for their help in finding superb materials and to Jessica Wegmann for her insightful suggestions and assistance in proofreading the manuscript.

DEDICATION

In Memoriam: Dr. Tom Wegmann (1941–1994),
passionate promoter of crosscultural education
in science, health, and other fields,
whose wisdom and
laughter lives on in the hearts of many.

Summary of Reading, Vocabulary, and Test-Taking Skills

Chapter	Reading Skills	Vocabulary Skills	Focus on Testing and Study Skills
one	• guessing new words from context • completing a summary • anticipating the reading: making predictions • scanning for specific information • skimming for main ideas • reading a shaded map	• guessing meaning by breaking down words • finding verbs with precise meanings • stories behind words: expressions associated with animals • word detective • understanding acronyms and abbreviations • enjoying quotations	• analyzing summary statements for a comprehension test
two	• skimming for the main idea • Identifying facts and opinions • using the encyclopedia to prepare a report • using predictions to aid comprehension • DRTA (Directed Reading/Thinking Activity)	• learning terminology for narrative writing • making inferences about character traits • useful slang expressions • using contextual clues to decipher unknown words	• recognizing the theme in an article or paragraph • summarizing a narrative piece of writing for an essay test
three	• distinguishing general from specific • recalling main ideas and details • drawing conclusions by using a chart • identifying facts and opinions • recognizing an ironic tone • recognizing point of view	• hearing the rhyme in poetry • coping with technical terms • stories behind words: some gender words	• improving your chances on multiple-choice examinations • fact/opinion practice questions • paragraph writing practice for short essay questions
four	• evaluating content: critical reading • skimming a narrative story • identifying support for a hypothesis	• matching key words to definitions • understanding abbreviations • using prefixes • analyzing words and phrases	• improving test scores on true/false questions • practice matching words and definitions for vocabulary tests

Chapter	Reading Skills	Vocabulary Skills	Focus on Testing and Study Skills
	• forming a line of argument • summarizing an article • finding out about mysterious phenomena	• scanning context for synonyms • stories behind words: mythology • learning about riddles	
five	• sequencing ideas into chronological order • learning to read an interview • finding support for main ideas • paraphrasing complicated passages • DRTA (Directed Reading/Thinking Activity • predicting action	• relating vocabulary to an idea • inferring attitudes and their causes • word parts study: the suffix -hood • interviewing a classmate • noting differences between British and American English • selecting adjectives for a context • Canadian and American spelling differences	• avoiding "traps" in standardized vocabulary tests
six	• comparing personal experience to a reading • applying concepts: mnemonic devices • finding support for or against a hypothesis • identifying elements of horror (in gothic fiction) • summarizing from a different point of view	• using charts and drawings to aid description • small differences between British, and North American English • reading 19th-century vocabulary • paraphrasing complex ideas	• underlining and marginal glossing as aids for memory • study mapping • practicing comprehension quizzes • reading for speed during tests

Summary of Reading, Vocabulary, and Test-Taking Skills

Chapter	Reading Skills	Vocabulary Skills	Focus on Testing and Study Skills
seven	• making inferences • applying inferences to specific situations • analyzing sentence structures • interpreting a table • distinguishing between general and specific • relating the reading to a new perspective	• vocabulary relating to business ethics • understanding idiomatic phrases • finding related nouns and verbs • inferring the meaning of key words and expressions	• reviewing study skills: underlining and marginal glossing
eight	• using clues to make inferences • summarizing the main point • using information to disprove false opinions • identifying a bias • matching general ideas and specific examples	• finding the visual metaphors • identifying technical vocabulary from context • fitting scientific terms into context • guessing the meaning of idioms and colloquial phrases • studying word derivatives: finding related words	• reading charts on tests • timed reading • reading diagrams on tests • timed reading
nine	• anticipating the reading: making predictions • making and supporting inferences • making inferences from a map • summarizing information about specific points • reading poetry for meaning	• guessing the meaning of words in context • expressing reactions to music • paraphrasing complex ideas • expressing reactions to paintings	• preparing for exams with study maps • timed reading • writing an instant summary
ten	• focusing on a key issue • guessing the meaning of new words from context • scanning to develop a contrast • building a summary from themes • relating facts to a specific part of a reading	• solving problems in groups • solving a crossword puzzle using medical terminology • adding color with verbs • learning legal terms in context • scanning for antonyms	• speaking in front of people (practice for oral examinations) • timed reading

Chapter	Reading Skills	Vocabulary Skills	Focus on Testing and Study Skills
eleven	• recalling major points of contrast • identifying and evaluating the point of view • relating the reading to a poem • recognizing historical significance • anticipating the reading: prediction • previewing an extended reading • summarizing the article • describing the author's point of view	• distinguishing shades of meaning • paraphrasing key ideas • matching the illness with the cure • matching definitions to technical terms • choosing the correct synonym	• answering short essay questions • practicing short essays • timed reading
twelve	• anticipating the reading: prediction • reading between the lines • reading a graph • making inferences • identifying an ironic point of view • finding a moral for the story	• relating prophesies to past, present, and future • experimenting with astrology and related terms • choosing the correct words to complete a summary	• writing an extemporaneous essay • practicing for a final exam • timed reading

CHAPTER one

Language and Learning

in this chapter

The author of the first selection describes his early encounters with learning English, the language that finally helped him to overcome his feelings of being an outsider in the dominant culture. The second selection discusses how to use the library. The third reading talks talks about the role of English in today's world.

SELECTION one

Native Americans

Before You Read

Guessing the Meaning of New Words from Context

 Try to guess the meanings of unfamiliar words as you read. One way of understanding a new word is to break it into smaller words, prefixes, and suffixes. Another way is to look for a synonym or explanation near the word. Practice these skills by writing your own definitions for the italicized words in the following sentences taken from the first reading selection. Use the hints to help you.

1. "We are born into a cultural *preconception* that we call reality and that we never question." (*Hint:* Do you know the meaning of the prefix *pre-* and the word *concept*?)

   preconception: _____

2. "We essentially know the world in terms of that cultural package or preconception, and we are so unaware of it that the most liberal of us go through life with a kind of *ethnocentricity*." (*Hint:* The word *ethnic* means "belonging to a particular culture or group." What do you think *centr-* means?)

   ethnocentricity: _____

3. "I grew up in a place that was called a *wilderness,* but I could never understand how that amazing ecological park could be called '*wilderness,*' something wild that needs to be harnessed." (*Hint:* What part of the sentence explains the meaning of *wilderness*?)

   wilderness: _____

4. "Nature is some sort of foe, some sort of *adversary,* in the dominant culture's mentality." (*Hint:* Because of the repetition of the words *some sort of,* you can see that there is another word that is very close in meaning to *adversary.* What word is this?)

   adversary: _____

 If you cannot break a word apart or find a nearby synonym or explanation, you simply have to guess a likely meaning to fit the context. Choose the best word to substitute for each italicized word in the following sentences from the selection.

1. "The bird had a very particular *significance* to me because I desperately wanted to be able to fly too."
   a. beauty
   b. meaning
   c. appearance
   d. name

2. "When I was ten years old, my life changed *drastically.* I found myself adopted forcefully and against my parents' will."
   a. slowly
   b. happily
   c. easily
   d. violently

3. ". . . They were considered *inadequate* parents because they could not make enough money to support me."
   a. unintelligent
   b. wealthy
   c. not suitable
   d. not interesting

4. ". . . I was even more confused when I found out that the meaning of the verb 'to duck' came from the bird and not *vice versa.*"
   a. the other way around
   b. from something else
   c. with many meanings
   d. written in a different way

5. ". . . We are so unaware of it that the most liberal of us go through life with a kind of ethnocentricity that automatically *rules out* all other ways of seeing the world."
   a. eliminates
   b. emphasizes
   c. includes
   d. improves

6. ". . . I could never understand how that amazing ecological park could be called 'wilderness,' something wild that needs to be *harnessed.*"
   a. changed
   b. set free
   c. controlled
   d. appreciated

7. "I grew up in a culture that considers us *literally* a part of the entire process that is called nature, to such an extent that when Black Elk called himself the brother of the bear, he was quite serious."
   a. in an imaginative way
   b. in reality
   c. intellectually
   d. poetically

8. "You can imagine my *distress* when I was ten years old to find out that synonyms for the word *earth—dirt* and *soil*—were used to describe uncleanliness on the one hand and *obscenity* on the other."

distress: **a.** fear
            b. joy
            c. suffering
            d. laughter

obscenity: **a.** correct speech and manners
            b. offensive language and actions
            c. religious customs
            d. objects considered beautiful

9. "I could not possibly understand how something that could be dirty could have any kind of negative *connotations.*"

  a. sounds connected to a word
  b. ideas associated with a word
  c. ways of spelling
  d. ways of writing

English is the official language of the United States and one of the two official languages of Canada (French is the other), but some people born in these countries do not grow up speaking it. For them, English is a second language that they learn at a later time. In some cases, this is because their parents are immigrants or because they grow up in an ethnic neighborhood where Spanish, Chinese, or another language is spoken by almost everyone. For a small percentage, it is because their ancestors were the original natives of this continent who were here before the arrival of the European settlers in the sixteenth century. Can you think of other parts of the world in which many people learn the official language of their country as a second language? Does this situation make a society weaker or stronger?

The author of the following selection, Jamake Highwater, is a Native American and a well-known author who writes in English. He speaks of the terrible shock that certain English words caused him when he first learned them at school. As you read, notice Highwater's attitudes toward the two languages and the two cultures that have formed him.

Native Americans

When I was about five years old, I used to watch a bird in the skies of southern Alberta from the Blackfeet Blood Reserve in northern Montana where I was born. I loved this bird; I would watch him for hours. He would glide effortlessly in that gigantic sky, or he would come down and light on the water and float there very majestically. Sometimes when I watched him he would creep into the grasses and waddle around not very gracefully. We called him *meksikatsi,* which in the Blackfeet language means "pink-colored feet"; *meksikatsi* and I became very good friends.

5

The bird had a very particular significance to me because I desperately wanted to be able to fly too. I felt very much as if I was the kind of person who had been born into a world where flight was impossible, and most of the things that I dreamed about or read about would not be possible for me but would be possible only for other people.

When I was ten years old, my life changed drastically. I found myself adopted forcefully and against my parents' will; they were considered inadequate parents because they could not make enough money to support me, so I found myself in that terrible position that 60 percent of Native Americans find themselves in: living in a city that they do not understand at all, not in another culture but between two cultures.

A teacher of the English language told me that *meksikatsi* was not called *meksikatsi,* even though that is what my people had called that bird for thousands of years. *Meksikatsi,* he said, was really "duck." I was very disappointed with English. I could not understand it. First of all, the bird didn't look like "duck," and when it made a noise it didn't sound like "duck," and I was even more confused when I found out that the meaning of the verb "to duck" came from the bird and not vice versa.

This was the beginning of a very complex lesson for me that doesn't just happen to black, Chicano, Jewish, and Indian children but to all children. We are born into a cultural preconception that we call reality and

Native Americans and native people of Canada celebrate their culture with traditional dances at annual pow-wows during the summer.

that we never question. We essentially know the world in terms of that cultural package or preconception, and we are so unaware of it that the most liberal of us go through life with a kind of ethnocentricity that automatically rules out all other ways of seeing the world.

As I came to understand English better, I understood that it made a great deal of sense, but I never forgot that *meksikatsi* made a different kind of sense. I realized that languages are not just different words for the same things but totally different concepts, totally different ways of experiencing and looking at the world.

As artists have always known, reality depends entirely on how you see things. I grew up in a place that was called a wilderness, but I could never understand how that amazing ecological park could be called "wilderness," something wild that needs to be harnessed. Nature is some sort of foe, some sort of adversary, in the dominant culture's mentality. We are not part of nature in this society; we are created above it, outside of it, and feel that we must dominate and change it before we can be comfortable and safe within it. I grew up in a culture that considers us literally a part of the entire process that is called nature, to such an extent that when Black Elk called himself the brother of the bear, he was quite serious. In other words, Indians did not need Darwin to find out that they were part of nature.

I saw my first wilderness, as I recall, one August day when I got off a Greyhound bus in a city called New York. Now that struck me as being fairly wild and pretty much out of hand. But I did not understand how the term could be applied to the place where I was from.

Gradually, through the help of some very unusual teachers, I was able to find my way into two cultures rather than remain helplessly between two cultures. The earth is such an important symbol to most primal people that when we use European languages we tend to capitalize the *E* in much the same way that the word *God* is capitalized by people in the dominant culture. You can imagine my distress when I was ten years old to find out that synonyms for the word *earth*—*dirt* and *soil*—were used to describe uncleanliness on the one hand and obscenity on the other. I could not possibly understand how something that could be dirty could have any kind of negative connotations. It would be like saying the person is godly, so don't go near him, and I could not grasp how these ideas made their way into the English language.

Jamake Highwater

After You Read

Completing a Summary

 exercise 1 Fill in the blanks of this summary with key words from the selection.

AN INDIAN BOY MEETS THE ENGLISH LANGUAGE

When Jamake Highwater was ten years old, he had to move from the

_____ to a _____. At school a teacher told him that the
　　　　1　　　　　　　　　　　2

meksikatsi he loved was really called a _____. He had grown up in a
　　　　　　　　　　　　　　　　　　　　　　3

culture that considered people as part of _____. He thought that he
　　　　　　　　　　　　　　　　　　　　　　　　4

saw his first "wilderness" when he went to _____. At first he felt he
　　　　　　　　　　　　　　　　　　　　　　　　5

was between two cultures, but he became part of both of them with the help of

some unusual _____ . He finally got over his shock at finding out
　　　　　　　　　　6

that in English synonyms for the word _____ had negative
　　　　　　　　　　　　　　　　　　　　　　7

_____: they were used to describe _____ on the one hand
　　　　8　　　　　　　　　　　　　　　　　　　　　9

and _____ on the other.
　　　　　10

Talking It Over

 activity In small groups, discuss the following questions.

1. Why did the duck have a special significance for Jamake Highwater when he was very young?
2. What drastic change occurred when he was ten years old? Why did he describe himself then as "between two cultures"?
3. Why didn't the author like the word *duck*? What are some English words that have surprised or displeased you? Explain.
4. According to Highwater, where was the wilderness? Explain.
5. Do you know who Charles Darwin is? (If not, how can you find out?) Why does the author say that the Indians did not need Darwin?
6. Why did it bother the author that in English obscene words and jokes are often referred to as "dirty" words and jokes? In some cultures, obscene jokes are referred to as "green stories." Is there any color associated with them in your culture? How are they referred to?
7. How did the author's attitude toward English change?

Finding Verbs with Precise Meanings

It is obvious that Jamake Highwater has mastered his second language well. Reread his description of the *meksikatsi* bird in the first paragraph and find the verbs that he used instead of the more ordinary ones given in the sentences that follow.

1. The bird would *fly* in the sky (without moving his wings): _____

2. Then he would come down and *land* on the water (gently and without making a splash): _____

3. Afterward the bird would *come* (slowly and carefully) into the grasses: _____

4. There he would *walk around* (swaying from side to side) not very gracefully: _____

Stories Behind Words: Expressions Associated with Animals

Highwater speaks of his disappointment with the verb *to duck*. Actually, many English words come from the names of animals. Usually some well-known characteristic of the animal provides the basis for the association. For example, people sometimes say they had "a *whale* of a good time." Since a whale is very big, the word *whale* intensifies the idea and means a *very* good time. Animals are also used in expressions such as "slow as a turtle" and "hungry as a bear." However, animals are often seen differently by different cultures, so the English expression "clumsy as an elephant" surprises people from India. They know elephants quite well and claim that they are among the most graceful of all animals. This caused some embarrassment for the Indian gentleman who once told an American lady that she "walked like an elephant." He couldn't understand why she got angry! Read the following sentences and guess the meanings of the italicized words. Try to explain what quality and animal are associated with each one.

1. He *wolfed* down his dinner with his eye on the clock.

   _____

   _____

2. The people *craned* their necks to see the famous actor.

   _____

   _____

3. She worked at the task with *dogged* determination.

_____

_____

4. A sparkling river *snaked* through the lush green valley below.

_____

_____

5. The teacher got angry because the students were *horsing* around.

_____

_____

6. That professor has an *elephantine* memory.

_____

_____

7. The new boy was a *bully* who liked to scare the other children.

_____

_____

8. She *fished* around in her purse until she found her glasses.

_____

_____

9. After winning the Nobel Prize, the scientist was *lionized* by the crowd of reporters.

_____

_____

exercise 4   Can you think of any other phrases like the ones in Exercise 1? If possible, give examples of words from the language of your culture that are associated with animals.

_____

_____

_____

_____

_____

_____

Library: The Buried Treasure

Before You Read
Anticipating the Reading

 *exercise* **1**

The following selection is taken from the book *Becoming a Master Student*. Judging from its title, why do you think people read this book? Looking at the title of the selection, what do you think the author means when he refers to "buried treasure"?

_____

_____

exercise **2**

Look at the photo and the headings in the selection. Then make a list of three specific pieces of information that you think you might learn from the article. When you finish, compare these items with those of your classmates.

1. _____

2. _____

3. _____

Libraries are one of the marks of civilization. They hold the accumulated wisdom of previous generations. Recent advances in technology are changing the modern library in remarkable ways. In the following article, you will read about some of them.

Library: The Buried Treasure

Books. That's what most people imagine when a library is mentioned. Books occupy a lot of space in a library, but they are only a small part of what is really there.

Most libraries have books. They also have—for your use—records, artwork, maps, telephone directories for major cities, audiovisual equipment, microfiche, slide programs, film strips, magazines, dictionaries and encyclopedias of all varieties, research aids, computer searches, and people.

The Best Resource Is Not Made of Paper

People who work in libraries are trained explorers. They know how to search out information that might be located in several different places. They can also act as guides for your own expedition into the data jungle. Their purpose is to serve you. Ask for help.

Recent advances in technology are changing the modern library in remarkable ways.

Most libraries have a special reference librarian who can usually let you know right away if the library has what you need. He or she may suggest a different library or direct you to another source, such as a business, community agency, or government office.

You can save hours by asking.

Any Book You Want

Most libraries now have nearly every book you could ever want through a service known as interlibrary loan. This sharing of materials gives even the smallest library access to millions of books on any subject you could imagine. Just ask that the book be ordered from another library. It often takes only a few days.

Periodicals

The magazines and newspapers a library carries depend mostly on the location and purpose of the library. A neighborhood branch of a public library may have copies of the local paper and magazines right from the grocery store aisle. A library in a business school is more likely to have the *Wall Street Journal* and trade journals for accountants and business managers. Law libraries subscribe to magazines that would probably bore the socks off a veterinarian.

Reference Material

The card catalog lists books available in that library and their location. It is an alphabetical listing that is cross-referenced by subject, author, and title. Each card carries the author's name, the title, the publisher, the date of publication, the number of pages and illustrations, the Library of Congress or Dewey decimal system number (for locating the book), and sometimes a brief description of the book. *Books in Print* is a list of most books currently in publication in the United States. Like the card catalog, it is organized by subject, author, and title.

The Reader's Guide to Periodical Literature catalogs articles found in most magazines. By subject, you can find titles of articles from a wide variety of magazines. The magazine name, date, and page numbers will be listed. If you want an older magazine, many libraries require that you fill out a form requesting the magazine so it can be retrieved from storage in closed stacks.

Other guides to what has been recently published include: *New York Times Index, Business Index, Applied Science and Technology Index, Accountants' Index, General Science Index, Education Index, Humanities Index, Art Index,* and many others. These indexes help you find what you want in a hurry.

Abstracts are publications that summarize current findings in specific fields. You can review condensed versions of specialized articles by reading *Chemical Abstracts, Psychological Abstracts,* or *Education Abstracts*. . . .

Resources listed in indexes or *Reader's Guide* but not available at a particular library are usually available through interlibrary loan.

General and specialized encyclopedias are found in the reference section. Find what you want to know about individuals, groups, places, products, words, or other books. Specialized examples include: *Encyclopedia of World Authors, Encyclopedia of Music and Musicians, Encyclopedia of Religion and Ethics, Encyclopedia of Associations, Thomas Register of American Manufacturers,* and *Encyclopedia of the Arts*.

Dictionaries of all sizes and specialties are also available in the library. Technical disciplines (medicine, computer science, engineering) often have their own dictionaries. Of special value to your writing projects is the thesaurus, a type of dictionary. You will find single words that have a very similar meaning to the word you look up (synonyms). Instead of standard definitions, a thesaurus provides fast relief when you just can't think of the word you want.

Computer networks now provide information and resource materials to most libraries. DIALOG, ORBIT, and BSR are the three major electronic

information vendors, and each contains several dozen data bases. Up-to-
the-minute reports (stock prices set in the past fifteen minutes, yesterday's
New York Times stories) can be retrieved almost instantly on a video
terminal.

Gaining familiarity with all these resources and services is crucial to
the success of most students. And to some, even more valuable than
access to information is the convenient, comfortable, quiet, and
dependable atmosphere for study to be found in a library.

David B. Ellis

Library at the *Universidad Nacional Autónoma de México* (National
Autonomous University of Mexico) in Mexico City. The mosaic tells the
story of the history of Mexico.

After You Read
Scanning for Specific Information

Can you tell in what library source you could find each of the pieces of information given below? If you took notes or have a very good memory, perhaps you can simply write down all of the correct information. If not, use the *scanning* technique.

To scan, move your eyes quickly over the article until you come to the specific piece of information that you want. If you remember that it is given in the middle or toward the end of the article, start your search there. Do not be distracted by other items. Concentrate. When you find what you are looking for, stop and immediately write it down. Then go on to the next point.

Write a correct source for each of the following pieces of information.

example: You are writing a report on acid rain for your political science class and need recent information on the subject:

The Reader's Guide to

Periodical Literature

1. You are preparing an exam in your music course and need to know the year in which the composer Beethoven wrote his famous ninth symphony: _____

2. You have bought some stock, and someone told you that just a few hours ago it jumped way up in price. You want to find out how much you have earned: _____

3. You once met a man from Vancouver on an airplane trip, and now you are planning to visit there. You remember his full name and that he lives near the university but would like to find out his phone number: _____

4. You will be having dinner with an engineer who works with super-conductors, and you want to read some recent information on this field: _____

5. You are writing an essay for your English course and have used the word *increase* four times and want to replace two of these with a synonym: _____

6. You have been assigned the topic "Television and Its Influence on Children" for your speech class and need to find some current magazine articles for background: _____

7. You have heard of a recent book on management techniques written by an author named Le Boeuf and would like to know the title:

_____

Talking It Over

In small groups, discuss the following questions.

1. What does the author mean when he says "the best resource is not made of paper"? When should you use this "resource"? How would you ask for help?
2. What is interlibrary loan? When would you use this service?
3. What services or sources have you used in the library? Have you had any trouble using them?
4. Why do you think that many people find the atmosphere of the library conducive to study? Which part of the library do you think is the best place to study?

Word Detective

Use clues and your *scanning* technique to find the words from the article that correspond to the descriptions. The words here and on the next page are given in the order of their occurrence.

1. A word of French origin that starts with an *m* and means "small sheets of film containing information that can be viewed under a special apparatus": _____

2. A word beginning with the letter *p* and used as one of the headings; it means "magazines and newspapers": _____

3. A slang expression consisting of a four-word phrase that means "be very uninteresting to": _____

4. A phrase of two words, each beginning with a *c*, that refers to the alphabetical listing of all the books in a library, by subject, author, and title: _____

5. A noun rhyming with the word *packs* that means the shelves used for the storage of books and other materials: _____

6. A word beginning with an *a* that refers to a brief summary of a scientific or technical article or of the current findings in a particular field:

   _____

7. An adjective beginning with a *c* and meaning "very important, decisive": _____

SELECTION **three**

English as a Universal Language

Before You Read

Guessing the Meaning of New Words

Choose the best meaning for the italicized words in the following sentences taken from the next reading selection. Guess the meaning of new words by breaking them apart—into smaller words or into prefixes and suffixes—or by using clues from the context.

1. English . . . has semiofficial *status* in many countries.
   a. difficulty
   b. rank
   c. statement
   d. enjoyment

2. There may be as many people speaking the various *dialects* of Chinese.
   a. words
   b. dialogs
   c. lists of rules
   d. ways of speaking

3. English is certainly more *widespread* geographically.
   a. restricted
   b. extended
   c. regional
   d. popular

4. By the year 2000, that figure is likely to *exceed* 1.5 billion.
   a. be more than
   b. be less than
   c. equal
   d. approach

5. English is not replacing other languages; it is *supplementing* them.
   a. proving its superiority over
   b. taking the place of
   c. being used in addition to
   d. being used exclusively by

6. English *prevails* in transportation and the media.
   a. exists
   b. preserves
   c. continues
   d. predominates

7. *Maritime* traffic uses flag and light signals, but vessels may at times communicate verbally.
   a. sea
   b. air
   c. ground
   d. rail

8. It is a foreign *tongue* for all six member nations.
   a. challenge
   b. body
   c. trade
   d. language

Skimming for Main Ideas

> Skimming is a useful way to get an overview of a reading selection. It is different from scanning. You scan for specific facts or details. You skim for general ideas.
>
> To skim, move your eyes quickly through the whole reading. Do not stop for details or worry about words you don't understand. Keep going like a fast-moving train from beginning to end. Afterward you will have a general idea of the contents. Then you can read the selection again with better comprehension.

Take two minutes and skim the next selection. Then look at the following list of ideas. Put a check in front of the ideas that are discussed in the reading.

_____ How English is taught in different countries

_____ Where English is taught

_____ The use of English among young people

_____ The use of English in literature and poetry

_____ The use of English in business, science, and diplomacy

_____ Comparisons of the use of English and the use of some other languages

Is English truly a "universal" language, or will it be at some time in the near future? The following selection from the book *Megatrends 2000* presents one opinion on this subject and supports it with numerous details and statistics. Read to see if you agree with the author's opinion.

English as a Universal Language

English is becoming the world's first truly universal language. It is the native language of some 400 million people in twelve countries. That is a lot fewer than the 800 million people or so who speak Mandarin Chinese. But another 400 million speak English as a second language. And
5 several hundred million more have some knowledge of English, which has official or semiofficial status in some sixty countries. Although there *may* be as many people speaking the various dialects of Chinese as there are English speakers, English is certainly more widespread geographically, more genuinely universal than Chinese. And its usage is growing at
10 an extraordinary pace.

English words and phrases are used throughout the world.

Today there are about 1 billion English speakers in the world. By the year 2000, that figure is likely to exceed 1.5 billion.

The world's most taught language, English is not replacing other languages; it is supplementing them:

- Two hundred and fifty million Chinese—more than the entire population of the United States—study English.
- In eighty-nine countries, English is either a common second language or widely studied.
- In Hong Kong, nine of every ten secondary school students study English.
- In France, state-run secondary schools require students to study four years of English or German; most—at least 85 percent—choose English.
- In Japan, secondary students are required to take six years of English before graduation.

Media and Transportation

English prevails in transportation and the media. The travel and communication language of the international airwaves is English. Pilots and air traffic controllers speak English at all international airports. Maritime traffic uses flag and light signals, but "if vessels needed to communicate verbally, they would find a common language, which would probably be English," says the U.S. Coast Guard's Werner Siems.

Five of the largest broadcasters—CBS, NBC, ABC, the BBC, and the CBC—reach a potential audience of about 300 million people through English broadcast. It is also the language of satellite TV.

The Information Age

The language of the information age is English. Computers talk to each other in English.

More than 80 percent of all the information stored in the more than 100 million computers around the world is in English.

Eighty-five percent of international telephone conversations are conducted in English, as are three-fourths of the world's mail, telexes, and cables. Computer program instructions and the software itself are often supplied only in English.

German was once the language of science. Today more than 80 percent of all scientific papers are published first in English. Over half the world's technical and scientific periodicals are in English, which is also the language of medicine, electronics, and space technology.

International Business

English is the language of international business.

When a Japanese businessman strikes a deal anywhere in Europe, the chances are overwhelming that the negotiations were conducted in English.

Manufactured goods indicate their country of origin in English: "Made in Germany," not *Fabriziert in Deutschland.* It is the language of choice in multinational corporations. Datsun and Nissan write international memorandums in English. As early as 1985, 80 percent of the Japanese Mitsui and Company's employees could speak, read, and write English. Toyota provides in-service English courses. English classes are held in Saudi Arabia for the ARAMCO workers and on three continents for Chase Manhattan Bank Staff.

Diplomacy

English is replacing the dominant European languages of centuries past. English has replaced French as the language of diplomacy; it is the official language of international aid organizations such as Oxfam and Save the Children as well as of UNESCO, NATO, and the UN.

Lingua Franca

English serves as a common tongue in countries where people speak many different languages. In India, nearly 200 different languages are spoken; only 30 percent speak the official language, Hindi. When Rajiv

Gandhi addressed the nation after his mother's assassination, he spoke in English. The European Free Trade Association works only in English even though it is a foreign tongue for all six member countries.

Official Language

75   English is the official or semiofficial language of twenty African countries, including Sierra Leone, Ghana, Nigeria, Liberia, and South Africa. Students are instructed in English at Makerere University in Uganda, the University of Nairobi in Kenya, and the University of Dar es Salaam in Tanzania.

80   English is the ecumenical language of the World Council of Churches, and the official language of the Olympics and the Miss Universe competition.

Youth Culture

    English is the language of international youth culture. Young people
85 worldwide sing the lyrics of U2, Michael Jackson, and Madonna songs without fully understanding them. "Break dance," "rap music," "bodybuilding," "windsurfing," and "computer hacking" are invading the slang of German youth.

Patricia Aburdene, John Naisbitt

After You Read
Scanning for Supporting Statistics

exercise **1**

The selection supports its ideas with many and varied statistics. Scan for the following information.

1. the number of English speakers in the world at the time the article was written: _____

2. the number of Chinese studying English: _____

3. the approximate number of computers in the world: _____

4. the percentage of scientific papers published first in English: _____

5. the number of different languages spoken in India: _____

6. the number of African countries in which English has official or semiofficial status: _____

Talking It Over

activity In small groups, discuss the following questions.

1. Why does the author feel that English is more universal than Chinese?
2. Where is English used as a common second language?
3. In your opinion, why do people in many parts of the world study English? Why are you studying English?
4. In what situations can you imagine that a knowledge of English could mean the difference between life and death?
5. How has technology helped to make English popular?
6. Can you explain the meaning of *lingua franca* (used as one of the subheads) in the selection? Is English a lingua franca or not? Why?
7. What English terms or phrases are common in your culture?

focus on testing

Analyzing Summary Statements

On reading comprehension tests, you may be given several statements and asked to select the one that best summarizes a selection. In order to do this, first read the statements and see if any of them is false or incorrect. If so, eliminate it. Next, look at the other statements and decide which one best expresses the main idea of the whole reading selection. This is a better summary than a statement that gives a secondary idea or expresses only some parts. If there are subheads in the selection, they can help to remind you of the important ideas and sections.

Look at the following exercise. Which of the statements is incorrect?_____

Which of the statements expresses a secondary idea and only refers to a

small part of the selection? _____

exercise To summarize (give a summary of) a reading selection is to express its contents in a shortened form. Choose the statement that best summarizes Selection Three. Then explain your answer.

a. English is replacing the dominant European languages of the past, and serves as a common means of communication in India and Africa and for scientists all over the world.
b. English is the most important language in the world for transportation, information, business, diplomacy, trade, and communication among the young.
c. English is the predominant language in the world because it is spoken by many more people than any other language and is used in most multinational companies.

Understanding Acronyms and Abbreviations

Acronyms are words formed from the first letters of a set phrase, such as *LASER* (**l**ightwave **a**mplification by **s**timulated **e**mission of **r**adiation) or *SCUBA* (**s**elf-**c**ontained **u**nderwater **b**reathing **a**pparatus). Abbreviations are letters pronounced separately to represent a phrase, such as NGO (**n**ongovernmental **o**rganization). Do you know the meaning of the following acronyms and abbreviations? The first eight were used in the selection. (If you do not know one, you can look it up in a good dictionary.)

1. CBS _____
2. NBC _____
3. ABC _____
4. BBC _____
5. CBC _____
6. UN _____
7. UNESCO _____
8. NATO _____
9. NAFTA _____
10. GATT _____

Reacting to a Different Opinion

In small groups, tell what you think about the following opinion. Do you agree with it or not? Explain. Compare the opinions of your group with those of other groups.

"This article expresses a very one-sided and nationalistic view in favor of the English language. There are many important languages in the world today. The author admits that French used to be the language of diplomacy and German used to be the language of science. Now it is the turn of English to be important in these two spheres, but it may be different in the future. No one can predict the future. Language reflects culture and there are many varied cultures on our planet. No one language can claim to be universal."

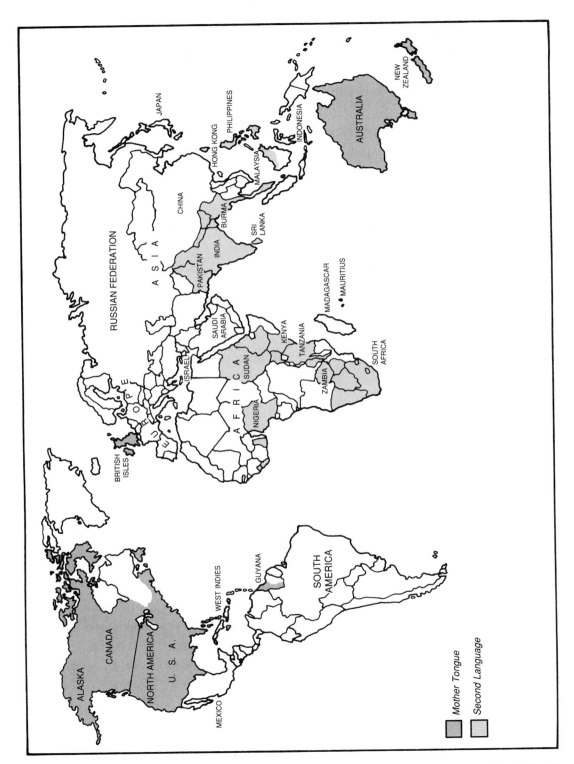

JAPAN
NEW ZEALAND
AUSTRALIA
PHILIPPINES
INDONESIA
HONG KONG
MALAYSIA
CHINA
BURMA
SRI LANKA
INDIA
RUSSIAN FEDERATION
ASIA
PAKISTAN
MADAGASCAR
MAURITIUS
SAUDI ARABIA
KENYA
TANZANIA
ISRAEL
SUDAN
SOUTH AFRICA
EUROPE
AFRICA
ZAMBIA
NIGERIA
BRITISH ISLES
WEST INDIES
GUYANA
SOUTH AMERICA
ALASKA
CANADA
NORTH AMERICA
U. S. A.
MEXICO

Mother Tongue
Second Language

24   Mosaic II • Reading

Reading a Shaded Map

 **exercise 3** Look at the map of the world on the opposite page, read its legend, and answer the following questions.

1. What do the shaded parts of the map indicate?

_____

_____

2. What is the difference between the two types of shading?

_____

_____

3. Looking at the map, tell on what continents English is spoken (in some countries) as the mother tongue.

_____

_____

_____

4. On what continents is English spoken as a second language?

_____

_____

_____

5. Which of these two groups is larger? Which is more important for the status of English as a *global* language?

_____

_____

_____

English today is spoken as a mother tongue by about 400 million people (see map opposite), and at least 400 million more who use it as a second language in societies—Africa, for instance—with dozens of competing languages. People in many European countries learn English as a second language. The Japanese and Chinese appear to be fascinated by English. It is also the language of international business and politics, transcending ideological and religious divisions. In total, there are probably more than a billion speakers of English, at least a quarter of the world's population.

Famous Quotations on Education

activity **3** Which of the following quotations relates most directly to your own personal ideas about education? Why? Share your ideas with your classmates.

Knowledge is power. —*Francis Bacon, 1561–1626*

Education is a thing of which only the few are capable. Teach as you will, only a small percentage will profit by your most zealous energy. —*George Gissing, 1857–1903*

We do not know what education could do for us, because we have never tried it. —*Robert Maynard Hutchins, 1899–1977*

'Tis Education forms the common mind:
Just as the twig is bent the tree's inclined.
—*Alexander Pope, 1688–1744*

There are two ways of spreading light: to be the candle or the mirror that reflects it. —*Edith Wharton, 1862–1937*

Experience is the best teacher. —*traditional proverb*

WHAT DO YOU THINK?

No English, S'il vous plaît

Attack on English

In 1994, the French Cultural Minister promoted a law requiring that 3,000 English words widely used in France be replaced by newly created French equivalents. He felt the French were losing an important part of their culture by using English words. This would mean changing "prime time" to *heure de grande écoute,* or calling a "corner" kick in soccer a *jet de coin.* Although government officials will have to follow the new laws, the French Constitutional Congress ruled that the law violates the "freedom of expression" of the general public. Do you think the minister was right in trying to keep foreign words out of the French language? Does your language include words of English origin? What are some examples? What words do you know in English that come from other languages?

CHAPTER **two**

Danger and Daring

in this chapter

Why take risks? Why face danger and death when you could stay home in safety and comfort? Throughout history, there have been many who dared: explorers, mountain climbers, travelers, soldiers, religious leaders. The first selection focuses on some present-day adventurers who are famous for their daring. Next, a short story examines some different attitudes toward risk taking. Then there is a true account of a Canadian naturalist and writer who lived among wild animals and made an important discovery—about himself.

Adventurers of Today

Before You Read
Anticipating the Reading

Helen Keller once wrote that a life without risk is not worth living. She had good reason to know. Blind and deaf from an early age, she became a renowned writer who later traveled and gave speeches in various parts of the world. Many people share her sentiments. In fact, today, more than ever, people attempt physical goals that are difficult to achieve. Consider marathon races, sky diving, and hang gliding. Why do you think so many of us are willing to attempt these feats? What character traits are necessary for people to take these risks?

In the space below, write about a risk taken by you or a friend in recent years. What happened? What was learned from this experience?

_____

_____

_____

Skimming for the General Idea and Organization

The following selection is an informative essay on modern adventurers based on recent items in the news. Before beginning to read, skim the selection to get a general idea of what it is about and its organization. Then answer the following questions.

1. What is the main idea of the article?

_____

_____

2. What are its main divisions?

_____

_____

Throughout the ages, human beings have searched for adventure. We have explored the longest deserts and climbed the highest mountains. We have gone to the depths of the sea and have flown far into the universe. What drives people to try dangerous deeds at the risk of injury or even death? Curiosity? Power? Wealth? Challenge? Notoriety? The following are examples of modern-day adventurers.

Adventurers of Today

Across the Tundra

March 1995

The fastest time ever in the Iditarod dogsled race was set by Doug Swingley of the United States. He completed the race in 9 days, 32 hours, and 43 minutes. The Anchorage to Nome, Alaska, race is 1,135 miles (1,827 kilometers) through long stretches of tundra, frozen lakes, and wastelands. Blizzards and below-zero temperatures are part of the race. Although the Iditarod has been practiced informally since 1910, the first official race was in 1967. The winner of that race, Dick Wilmarth, completed the race in 20 days, 49 minutes, and 41 seconds.

The first woman to win the race was a 28-year-old Canadian named Libby Riddles on March 20, 1985. After nearly 18 days on the trail, Riddles and her thirteen huskies beat sixty teams for the $50,000 top prize. Riddles had taken the lead during the final days of the race by pushing into a snowstorm that other contestants decided to sit out. She crossed the finish line some three hours ahead of the second-place finisher. Another woman, Susan Butcher, won three consecutive Iditarods: 1986–1988. American Rick Swenson is the all-time champion with a record of five Iditarod wins.

The longest dogsled race in the world, however, is in Russia. The 1,243-mile (2,000 kilometers) Bernegnia Trail is from Esso to Markovo, Russia. The 1991 race was won by Pavel Lazarev in 10 days, 18 hours, 17 minutes, and 56 seconds.

Mushers race dog-sleds across the finish line of the Iditarod.

Above the Earth

December 23, 1986

Dick Rutan, 48, and Jeanna Yeager, 34, became the first pilots to circle the world without making a stop or refueling. Their plane, the *Voyager,* designed by Dick's brother, Burt Rutan, made the 25,012-mile (40,254-kilometer) flight in nine days. Five times during their flight, typhoons and other storms had forced them to change course or climb to a higher altitude. Occasionally, the lightweight craft had been tossed about as if it were a toy.

The most frightening five minutes of the journey came seven and a half hours away from landing, when the plane plummeted some 3,500 feet (1,000 meters) from its altitude of 8,500 feet (2,600 meters) over the coast of California. The rear engine had stalled upon drawing in air from a near-empty fuel tank, and the pilots had had to switch to the front engine to save the plane.

The journey was the longest flight made without a stop, and the continuous nine days, three minutes, and forty-four seconds the two pilots spent in the air set an aviation endurance record.

September 24, 1993

Eleven-year-old Vicki Van Meter became the youngest girl to fly across the United States. She was accompanied by an instructor, Bob Baumgartner, but did all the flying and navigating herself. Van Meter flew a single-engine Cessna 172 from Augusta, Maine, to San Diego, California. The flight lasted from September 20 to September 23 with four stops for refueling.

Through Empty Space

April 1987

Skydiver Gregory Robertson, 35, made one of the most daring rescues in skydiving history. Fellow skydiver Debbie Williams, 31, while attempting to join three other divers in a hand-holding ring formation, slammed into the backpack of another chutist and was knocked unconscious. She was floating through the air like a limp rag doll.

Within seconds, Robertson, a veteran instructor with 1,700 jumps to his credit, assessed the situation and decided to attempt rescue. Assuming a rocket-like vertical position, Robertson pinned his arms to his body, crossed his ankles and plummeted in a "no-lift" dive at a speed of around 200 miles per hour toward Williams. At 3,500 feet, about ten seconds before impact, Robertson caught up with Williams and angled her in the right position so that her chute could open. With six seconds

Skydivers in ring formation.

left, at 2,000 feet, Robertson yanked the ripcord on Williams' emergency chute, then pulled his own. The two sky divers floated to the ground. Williams landed on her back and suffered injuries, but thanks to Robertson's daring rescue, she is alive and has recovered.

December 1993

The seven-member crew of the space shuttle *Endeavor* set out on an eleven-day mission to repair the damaged Hubble Space telescope. During a record five space walks, astronauts Story Musgrave, Claude Nicollier, Jeffrey Hoffman, Kathryn Thornton, and Tom Akers repaired the telescope. While floating in space, they inserted a new camera and other instruments intended to compensate for the telescope's primary mirror. They virtually restored full vision to the telescope. Scientists were able to resume a number of space projects including the search for black holes.

February 2, 1995

Lieutenant Eileen M. Collins of the U.S. Air Force became the first woman astronaut to pilot a shuttle into space. She led the *Discovery* to a historic rendezvous with the Russian space station *Mir*. The two vessels passed within thirty-five miles of each other but did not link up on this mission. Although Lieutenant Collins was the first female astronaut pilot, the presence of women in space leads back to an earlier time. The first woman on a space flight was Valentina Tereskova, who was part of a

Lieutenant Eileen M. Collins, the first woman to pilot a shuttle into space

Soviet space crew in 1963. Two other women astronauts, research scientist Judith Resnik and high school teacher Christa McAuliffe, lost their lives in the ill-fated explosion of the space shuttle *Challenger* in 1986.

Into the Deep Ocean
1995

Jacques Cousteau, 85, the French oceanographer, author, and motion picture producer, celebrated over fifty years of exploration of the world's oceans. In 1943, he helped invent the Aqualung, a device that evolved into modern scuba equipment for underwater diving. He also developed the underwater diving station and an underwater observation vehicle called the diving saucer. Aboard his research ship *Calypso,* Cousteau and his crews explored many of the world's waterways. He's written many books and articles, and made television specials calling attention to the need for conservation of ocean life. During his underwater ventures, he was often joined by his sons, Jean Michel and Phillipe. During a 1979 exploratory mission, Phillipe, the younger son, was killed in a seaplane accident.

Jacques Cousteau, underwater adventurer

February 1995

Frenchman Guy Delage, 42, swam 2,400 miles from Cape Verde, Africa, to the Caribbean island of Barbados. He completed his journey across the Atlantic Ocean in less than two months. Swimming ten hours a day, often in the company of sharks, Delage would climb aboard an accompanying raft to rest at night. Equipped with a wet suit, flippers, and radar-guided kickboard, Delage was often seasick. Ridiculed as the "mad swimmer" by some, and the "long-distance bather" (because of the use of the raft) by others, Delage nevertheless received a hero's welcome by a large crowd in Barbados. The crowd included his wife and two young children.

Upon the Highest Peaks
July 20, 1986

Teiichi Igarashi, born September 21, 1886, climbed the snowcapped Mt. Fuji at age 99 years, 302 days. Igarashi topped the 12,388-foot mountain to become the oldest climber on record to achieve such a remarkable feat.

May 1991

115

Timothy John Macartney-Snape, 35, traversed Mt. Everest's entire altitude from sea level to summit. Starting from the Bay of Bengal near Calcutta, India, on February 5, 1990, he walked, climbed, and reached the summit of Mt. Everest on May 11, 1991. The Australian had walked

120

approximately 745 miles.

M. Prijic

After You Read

Using Facts to Explode Myths

 People often have opinions on subjects without knowing many of the relevant facts. Tell what facts from the article contradict the following opinions.

1. Only the young participate in dangerous activities; older people are too concerned with safety and security.
2. Nowadays people are too selfish to risk their lives for the benefit of others.
3. Children are too young for important achievements.
4. Men are stronger and braver than women, so real acts of danger and daring are performed only by men.
5. No airplane will ever circle the globe without refueling, because if it is light enough to attain the required speed, it will not withstand the winds and storms.
6. The honor of being an astronaut in the American space program is reserved for male WASPs (White Anglo-Saxon Protestants).
7. Marriage and children mean the end to adventure.

Making Inferences About Character Traits

 Inferences are conclusions we draw from facts. For example, if someone is frowning, we infer that he or she is sad or angry. The article discusses a number of modern-day adventurers. It does not say what traits (qualities) of character they have, but it does give you information about what they have done. Look at the following list of traits. Do you know what all the words mean? Tell which traits you think the adventurers have and from what information you have inferred this.

persistence	decisiveness
self-confidence	timidity
laziness	intelligence
ambition	imagination
courage	

Talking It Over

In small groups, discuss the following questions.

1. Which of the adventures mentioned in the article do you think is the most interesting? Which of the people described is the most worthy of admiration? Why?
2. Have you ever done something dangerous or daring? If so, what was it and why did you do it? Give an example of something adventurous you might like to do someday.
3. What do you think of the American space program? Should it be discontinued and the money used for something else? Should the focus be changed to unmanned missions? Explain your opinion.
4. The most famous quotation about the dangerous sport of mountaineering is from adventurer George Leigh Mallory. On a lecture tour in 1923, he was asked, "Why do you want to climb Mt. Everest?" Mallory replied, "Because it is there." What do you infer about Mallory from this quotation?

Using the Encyclopedia to Prepare a Class Report

Research a person who has performed an important act of danger and daring and prepare a class report, answering the following questions.

1. What dangerous act did he or she perform?
2. Why was it important?
3. When did it happen?
4. How old was he or she at the time?
5. Why do you think he or she did it? For fame? For fortune? For knowledge? For religious or political convictions?

The easiest way to find out this information is probably to go to an encyclopedia, look up the person's name, and scan the article about him or her until you find what you want. Don't copy the phrases word for word from the encyclopedia. Instead, put the answers into your own words. Here are some suggestions for your research.

Gonzalo Pizarro	Mohandas Gandhi
Martin Luther King, Jr.	Amelia Earhart
Leif Ericsson	Cleopatra
Mata Hari	Houdini
Louis Riel	Tadeusz Kosciuszko
Ibn Battuta	Alexandra David Neal

SELECTION two
A High Dive

Before You Read
Learning Narrative Terms

A narrative is a story. It has characters, setting (the time and place), and plot. The plot is the action, the chain of events making up the story line. Learning the typical development of a plot can help you to read most stories. Usually, a plot follows four steps.

1. **conflict:** the problem or difficult situation at the beginning. (After all, if everything were going fine, there would be no movement, no real story to tell.)
2. **complication:** the group of events or other factors that increase the conflict and make it more difficult.
3. **climax:** the high point or turning point of the action that occurs toward the end.
4. **resolution:** the ceasing or solution of the problem for better or worse. Sometimes there is a happy ending and sometimes a sad one, depending on the author's view of reality and the point he or she wants to make.

   Typical conflicts in fictional stories involve a struggle between a character and nature (a mountain to climb, a jungle to cross), between the main character and other characters (a detective against a criminal, a hero against evildoers), between a character and a social or economic situation, or between a character and himself or herself (a person who fights his or her own fear, ambition, ignorance, and so on). Sometimes there is more than one conflict in the same story.

exercise 1   Read the first paragraph of the story "A High Dive." Then write a brief description of the conflict.

_____

_____

_____

_____

_____

Thinking Ahead and Predicting the Action

As you read, try to think ahead of the story. Don't worry about the words you don't understand. Simply follow the main steps of the plot and pick up clues from the context to help you predict what is going to happen next. The story will be interrupted at a few points and you will be asked some questions to guide you.

The following story is fiction, which means that it did not really happen but was invented by the author. However, most writers of fiction are keen observers, and so their stories contain a good deal of truth based on observation. The following story is about danger and risk. What book or film do you know of that involves danger and risk?

A High Dive

The circus manager was worried. Attendances had been falling off and such people as did come—children they were, mostly—sat about listlessly, munching sweets or sucking ices, sometimes talking to each other without so much as glancing at the show. . . . What did people
5 want? Something that was, in his opinion, sillier and more pointless than the old jokes; not a bull's-eye on the target of humor, but an outer or even a near miss—something that brought in the element of futility and that could be laughed at as well as with; an unintentional joke against the joker.

10 The clowns were quick enough with their patter but it just didn't go down; there was too much sense in their nonsense for an up-to-date audience, too much articulateness. They would do better to talk gibberish perhaps. Now they must change their style, and find out what really did make people laugh, if people could be made to; but he, the manager, was
15 over fifty and never good himself at making jokes, even the old-fashioned kind. What was this word that everyone was using—"sophisticated"? The audiences were too sophisticated, even the children were: They seemed to have seen and heard all this before, even when they were too young to have seen and heard it.

20 "What shall we do?" he asked his wife. They were standing under the Big Top, which had just been put up, and wondering how many of the empty seats would still be empty when they gave their first performance.

"I don't see what we can do about the comic side," she said. "It may come right by itself. Fashions change, all sorts of old things have returned
25 to favor, like old-time dances. But there's something we could do."

"What's that?"

"Put on an act that's dangerous, really dangerous. Audiences are never bored by that. I know you don't like it, and no more do I, but when we had the Wall of Death—"

Her husband's big chest muscles twitched under his thin shirt.

30

> **Prediction**   What possible solution to the conflict does one of the characters offer? What do you think the "Wall of Death" was? Will the man and woman probably agree or disagree as they talk about it?

"You know what happened then."

"Yes, but it wasn't our fault; we were in the clear."

He shook his head.

"Those things upset everyone. I know the public came after it happened—they came in shoals.* They came to see the place where someone had been killed. But our people got the needle and didn't give a good performance for I don't know how long. If you're proposing another Wall of Death I wouldn't stand for it—besides, where will you find a man to do it?—especially with a lion on his bike, which is the great attraction."

35

40

"But other turns are dangerous too, as well as dangerous looking. It's being dangerous that is the draw."

"Then what do you suggest?"

Before she had time to answer a man came up to them.

"I hope I don't butt in," he said, "but there's a man outside who wants to speak to you."

45

"What about?"

"I think he's looking for a job."

"Bring him in," said the manager.

> **Prediction**   What do you think is meant by the word *draw* in this context? What has happened to complicate the plot? What do you imagine the new character will propose?

The man appeared, led by his escort, who then went away. He was a tall, sandy-haired fellow with tawny leonine eyes and a straggling

50

---

shoals   large groups, throngs, droves

moustache. It wasn't easy to tell his age—he might have been about thirty-five. He pulled off his old brown corduroy cap and waited.

"I hear you want to take a job with us," the manager said, while his wife tried to size up the newcomer. "We're pretty full up, you know. We don't take on strangers as a rule. Have you any references?"

"No, sir."

"Then I'm afraid we can't help you. But just for form's sake, what can you do?"

As if measuring its height the man cast up his eyes to the point where one of the two poles of the Big Top was embedded in the canvas.

"I can dive sixty feet into a tank eight feet long by four feet wide by four feet deep." The manager stared at him.

"Can you now?" he said. "If so, you're the very man we want. Are you prepared to let us see you do it?"

"Yes," the man said.

"And would you do it with petrol burning on the water?"

"Yes."

"But have we got a tank?" the manager's wife asked.

"There's the old Mermaid's tank. It's just the thing. Get somebody to fetch it."

While the tank was being brought the stranger looked about him.

"Thinking better of it?" said the manager.

"No, sir," the man replied. "I was thinking I should want some bathing trunks."

"We can soon fix you up with those," the manager said. "I'll show you where to change."

Leaving the stranger somewhere out of sight, he came back to his wife.

"Do you think we ought to let him do it?" she asked.

"Well, it's his funeral. You wanted us to have a dangerous act, and now we've got it."

"Yes, I know, but . . ." The rest was drowned by the rattle of the trolley bringing in the tank—a hollow, double cube like a sarcophagus. Mermaids in low relief sported on its leaden flanks. Grunting and muttering to each other the men slid it into position, a few feet from the pole. Then a length of hosepipe was fastened to a faucet and soon they heard the sound of water swishing and gurgling in the tank.

"He's a long time changing," said the manager's wife.

"Perhaps he's looking for a place to hide his money," laughed her husband, and added, "I think we'll give the petrol a miss."

90   At length the man emerged from behind a screen and slowly walked toward them. How tall he was, lanky and muscular. The hair on his body stuck out as if it had been combed. Hands on hips he stood beside them, his skin pimpled by gooseflesh. A fit of yawning overtook him.

    "How do I get up?" he asked.

95   The manager was surprised, and pointed to the ladder. "Unless you'd rather climb up, or be hauled up! You'll find a platform just below the top, to give you a foothold."

    He had started to go up the chromium-plated ladder when the manager's wife called after him: "Are you still sure you want to do it?"

100   "Quite sure, madam."

    He was too tall to stand upright on the platform; the awning brushed his head. Crouching and swaying forty feet above them he swung his arms as though to test the air's resistance. Then he pitched forward into space, unseen by the manager's wife, who looked the other way until she

105 heard a splash and saw a thin sheet of bright water shooting up.

    The man was standing breast-high in the tank. He swung himself over the edge and crossed the ring toward them, his body dripping, his wet feet caked with sawdust, his tawny eyes a little bloodshot.

    "Bravo!" said the manager, taking his shiny hand. "It's a first-rate act,

110 that, and will put money in our pockets. What do you want for it, fifteen quid a week?"

    The man shook his head. The water trickled onto his shoulders, oozed from his borrowed bathing suit and made runnels[*] down his sinewy thighs. A fine figure of a man: the women would like him.

115   "Well, twenty then." Still the man shook his head.

    "Let's make it twenty-five. That's the most we give anyone."

    Except for the slow shaking of his head the man might not have heard. The circus manager and his wife exchanged a rapid glance.

---

[*]*runnel*   a small stream, brook, rivulet

Prediction   Were you right about the climax? Why do you think that the man is not responding? Do you predict that he will become a member of the circus or not? Why? How do you think the story will end?

120 "Look here," he said. "Taking into account the draw your act is likely to be, we're going to make you a special offer—thirty pounds a week. All right?"

Had the man understood? He put his finger in his mouth and went on shaking his head slowly, more to himself than at them, and seemingly unconscious of the bargain that was being held out to him. When he still 125 didn't answer, the knot of tension broke, and the manager said, in his ordinary, brisk voice, "Then I'm afraid we can't do business. But just as a matter of interest, tell us why you turned down our excellent offer."

The man drew a long breath and breaking his long silence said, "It's the first time I done it and I didn't like it."

130 With that he turned on his heel and walked off unsteadily in the direction of the dressing room.

The circus-manager and his wife stared at each other.

"It was the first time he'd done it," she muttered. "The first time." Not knowing what to say to him, whether to praise, blame, scold or sympa-135 thize, they waited for him to come back, but he didn't come.

"I'll go and see if he's all right," the circus manager said. But in two minutes he was back again. "He's not there," he said. "He must have slipped out the other way, the crack-brained fellow."

L. P. Hartley

After You Read
Talking It Over

In small groups, discuss the following questions.

1. Were most of your predictions about the action correct? Did any part of the story surprise you?
2. By the way the younger man speaks, you can tell that he is not very well educated. What grammar mistake does he make toward the end of the story that shows you this?
3. Will the diver return? Explain your answer.
4. Why do you think the circus manager kept on making higher offers to the diver? What lesson does this teach us about bargaining? Do you think it is usually appropriate to bargain for a salary or not? On which of the following occasions would it be appropriate to bargain in North American society? In your culture?

   - purchasing food at the supermarket
   - buying a new or used car
   - arranging to sublet an apartment
   - ordering dinner at a restaurant
   - buying clothes at a department store
   - buying second-hand furniture (or a used bicycle) that was advertised in the newspaper or on a bulletin board

Choosing a Theme Statement

> Besides characters, plot, and setting, a story also has a *theme:* the general idea or main point of the story. An author combines the characters, plot, and setting in a particular way to show something. To find the theme of a story, you can ask yourself: Does the story express a particular opinion or belief? Perhaps it makes some statement about the meaning of courage or the true definition of love.

The preceding story deals with the need for making money and for taking risks. Which of the following statements do you think expresses the theme of the story best? If you do not like any of them, write your own statement of the theme below.

1. No amount of money is worth the risk of losing a human life.
2. Only the person who takes a risk can judge how much it is worth.
3. It takes courage as well as skill to confront danger successfully.

4. _____

   _____

   _____

Word Detective

Follow the clues to find the words and phrases in the article.

1. a hyphenated word in the first paragraph that refers to a part of an animal and means "an exact hit right in the center":

   _____

2. an adjective used twice in the second paragraph; it begins with the letter *s* and means the opposite of "simple" or "naive":

   _____

3. a two-word phrase, used in the third paragraph and after, that means "the large tent used for circuses":

   _____

4. a noun used to describe the tank that is brought in toward the middle of the story; it begins with *s* and means "a coffin (box that holds a dead body for burial) used in ancient times":

   _____

5. an *-ing* word that begins with *c* and is used to describe the way the diver stood at the top of the platform under the tent because he was too tall to stand up straight:

   _____

6. a verb used in the second-to-last paragraph that means "to share the feelings (of someone)":_____

Some Slang Used to Refer to Money

You can tell that this story takes place in Great Britain because the circus manager makes offers in pounds rather than in dollars. What slang word does he use to refer to pounds when he makes his first offer?

_____

Do you know the meaning of the italicized slang words in the following sentences? They refer to money in Canada and in the United States.

1. You say the price is ten *bucks*. Why, that's outrageous!
2. I wouldn't give you *two bits* for that! Well . . . okay, for *six bits,* I'll take it.
3. Can you trust me until tomorrow? I don't have any *bread* on me now.
4. Let's go to a restaurant that accepts *plastic.*

SELECTION three
The World We Lost

Before You Read

Guessing the Meaning of New Words from Context

 Read the following excerpts from the next selection and choose the best definition for each italicized word. Use the hints in parentheses to aid you.

1. "In order to round out my study of wolf family life, I needed to know what the *den* was like inside—how deep it was, the diameter of the passage, the presence (if any) of a nest at the end of the *burrow,* and such related information."

The *den* is the place where the wolves go to:
a. hunt
b. sleep
c. die

A *burrow* is:
a. a pile of sticks and mud
b. a young wolf or dog
c. a hole dug by an animal

2. "The *Norseman* came over at about fifty feet. As it roared past, the plane waggled its wings gaily in salute, then lifted to skim the crest of the wolf *esker,* sending a blast of sand down the slope with its propeller wash."

A *Norseman* is a type of:
a. animal
b. wind
c. plane

(*Hint:* The word *esker* is not well known even to English speakers, but the reader can use clues from the context: the word *crest,* your knowledge of where the man is going, what happens when the propeller gets near the esker.)

An *esker* is:
a. a ridge of sand
b. a small river
c. a kind of fruit tree

3. "My mouth and eyes were soon full of sand and I was beginning to suffer from *claustrophobia,* for the tunnel was just big enough to admit me."
(*Hint: Phobia* is a term used in psychology to refer to a deep, irrational fear. If you remember that the word *for* means "because" when it starts a

secondary clause, you will understand what fear is referred to by this word.)

Claustrophobia is the unreasonable fear of:
a. high, open places
b. small, enclosed places
c. wild animals

4. "Despite my close *familiarity* with the wolf family, this was the kind of situation where irrational but deeply ingrained *prejudices* completely overmaster reason and experience."

In this context, *familiarity* means:
a. similarity
b. hatred
c. acquaintance

(*Hint:* If you break up the word *prejudice,* you get the prefix *pre-* meaning "before," and the root *jud,* which also appears in words such as *judge* and *judgment.*)

Prejudices are:
a. strong and warm emotions
b. opinions formed with no basis in fact
c. conclusions drawn from observation and action

5. "It seemed *inevitable* that the wolves *would* attack me, for even a *gopher* will make a fierce defense when he is cornered in his den." (*Hint:* The word *even* is your best clue to the meaning of both the italicized words.)

Inevitable means:
a. certain
b. highly unlikely
c. possible

A *gopher* is an animal that is:
a. large and dangerous
b. small and defenseless
c. similar to a wolf

6. "I was *appalled* at the realization of how easily I had forgotten, and how readily I had denied, all that the summer *sojourn* with the wolves had taught me about them . . . and about myself."

Appalled means:
a. pleased
b. shocked
c. relieved

Sojourn means:
a. reading
b. weather
c. stay

Do you ever have nightmares? What is your secret fear? Poisonous snakes? Earth-quakes? Water? Fire? Everyone is afraid of something, and wild animals appear high on the list of horrors for many people. Farley Mowat, the world-famous Canadian writer and adventurer, shared this fear even though he accepted a job that meant living alone in the far north for many months in direct contact with packs of wolves. The Wildlife Service of the Canadian government hired him to investigate claims that hordes of blood-thirsty wolves were killing the arctic caribou (large animals of the deer family). Much to his surprise, Mowat discovered that the wolves were not savage killers, but cautious and predictable animals that usually tried to stay out of people's way. He gave names to the wolves he studied (Angeline, George, and so forth), and even became fond of them.

Later he wrote a book called *Never Cry Wolf* about his experiences. It became a best-seller and was made into a popular movie that has changed many people's ideas about wolves, although extermination campaigns against wolves still continue. The following selection is the last chapter of his book. It tells of an incident that led the author to an important discovery, not about the wolves but about himself. What do you think the title might mean? See if your idea of it changes as you read the story.

The World We Lost

In order to round out my study of wolf family life, I needed to know what the den was like inside—how deep it was, the diameter of the passage, the presence (if any) of a nest at the end of the burrow, and such related information. For obvious reasons I had not been able to make the

5   investigation while the den was occupied, and since that time I had been too busy with other work to get around to it. Now, with time running out, I was in a hurry.

I trotted across country toward the den and I was within half a mile of it when there was a thunderous roar behind me. It was so loud and

10 unexpected that I involuntarily flung myself down on the moss. The Norseman came over at about fifty feet. As it roared past, the plane waggled its wings gaily in salute, then lifted to skim the crest of the wolf esker, sending a blast of sand down the slope with its propeller wash. I picked myself up and quieted my thumping heart, thinking black thoughts

15 about the humorist in the now rapidly vanishing aircraft.

The den ridge was, as I had expected (and as the Norseman would have made quite certain in any case), wolfless. Reaching the entrance to the burrow I shed my heavy trousers, tunic, and sweater, and taking a flashlight (whose batteries were very nearly dead) and measuring tape

20 from my pack, I began the difficult task of wiggling down the entrance tunnel.

The flashlight was so dim it cast only an orange glow—barely sufficient to enable me to read the marks on the measuring tape. I squirmed onward, descending at a forty-five-degree angle, for about eight feet. My mouth and eyes were soon full of sand and I was beginning to suffer from claustrophobia, for the tunnel was just big enough to admit me.

At the eight-foot mark the tunnel took a sharp upward bend and swung to the left. I pointed the torch in the new direction and pressed the switch.

Four green lights in the murk ahead reflected back the dim torch beam.

In this case green was not my signal to advance. I froze where I was, while my startled brain tried to digest the information that at least two wolves were with me in the den.

Despite my close familiarity with the wolf family, this was the kind of situation where irrational but deeply ingrained prejudices completely overmaster reason and experience. To be honest, I was so frightened that paralysis gripped me. I had no weapon of any sort, and in my awkward posture I could barely have gotten one hand free with which to ward off an attack. It seemed inevitable that the wolves *would* attack me, for even a gopher will make a fierce defense when he is cornered in his den.

The wolves did not even growl.

Save for the two faintly glowing pairs of eyes, they might not have been there at all.

Two baby wolves at the entrance to their den

The paralysis began to ease and though it was a cold day, sweat broke out all over my body. In a fit of blind bravado, I shoved the torch forward as far as my arm would reach.

It gave just sufficient light for me to recognize Angeline and one of the pups. They were scrunched hard against the back wall of the den; and they were as motionless as death.

The shock was wearing off by this time, and the instinct for self-preservation was regaining command. As quickly as I could I began wiggling back up the slanting tunnel, tense with the expectation that at any instant the wolves would charge. But by the time I reached the entrance and had scrambled well clear of it, I had still not heard nor seen the slightest sign of movement from the wolves.

I sat down on a stone and shakily lit a cigarette, becoming aware as I did so that I was no longer frightened. Instead an irrational rage possessed me. If I had had my rifle I believe I might have reacted in brute fury and tried to kill both wolves.

The cigarette burned down, and a wind began to blow out of the somber northern skies. I began to shiver again; this time from cold instead of rage. My anger was passing and I was limp in the aftermath. Mine had been the fury of resentment born of fear: resentment against the beasts who had engendered naked terror in me and who, by so doing, had intolerably affronted my human ego.

I was appalled at the realization of how easily I had forgotten, and how readily I had denied, all that the summer sojourn with the wolves had taught me about them . . . and about myself. I thought of Angeline and her pup cowering at the bottom of the den where they had taken refuge from the thundering apparition of the aircraft, and I was shamed.

Somewhere to the eastward a wolf howled; lightly, questioningly. I knew the voice, for I had heard it many times before. It was George, sounding the wasteland for an echo from the missing members of his family. But for me it was a voice which spoke of the lost world which once was ours before we chose the alien role; a world which I had glimpsed and almost entered, . . . only to be excluded, at the end, by my own self.

Farley Mowat

After You Read

Talking It Over

In small groups, discuss the following questions.

1. Would you be afraid to study wild animals? Would you be able to spend a summer completely alone, away from all human company? What character traits (qualities) must a person have to do these things?
2. Farley Mowat writes in a personal, down-to-earth style. He is not afraid to tell about his faults and his feelings. In your opinion, what does this indicate about his character?
3. At a dramatic point in his story, Mowat interjects a bit of humor. He says, "In this case green was not my signal to advance." What does he mean by this? The use of humor at a very serious moment is called *comic relief*. What do you think of this technique?
4. How can you tell that Mowat has gotten to know the wolves as individuals and that he feels affection for them?
5. Have you ever seen wolves? Do you know of places other than Canada where they live?
6. In your opinion, should wolves be exterminated or not? Why?

focus on testing

Summarizing a Narrative

On essay tests, you may need to write the summary of a narrative. Most stories cannot be summarized in a single sentence, so the summary will have to be longer than a summary statement. Good summaries are brief and include all essential elements. So the best one tells *the most* in *the fewest words*.

Generally, narratives (fiction or non-fiction) follow the four steps for plot development described on page 36. Use these steps as guidelines to write narrative summaries. It is not easy to write a summary, so many writers do a rough copy first on a separate sheet of paper. Then they read it over and cross out the parts that are not essential. Finally, they write the final version on the test paper. Try this technique in the following exercise. Afterward, compare your summary with those of your class-mates. Who has said the most in the fewest words? That person has the best summary.

**exercise 1**   Write a summary of Mowat's story in eight sentences (or fewer) by completing the following outline.

"THE WORLD WE LOST": A SUMMARY

1. *(conflict)* In the far north, the Canadian writer Farley Mowat . . .
2. *(complications)* When he was within half a mile of his goal . . .
3. *(climax)* Suddenly in the darkness he saw . . .
4. *(resolution)* Afterward, Mowat realized . . .

Expressing the Theme

**exercise 2**   Mowat's story was based on true experience, but he chose, from among many true events, certain ones to tell for a particular reason, to show a certain general idea, or *theme*. Describe in one or two sentences what you consider the theme of the selection.

Thinking Your Way Out of Danger

**activity 2**   Many times the only way to get out of a dangerous spot is with your brain. Read over the following imaginary situations; then work together in small groups and try to figure out how you would escape from each of them.

SITUATION A: THE WINDOWLESS PRISON

While participating in a revolution against an unjust tyrant, you are caught and thrown into a prison cell that has a dirt floor, thick stone walls, and no windows. There is only a skylight, very high above, to provide light and air. To prevent escape, there are no tables or chairs, only a very small mattress on the floor. Just before you are locked in, a comrade whispers to you that it is possible to escape through the skylight by digging a hole in the floor. How can you do this?

SITUATION B: THE CAVE OF THE TWO ROBOTS

Having entered a time machine, you have been whisked one thousand years into the future to find yourself at the mercy of a superior civilization. These creatures of the future choose to amuse themselves by playing games with you. They set you in a cave that has two doors at the end of it: One leads back to the time machine that would transport you safely home, and the other leads to a pit filled with horrible monsters. There are also two robots in the cave. They know the secret of the doors. One always tells the truth and one always lies, and you do not know which is which. According to the rules of their game, you are allowed to ask one question to one of the robots. What question should you ask? How can you know which door to choose?
(Solutions on page 342.)

WHAT DO YOU THINK?

Courting Danger

Many activities can be dangerous: mountain climbing, sky diving, bungee jumping, scuba diving. Even sports like downhill skiing, football, rollerblading, and horseback riding are dangerous at times. Do you participate in any of these activities, or do you have friends or relatives who do? Which do you consider the most dangerous? Why? In your opinion, when is it irresponsible to participate in dangerous activities? Explain.

Bungee jumping has become a popular way of "courting" danger.

Man and Woman

in this chapter

Down through the ages, the eternal "battle of the sexes" has been a popular topic. This chapter begins with a discussion of how technology and tradition blend to aid romance in today's Japan. Then a poem gives one man's view of the transforming power of love. An analysis of the differences between men and women follows, comparing the sexes with regard to sports, health, aggression, crime, child care, and brain structure, and drawing conclusions that may surprise you. Finally, an essay written by a feminist with a good sense of humor expresses a number of serious opinions about marriage in an ironic and lighthearted style.

For Better or Worse, Arranged Marriages Still Thrive in Japan

Before You Read

Distinguishing the General from the Specific

The following article is from the *Wall Street Journal,* a newspaper best known for its business and financial news. This, however, is a feature article, one that deals with a topic of general human interest. Like many feature articles, it alternates between *general* statements (large, broad ideas) and *specific* information (small points, details, statistics, particular cases, and examples that illustrate or support the general statements). Take three minutes to skim the selection. Then answer the following questions about its overall organization.

1. Does the article begin with the general or the specific? Why do you think it begins this way?

_____

_____

2. At what point does it change?

_____

3. How does it end?

_____

4. How could you briefly describe its organization?

_____

_____

What is the best way to find a husband or a wife? Should you let your family select a mate for you or should you date many people and try to "fall in love"? Many cultures have the tradition of arranged marriages. These are brought about by "matchmakers" who find and introduce possible candidates to a young person at the family's request and for a fee. What do you think of this practice? Judging by the title of the selection, do you think this tradition is popular in Japan? What does the first phrase of the title tell you about the author's point of view? In the article you will find out what the Japanese mean by being "wet" or "dry" when making a decision and how modern technology is aiding romance. Read for main ideas and see if you change some of your opinions about the best way to select a mate.

For Better or Worse, Arranged Marriages Still Thrive in Japan

"**H**e was a banker," Toshiko says of the first young man her parents set her up with. "He was *so-o-o-o-o* boring."

The second was an architect. He tried to impress her with his knowledge of the historic hotel where they had coffee. "He was wrong on almost every point," she sniffs.

The third, for some reason, "asked me a lot of questions about the French Revolution."

Seven more followed. She turned them all down. Just twenty-six, and seeing on the sly a boyfriend from the wrong side of the tracks, Toshiko was in no hurry to get married. With her Yale diploma, her colloquial English, and her very modern outlook on life, this rich family's daughter from Tokyo could almost pass for a rich family's daughter from Greenwich, Connecticut.

But Tokyo isn't Greenwich. Like most unmarried women here, Toshiko (it's not her real name; her parents read this newspaper) still lives with her mother and father. And like most parents here, they think that by the time a young woman reaches her mid-twenties she ought to be married. About a year ago, they began to pressure her to go through *omiai,* the ceremonial first meeting in the traditional Japanese arranged marriage.

Meet and Look

"It was such a drag to get up in the morning, because I knew at breakfast we would have another fight about this," Toshiko says. "I did my first *omiai* so I could have some peace at home."

These days lots of young Japanese do *omiai,* literally, "meet and look." Many of them, unlike Toshiko, do so willingly. In today's prosperous and increasingly conservative Japan, the traditional *omiai kekkon,* or arranged marriage, is thriving.

But there is a difference. In the original *omiai,* the young Japanese couldn't reject the partner chosen by his parents and their *nakodo,* or middleman. After World War II, many Japanese abandoned the arranged marriage as part of their rush to adopt the more democratic ways of their American conquerors. The Western *ren'ai kekkon,* or love marriage, came into vogue; Japanese began picking their own mates by dating and falling in love.

But the Western way was often found wanting in an important respect: It didn't necessarily produce a partner of the right economic, social, and educational qualifications. "Today's young people are quite calculating," says Chieko Akiyama, a social commentator.

No Strings

What seems to be happening now is a repetition of a familiar process in the country's history, the "Japanization" of an adopted foreign practice. The Western ideal of marrying for love is accommodated in a new *omiai* in which both parties are free to reject the match. "*Omiai* is evolving into a sort of stylized introduction," Mrs. Akiyama says.

Many young Japanese now date in their early twenties, but with no thought of marriage. When they reach the age when society decrees they should wed—in the middle twenties for women, the late twenties for men—they increasingly turn to *omiai*. Some studies suggest that as many as 40 percent of marriages each year are *omiai kekkon*. It's hard to be sure, say those who study the matter, because many Japanese couples, when polled, describe their marriage as a love match even if it was arranged.

These days, doing *omiai* often means going to a computer matching service rather than to a *nakodo*. The *nakodo* of tradition was an old woman who knew all the kids in the neighborhood and went around trying to pair them off by speaking to parents; a successful match would bring her a wedding invitation and a gift of money. But Japanese today find it's less awkward to reject a proposed partner if the *nakodo* is a computer.

Japan has about five hundred computer matching services. Some big companies, including Mitsubishi, run one for their employees. At a typical commercial service, an applicant pays $80 to $125 to have his or her personal data stored in the computer for two years and $200 or so more if a marriage results. The stored information includes some obvious items, like education and hobbies, and some not-so-obvious ones, like whether a person is the oldest child. (First sons, and to some extent first daughters, face an obligation of caring for elderly parents.)

The customer also tells the computer service what he or she has in mind. "The men are all looking for good-looking women, and the women are all looking for men who can support them well," says a counselor at one service.

Whether generated by computer or *nakodo,* the introduction follows a ritual course. The couple, who have already seen each other's data and picture, arrive at a coffee shop or computer-service meeting room accompanied by their parents and the *nakodo* or a representative of the service. After a few minutes of pleasantries, the two are left to themselves. A recent comedy movie had such a couple heading directly to one of Japan's "love hotels," which offer rooms by the hour; but ordinarily it takes love a good bit longer to flower, if it does at all.

Japanese wedding banquet

And there still are those Japanese who consider love and marriage to be quite separate things. Here, in brief, are how three arranged marriages of the past twenty-five years unfolded.

The Asamis

Munehiro Asami was a twenty-eight-year-old office worker at a machine-parts company. "I had a friend from childhood whose mother was very pushy," he says. "One day she stomped into my room and took a picture of me out of my picture album. She also left an *omiai* picture of a lady. I was to meet this girl and I didn't want to go."

Neither did the woman. She was Reiko Ohtsuka, a twenty-three-year-old part-time office worker. She recalls how she "half jokingly" agreed to the meeting, then asked if it was too late to change her mind. It was.

But all was for the best, apparently. Mr. Asami warmly remembers the ritual as "like being introduced to a cute girl by your friend." Miss Ohtsuka discovered that her worries about what to talk about were unfounded. "We dated for four months," she says, "fell in love, and got married."

The Watanabes

In 1972 he was five years out of Tokyo University, Japan's Harvard. He was working for a big Tokyo bank. And, reflecting his heavy work schedule and a certain Japanese shyness, he had never had a date.

Mr. Watanabe—he doesn't want to be identified further—always intended to marry through *omiai*. "It's a good system," he says, because the partners don't waste time on someone who doesn't meet their specifications. It's also realistic, he adds: "In love marriages, the two look only at each other's good points: We calculate the bad as well."

Mr. Watanabe was looking for a wife who, first and foremost, "would get along well with my father." To that end, he asked for someone from his home prefecture of Yamanashi. He also wanted a wife who wouldn't have to support her parents. Being himself a second son, he could qualify for a woman who was also looking for a mate free of parental obligations.

Thus, after an introduction through his uncle, did Mr. Watanabe marry a second daughter from his home town in early 1973. They now have two children. "Everyone wants to get married through love, but not everyone can," Mr. Watanabe says.

The Japanese like to think they are "wet" (emotional) compared with "dry" (rational) Westerners. But Mr. Watanabe thinks that "when it comes to marriage, we Japanese are dry."

The Azumas

Kikuko Azuma, who found her husband through *omiai* twenty-five years ago, says the custom is still "the shortest, most convenient way." She is recommending it to her twenty-two-year-old daughter.

Japanese bride in traditional dress

Mosaic II • Reading

Princess Masako and Prince Naruhito

Masako Owada, the new Japanese princess, was not chosen through the process of *omiai*. A career diplomat in the Foreign Ministry, Owada took six years to decide to marry into the traditional life of a Japanese princess. Some Japanese, especially women, were disappointed that she gave up her pioneering role as a diplomat for a strictly traditional way of life. Others think that Masako may change the role of Japanese princess.

120   Mrs. Azuma was only twenty and just out of junior college when she wed. But she was eager to study in the United States and by coincidence was introduced to a twenty-seven-year-old trading company executive about to be transferred to New York. He was from a well-to-do family, and Mrs. Azuma recalls being chauffeured to the *omiai* at an expensive
125 Western restaurant. "I admired his social status," she says.

    Then too, her own parents were having marital difficulties, and she feared that if they divorced she would seem a less desirable catch in a future *omiai.* So she had to move quickly, even though "at twenty I hadn't given much thought to getting married."

130   Did she love him? "Love and marriage are different," Mrs. Azuma replies firmly. "I think after you get married, love eventually emerges." Does her husband of twenty-five years agree? "I don't know," she says. "I don't really know him very well."

There is one other *omiai* success story to report. It is about Toshiko, the
135 young sophisticate who opened this article. After coolly dismissing ten
young men sent her way, she was intrigued by Number 11, a physician
who had worked in Africa. A friend says he was the first guy Toshiko had
met whom she found "intellectually compatible" and who, more importantly, wasn't intimidated by her.
140 Toshiko herself isn't available for comment. She is in Fiji making
wedding preparations.

Urban C. Lehner

After You Read

focus on testing

Improving Your Chances on Multiple-Choice Exams

Multiple choice is a common format on objective exams. You can use the
following exercise to practice your strategy for this type of test. Do the
exercise without looking back at the reading, as if it were an exam. Here
are some tips to help you.

1. There is usually a time limit during a test, so first quickly look through
the whole exercise and do the items you are sure of.
2. Next, *if there is no penalty for guessing,* take a guess at the remaining
ones. Generally, if you are uncertain, choose an option in the middle,
either *b* or *c,* rather than *a* or *d.* These tend to be used more for
correct answers. If you are just guessing, keep the same letter consistently. Long statements in multiple choice tend to be true.
3. Afterward, go back to the reading, scan for the answers, and correct
your work.

exercise: Choose the best way of finishing each statement, based
on what you have just read.

1. The literal translation of the Japanese word *omiai* is:
   a. ceremonial introduction
   b. meet and look
   c. computer wedding
   d. arranged marriage

2. After World War II, a new practice that came into fashion in Japan was:
  a. divorce
  b. arranged marriage
  c. love marriage
  d. church wedding

3. In order to use the new commercial services for *omiai,* a person must:
  a. pay money
  b. belong to a noble family
  c. go to a "love hotel"
  d. all of the above

4. Many Japanese do not want to marry:
  a. an oldest child
  b. a youngest child
  c. a middle child
  d. a twin

5. The reason that this position in the family makes the person a less desirable marriage partner is that he or she:
  a. is usually very spoiled and arrogant
  b. does not inherit any money or property
  c. has to take care of his or her parents when they are older
  d. must make all the food

6. In comparison with the time right after World War II, the practice of arranged marriages in Japan now seems to be:
  a. decreasing
  b. increasing
  c. about the same
  d. completely finished

Finding Support for General Ideas

Find specific facts, statistics, and examples from the article to support the following general ideas here and on the next page.

1. "In today's prosperous and increasingly conservative Japan, the traditional *omiai kekkon,* or arranged marriage, is thriving."

_____

_____

_____

2. "What seems to be happening now is a repetition of a familiar process in the country's history, the 'Japanization' of an adopted foreign practice."

_____

_____

_____

3. "The Japanese like to think they are 'wet' (emotional) compared with 'dry' (rational) Westerners. But Mr. Watanabe thinks that 'when it comes to marriage, we Japanese are dry.'"

_____

_____

_____

Drawing Conclusions from a Chart

You can find specifics to support generalizations or you can do the reverse: make generalizations on the basis of specifics. The chart *Months for Weddings in the U.S.* gives specific statistics. Read the chart and write *C* in front of the one generalization that correctly describes the data. Write *I* in front of the others, which are incorrect.

1. _____ Most Americans get married at Christmastime.

2. _____ Americans do not care which month they get married in.

3. _____ Americans prefer to marry in months that begin with the letter *J*.

4. _____ Americans prefer warm weather for weddings.

5. _____ Americans prefer cold weather for weddings.

TOP 10			
MONTHS FOR WEDDINGS IN THE US			
Month	**Weddings**	**Month**	**Weddings**
1 June	256,000	6 October	221,000
2 August	242,000	7 December	184,000
3 May	231,000	8 April	175,000
4 July	228,000	9 November	174,000
5 September	227,000	10 February	166,000

Source: National Center for Health Statistics

Figures are for 1992 from a US total of some 2,362,000 weddings, a decrease of 9,000 from 1991. March is at No. 11 with 145,000, and January is last with 112,000.

A wedding at Christmastime

Talking It Over

In small groups, discuss the following questions.

1. According to the article, at what age is a woman expected to marry in Japan? A man? Is it the same in your culture? What do you think is the ideal age to marry? Why?
2. What are some of the advantages of arranged marriages? What are some of the disadvantages?
3. Do you think that arranged marriages are more or less likely to end in divorce? Why?
4. Did reading the article give you any new information? Did it change your views on how to select a marriage partner? Explain.

Looking at Love

Take a fresh look at love by reading the following poem by the English poet Alfred Edward Housman (1859–1936). Like many English poems, this one uses rhyme, the use of the same sounds at the end of the last words in certain lines (for example: *you* / *grew, brave* / *behave*). Read it aloud to enjoy the rhyme and rhythm and take care to pronounce the word *again* in the second stanza in the British way (∂´geɪn) so that it will rhyme correctly.

Oh, When I Was in Love with You

Oh, when I was in love with you,
    Then I was clean and brave,
And miles around the wonder grew
    How well I did behave.

5   And now the fancy passes by,
    And nothing will remain,
And miles around they'll say that I
    Am quite myself again.

A. E. Housman

Talking It Over

In small groups, discuss the following questions.

1. Do you think that love can transform a person? How? In the poem, is the transformation permanent or temporary? Do you agree?
2. Is there a regular pattern of rhyme in the poem? Why do you think the poet used rhyme? What effect does it have on a reader?
3. How would you describe the tone of the poem? Do you think a woman would use this tone when talking about love? Why or why not?

A POPULAR SAYING

A man chases a woman until she catches him.

SELECTION two

The Sexes: Anatomy of a Difference

Before You Read
Coping with Technical Terms

With a long article like this one, which uses a number of technical terms, your best strategy is to skim it, skipping over any words you don't understand. Then read it a second time and pay more attention to some of the terms—the ones that are used several times or that seem important for understanding the main ideas. Often you can figure these out from the context. Practice this skill with the following terms taken from the reading.

1. *Sex hormones.* This is obviously an important term since it occurs many times and in many different parts of the article. It occurs first in line 53. No definition is given, but you can tell from the context that it refers to substances or chemicals in the body, and you are told what they do. Look at lines 55–58 and complete the following definition.

   sex hormones: substances that _____

   _____

2. *Testosterone.* This term is also used many times and appears first in line 50. If you skip over it during the first reading, you will find that it is defined for you in lines 98–99. Look there now and write a definition.

   testosterone: _____

   _____

3. *Feedback.* This word is used only twice, but it is important for the under-standing of a key idea: the relationship between testosterone and aggression. Like the words *program* and *programming, feedback* comes from the field of electronics but is now used in a broader way in general language. Read lines 64–73 carefully; then write the best definition you can. (This may be hard, but it isn't impossible even if you know nothing about electronics.)

   feedback: _____

   _____

4. *Estrogen.* This term appears first in line 106, where its definition can be guessed from the context. If you have understood terms 1 and 2, this should be easy.

estrogen: _____

_____

5. *Autism, hyperactivity, stuttering, dyslexia, aphasia.* All of these terms appear in one sentence in lines 88–89, where two of them are defined. Why do you think the author did this when writing for an English-speaking audience? Why isn't it necessary to know all these terms in order to understand the basic point of the sentence? Scan the paragraph for the two definitions and write them below. Then write a general description that refers to all of them.

1: _____

2: _____

general description: _____

_____

6. *Chromosome, genes, immune system.* These three terms come from biology, and you probably either know all three or you don't know any of them. You need to understand them in order to grasp the idea presented in lines 95–102, so this might be a time to go to the dictionary. If you look up the first term, you may be able to guess the others from a careful reading of the last sentence of the paragraph.

chromosome: _____

gene: _____

immune system: _____

7. *Visual, spatial.* These two terms are first used together in hyphenated form in the second-to-the-last paragraph; they modify the word *abilities*. They are used in the last paragraph in ways that hint at their meaning, but the best clues are right in the first three letters of each word.

visual and spatial abilities: abilities to _____

_____

Here are some interesting questions:

Are men stronger than women?_____

Are they better at sports?_____

Do women shoot guns as well as men do?_____

Will a woman ever win an important marathon race (twenty-six

miles)?_____

Which of the sexes commits more violent crimes?_____

Which one is more susceptible to disease?_____

Can men take care of babies as well as women can?_____

Can women be good engineers?_____

These are *controversial* questions, questions that cause a good deal of discussion because people tend to have differing opinions and strong emotions concerning them. Take a moment to think about them and write *yes* or *no* in the blanks. After you read the following article on sexual differences, look back at these questions to see whether any of your views has changed. The article, taken from *Health* magazine, is written in the form of commonly asked questions about male-female differences, with answers provided by the author, a popular writer on health and science topics.

The Sexes: Anatomy of a Difference

How much do we really know about the differences between the sexes? Can we separate nature (biology) from nurture (social training and expectations)? Though there are no definite conclusions, science *has* come up with some fascinating new answers to these and other age-old
5 questions about *"la différence."*

Can a woman match—or beat—a man in any sport?

If you're a woman and you want to challenge a man to a test of strength, your best bet would be either a contest to see who can do the most sit-ups, or leg wrestling (which works just like arm wrestling except
10 that you lie on your back, hook ankles, and try to pull the other person over). Pound for pound, a woman can be as strong in the abdominal and leg muscles as a man because her relatively larger pelvis has plenty of room for muscle attachments. A woman's pelvis also gives her more leverage in leg wrestling.
15 Women's joints are more flexible and less tightly hinged than men's, so women get thrown about more in figure skating and ballet by men, whose upper-body strength is useful in lifting, holding, and throwing them. And in sports where strength is not a factor—skydiving, parachuting, sharpshooting—men and women perform and compete
20 equally. Olympic rifle shooting has no separate categories for men and women.

If women have such strong legs, how come the fastest runners are still men?

In endurance events like running and long-distance swimming, women
25 actually do very well. Grete Waitz beat 11,705 men in the 1982 New York

Isabelle Mouhan of France waves a French flag as she crosses the finish line in Nice to win the first long-distance triathlon World Championship.

City Marathon; only 124 men managed to beat her. In long-distance swimming, a woman's body fat becomes an advantage, providing both buoyancy and insulation against the cold. Women have traditionally done better than men in English Channel swimming, for instance.

To serve his greater muscle mass, a man has a larger heart and lungs, more oxygen-carrying hemoglobin in his blood, and a larger stroke volume. Muscles depend on oxygen to work; the more oxygen you can get to them, the more energy you have. And a man's cardiovascular system more than fills his oxygen needs.

Training increases stroke volume and cuts down body fat; Grete Waitz's levels in both, not to mention her pelvic width, are undoubtedly much closer to runner Alberto Salazar's than to mine. Nevertheless, in 1982 Salazar beat Waitz in the marathon by seventeen minutes, fifty-four seconds. The oxygen factor is probably the greatest male advantage, but the difference between men's and women's time has been getting smaller, and some experts think that the best women will one day equal the best men in events like marathons.

OK, so the physical differences between men and women balance out. But are women as aggressive as men? Why is it usually men who commit violent crimes?

In everything from dreams and fantasies to play and crime, males of all ages seem to be more aggressive than females. The difference is one of the few that has been generally accepted by experts, but nobody really knows exactly how aggression works. There is a clear correlation between male aggression and high testosterone levels; by far the majority of violent crimes, for instance, are committed by young men, whose testosterone levels are much higher than those of older men.

Sex hormones program our bodies to develop as male or female, and many researchers now think that hormones program our brains as well. For instance, the same part of the brain that regulates the production of sex hormones also regulates the basic patterns of *some* of our behavior in courtship and sex, aggression and nurturing—behavior, in short, in which men and women act very differently.

The problem is that it isn't always clear which comes first, testosterone or the aggression. For example, it's been found that after a competition, a wrestler will have more testosterone in his bloodstream if he has won than if he has lost. Male hormone levels rise during a fight, as they do during sex, but are they responsible for starting the fight in the first place?

What seems most likely is that there is a continuous feedback loop among hormones, the environment, and social programming, just as there's feedback between body and brain. Male violence against women, for instance, is fairly common in many societies. A man is more likely to respond to jealousy by blaming his partner, getting angry, and using violence, but a woman is more likely to blame herself. The man's reaction could be connected to the fact that testosterone levels rise with desire, so the hormonal trigger for violence is ready to pull if other elements such as jealousy, frustration, or rejection are present. But not every man beats his wife; ultimately it's the man, not the hormones, who's responsible.

Today, from the office to the tennis court, we expect women to be more aggressive than we did twenty years ago; not surprisingly, women have also been committing more—and more violent—crimes, although still far fewer than men.

Why do women live longer than men?

No one really knows. The difference is in the genes, and one suggestion has been that there was originally no evolutionary reason for men to live past the age when they are useful as hunters, while women, the social center of the group, remained useful for child care, housekeeping, and food gathering even after their own childbearing years were over.

Men are much more vulnerable than women in a number of ways. Boy babies inherit more birth defects and suffer more birth traumas. In childhood, boys have more accidents, and they are far more likely than girls to suffer from autism, hyperactivity, stuttering, dyslexia (difficulty in reading), or aphasia (the loss of the ability to use words as symbols). In young adulthood they are particularly prone to violent deaths, and in middle age they are more likely to develop digestive disorders and kidney disease. They remain more vulnerable to viral infections of all kinds, and if they *do* avoid all the risks and make it to old age, they generally still die sooner than their female peers.

What makes men so vulnerable? Boys may owe their susceptibility to diseases to the fact that they have only one X chromosome. The other, the Y, determines their sex and is the most basic difference between men and women. It contains genes which program for the production of testosterone and the other hormones which produce the male body. The X chromosome includes genes that control the immune system; women, with two Xs, have a "backup" set of genes and, it may be, greater protection.

Is there a maternal instinct that makes it more natural for a woman to mother than a man? Can men take care of babies?

Unlike testosterone and male aggression, there is no clear correlation between estrogen and the desire or ability to be a good mother. In fact, experiments on primates suggest that mothering is very much a learned activity. Monkeys and chimpanzees raised in isolation aren't very good at it.

Women are certainly physiologically designed and hormonally prepared to bear and nurse infants. They go through complex monthly hormonal cycles which prepare their bodies for conception. During pregnancy their estrogen levels rise dramatically, then drop just before birth. Other hormones, *prolactin* and *oxytocin,* start milk production and release it in response to an infant's cry.

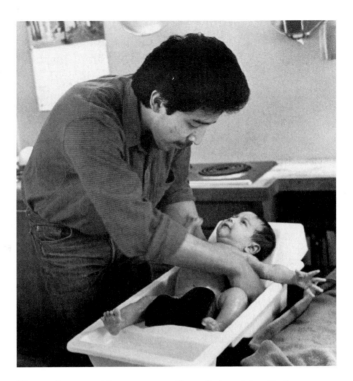

Men today are taking a more active role in raising their children.

But adoptive mothers, who don't go through all these changes, still do a very good job of mothering, while some biological mothers don't. And fathers who care for their babies and children report high levels of "maternal" feelings. All this suggests that maternal feelings in both sexes develop through closeness and caretaking rather than through biological programming.

How come most of the engineers and computer experts are men?

Women are, on the whole, more verbal than men. They are good at languages and verbal reasoning, while men tend to excel at tasks demanding visual-spatial abilities. In fact, along with aggression, these are the most commonly accepted differences between the sexes.

Words are tools for communicating with other people, especially information about people. They are mainly social tools. Visual and spatial abilities are good for imagining and manipulating objects and for communicating information about them. Are these talents programmed into the brain? In some of the newest and most controversial research in neurophysiology, it has been suggested that when it comes to the brain, males are specialists while women are generalists.

Chapter 3 • Man and Woman

But no one knows what, if anything, this means in terms of the abilities
of the two sexes. Engineering is both visual and spatial, and it's true that
there are relatively few women engineers. But women become just as
skilled as men at shooting a rifle or driving a car, tasks that involve visual-
spatial skills. They also do equally well at programming a computer, which
is neither visual nor spatial. Women do, however, seem less likely to fall in
love with the objects themselves. We all know men for whom machines
seem to be extensions of their identity. A woman is more likely to see her
car, rifle, or computer as simply a tool—useful, but not in itself fascinating.

135

140

Signe Hammer

After You Read

Separating Fact from Opinion

The difference between fact and opinion is not always clear, but some general
rules can help you distinguish between them.

1. General statements (which could be verified in an encyclopedia or other
   reference book) about past or present events are usually facts; statements
   about the future are usually opinions, since the future by its nature is
   uncertain.
2. Statements that include the modals *may, might,* or *could,* or qualifiers such as
   perhaps, maybe, possibly, or *probably* are opinions.
3. Statements based on evidence (research, case studies, experiments, question-
   naires) need to be evaluated. If they are based on only one person's research,
   they should be considered opinions. If they are based on a great deal of
   research and if most experts agree, then they can be considered facts.
4. It is also important to remember that the difference between what is
   considered fact and opinion depends on the limits of our knowledge. Time,
   place, and culture influence these limits for all societies. At one time it was
   considered a fact to say that the earth was flat. Today, we say that the earth is
   round. Is it really? Well, it's somewhat round, and certainly it is more round
   than flat. The line between fact and opinion is sometimes open to discussion.

 *exercise*

Tell whether each of the following statements based on the article is fact (F) or
opinion (O). You might need to look at its context. Since the statements are not
presented exactly as they appear in the text, the line numbers are given.

1. _____ In endurance events such as running and long-distance swimming,
women do very well. (lines 24–25)

2. _____ Men have greater muscle mass and larger hearts and lungs than
women. (lines 30–32)

3. _____ The best women runners will one day equal the best men runners in events such as the marathon. (lines 39–42)

4. _____ Males are more aggressive than females. (lines 46–52)

5. _____ Sex hormones program our bodies to develop as male or female. (lines 53–58)

6. _____ Men's violent actions against women are related to the fact that testosterone levels rise with desire. (lines 66–73)

7. _____ Men commit more violent crimes than women. (lines 74–77)

8. _____ On the average, women live longer than men because in the past, old women were more useful to the social group than old men. (lines 79–84)

9. _____ In general, men are more vulnerable to birth defects, disease, and accidents than women. (lines 85–94)

10. _____ Boys are more susceptible to disease than girls because they have only one X chromosome. (lines 95–102)

11. _____ Mothering is an activity that is learned, not inborn. (lines 105–109)

12. _____ Women are more verbal than men, while men are better than women at visual-spatial activities. (lines 123–126)

13. _____ There are very few women engineers. (lines 134–136)

14. _____ Women are just as good as men at driving a car. (lines 136–138)

Talking It Over

 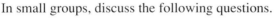 In small groups, discuss the following questions.

1. Does the article discuss only physical differences between the sexes? Or are other types of differences mentioned too? Explain.
2. Are there some opinions expressed in the article that you do not agree with? Explain.
3. In your opinion, are men and women treated equally in society? Should they be?
4. Look back at the questions given before the article. Which ones would you answer differently now? Why?
5. Because of recent advances in technology, it is now possible to determine, with a fair degree of accuracy, the sex of a child before its birth. Should this technology be made available to everyone or not? Explain.

Drawing Conclusions from a Chart

 exercise **2**

Read the two charts about the fastest swimmers to cross the English Channel. Then choose one of the following statements and explain your choice.

  A. These charts support what the article says about men and women in sports.
  B. These charts do *not* support what the article says about men and women in sports.
  C. These charts have no relevance to what the article says about men and women in sports.

TOP 10
FIRST CROSS-CHANNEL SWIMMERS

	Swimmer	Nationality	Time hr:min	Date
1	Matthew Webb	British	21:45	Aug 24–25, 1875
2	Thomas Burgess	British	22:35	Sep 5–6, 1911
3	Henry Sullivan	American	26:50	Aug 5–6, 1923
4	Enrico Tiraboschi	Italian	16:33	Aug 12, 1923
5	Charles Toth	American	16:58	Sep 8–9, 1923
6	Gertrude Ederle	American	14:39	Aug 6, 1926
7	Millie Corson	American	15:29	Aug 27–28, 1926
8	Arnst Wierkotter	German	12:40	Aug 30, 1926
9	Edward Temme	British	14:29	Aug 5, 1927
10	Mercedes Gleitze	British	15:15	Oct 7, 1927

TOP 10
FASTEST CROSS-CHANNEL SWIMMERS

	Swimmer	Nationality	Year	Time hr:min
1	Penny Lee Dean	American	1978	7:40
2	Philip Rush	New Zealander	1987	7:55
3	Richard Davey	British	1988	8:05
4	Irene van der Laan	Dutch	1982	8:06
5	Paul Asmuth	American	1985	8:12
6	Anita Sood	Indian	1987	8:15
7	Monique Wildschutt	Dutch	1984	8:19
8	Eric Johnson	American	1985	8:20
9	Susie Maroney	Australian	1990	8:29
10	Lyndon Dunsbee	British	1984	8:34

Stories Behind Words: Mothering, Fathering, and Other Gender Terms

Many people today feel that historically women have not been treated as well as men in most cultures. In the Western world, as recently as a hundred years ago, they were not allowed to vote in elections and were excluded from most professions. The attitude of favoring one sex over another (in this case, favoring the male) is called *sexism,* which is thought by many to be present in the very language we speak. For example, the verb *to mother,* used in the latter part of the article, generally means "to care for, protect" (for example, "That teacher *mothers* all her students."); whereas the verb *to father* usually means simply "to engender or originate" (for example, "He *fathered* three sons."). Here the idea that women, not men, should take care of children is locked into our everyday speech.

Feminists (people who fight for the rights of women) claim that there are examples of sexism in the vocabulary and even in the grammar of the English language. A common example is the use of the word *man* or *mankind* to refer to the whole human species: "*Man* is the only tool-using animal. . . . The achievements of *mankind* after the agricultural era began. . ." Certain critics of the feminists have argued that this usage doesn't really matter because everyone knows that the words *man* and *mankind* also refer to women. Feminists, however, generally believe that this manner of speaking has created the idea that men have been the active participants in history—working, building, exploring, inventing— while women have sat quietly on the sidelines, helping them. Some people favor language reform and think that the words *people* or *humanity* should be used in these contexts. Others say, "Well, let's be honest! Men *have* been the active ones throughout history."

SELECTION three
I Want a Wife

Before You Read
Identifying an Ironic Tone

> Everyone knows that a person's tone of voice can influence us a great deal. The sentence "Will you open the window?" can be said in a soft, pleasing way or with a harsh, demanding tone that makes us angry. We also speak of the *tone* of an essay, speech, or article. It might be formal or informal, serious or humorous, angry or playful. The important thing is that it is appropriate to the author's subject, audience, and purpose. For what kind of topic and audience do you think that an angry tone would be appropriate and effective?
>
> The following essay is written in an *ironic tone.* This means that the author says something very different from (at times, even opposite to) what she means. *Irony* is a very common device, even in everyday conversation, and it usually has a humorous effect. For example, when it rains on the day of a school picnic, someone might say *ironically,* "What lovely weather!"

 Take two minutes to skim the following essay for the main idea and the tone. Then answer the following questions.

1. At what point do you first notice that the tone seems ironic?

_____

2. What are some statements that seem to express something different from what the author really means?

_____

_____

_____

What qualities are needed to be a perfect wife? Do our modern views on this subject differ greatly from those of our grandparents? The following selection talks about what a wife should be. Written by a contemporary American writer, this humorous essay has become quite popular, chiefly because of the author's clever use of *irony,* which is discussed in the following exercise. Pay attention to the author's style, or way of writing, and see if you can understand the message beneath the humor.

I Want a Wife

I belong to that classification of people known as wives. I am a Wife. And, not altogether incidentally, I am a mother.

Not too long ago a male friend of mine appeared on the scene fresh from a recent divorce. He had one child, who is, of course, with his ex-wife. He is obviously looking for another wife. As I thought about him while I was ironing one evening, it suddenly occurred to me that I, too, would like to have a wife. Why do I want a wife?

I would like to go back to school so that I can become economically independent, support myself, and, if need be, support those dependent upon me. I want a wife who will work and send me to school. And while I am going to school I want a wife to take care of my children. I want a wife to keep track of the children's doctor and dentist appointments. And to keep track of mine, too. I want a wife to make sure my children eat properly and are kept clean. I want a wife who will wash the children's clothes and keep them mended. I want a wife who is a good nurturant attendant to my children, who arranges for their schooling, makes sure that they have an adequate social life with their peers, takes them to the park, the zoo, etc. I want a wife who takes care of the children when they are sick, a wife who arranges to be around when the children need special care, because, of course, I cannot miss classes at school. My wife must arrange to lose time at work and not lose the job. It may mean a small cut in my wife's income from time to time, but I guess I can tolerate that. Needless to say, my wife will arrange and pay for the care of the children while my wife is working.

I want a wife who will take care of my physical needs. I want a wife who will keep my house clean. A wife who will pick up after me. I want a wife who will keep my clothes clean, ironed, mended, replaced when need be, and who will see to it that my personal things are kept in their proper place so that I can find what I need the minute I need it. I want a wife who cooks the meals, a wife who is a *good* cook. I want a wife who will plan the menus, do the necessary grocery shopping, prepare the meals, serve them pleasantly, and then do the cleaning up while I do my studying. I want a wife who will care for me when I am sick and sympathize with my pain and loss of time from school. I want a wife to go along when our family takes a vacation so that someone can continue to care for me and my children when I need a rest and change of scene.

I want a wife who will not bother me with rambling complaints about a wife's duties. But I want a wife who will listen to me when I feel the need to explain a rather difficult point I have come across in my course of studies. And I want a wife who will type my papers for me when I have written them.

I want a wife who will take care of the details of my social life. When my wife and I are invited out by my friends, I want a wife who will take care of the babysitting arrangements. When I meet people at school that I like and want to entertain, I want a wife who will have the house clean, will prepare a special meal, serve it to me and my friends, and not interrupt when I talk about the things that interest me and my friends. I want a wife who will have arranged that the children are fed and ready for bed before my guests arrive so that the children do not bother us. I want a wife who takes care of the needs of my guests so that they feel comfortable, who makes sure that they have an ashtray, that they are passed the hors d'oeuvres, that they are offered a second helping of the food, that their wine glasses are replenished when necessary, that their coffee is served to them as they like it. And I want a wife who knows that sometimes I need a night out by myself.

If, by chance, I find another person more suitable as a wife than the wife I already have, I want the liberty to replace my present wife with another one. Naturally, I will expect a fresh, new life: My wife will take the children and be solely responsible for them so that I am left free.

When I am through with school and have a job, I want my wife to quit working and remain at home so that my wife can more fully and completely take care of a wife's duties.

My God, who *wouldn't* want a wife?

Judy Syfers

After You Read
Recalling Information

 Put a + in front of the actions and attitudes that, according to the essay, are part of being a wife. Put a 0 in front of those that, according to the essay, would *not* be part of being a wife.

1. _____ work and earn money so that her husband can go to school

2. _____ keep track of doctor's and dentist's appointments for her husband and children

3. _____ lose time at her job if necessary so that she can care for the children when they are sick

4. _____ hire someone to clean the house, iron, and mend clothes so that she can do well in her professional work

5. _____ share with her husband the responsibility for cooking good meals

6. _____ take a vacation from time to time so that she can get away from child care and have a change of scene

7. _____ listen to her husband when he wants to talk and keep quiet about the problems that are bothering her

8. _____ entertain her husband's friends and make sure that the children do not bother them

9. _____ have a night out by herself from time to time

10. _____ allow her husband to leave and marry a younger woman if he wants to

11. _____ quit working and forget about her career when her husband gets a job and wants her to stay home

Recognizing the "Real" Point of View

 In small groups, discuss the following questions.

1. What do you think is the *real* point of view of the author on the role of a wife? On a wife's attitude toward her career? On housework and child care? On entertaining friends? On getting a divorce?

2. If the author does not really believe that a wife should be the way she describes one in the essay, why does she describe her that way? Why doesn't she say directly what she means?

Talking It Over

Interview a classmate by asking him or her the following questions.

1. What do you think is the ideal arrangement for a couple when both work outside the home? Which household duties can be shared? Are certain chores "men's work" and others "women's work"? Explain.
2. Are married people happier than single people?
3. Do you notice any differences between North American marriages and marriages in your culture?
4. What do you think of the "women's liberation" movement? Is there such a movement in your culture?

Expressing Your Own Point of View in a Summary Style

How do you see the perfect wife or the perfect husband? Write a paragraph (from five to ten sentences) on this subject, according to the following plan. Your teacher might ask you to read your paragraph to the class.

First (topic) sentence:	*In my opinion, the ideal (wife/husband) is . . .*
Three to eight sentences:	Give examples of what this person does or says.
Last sentence (conclusion):	Express some personal reaction or opinion regarding the person you described. For example: *I doubt that this kind of (wife/husband) really exists!* or *Now you can see why I am looking for someone like this!*

WHAT DO YOU THINK?

How Men and Women Communicate

A well-known "pop (popular) psychology" book in North America is called *Women Are from Venus, Men Are from Mars.* The book talks about the difference in the styles of communication between the sexes and why they have such difficulty understanding one another. Venus (women), says author John Gray, have different values from Mars (men). "A woman's sense of self is defined through her feelings and the quality of her relationships." But "Martians (men) value power, competency, efficiency, and advancement. Their sense of self is defined through their ability to achieve results." What do you think of these definitions? Would they be correct for men and women in your culture? Why do you think men and women have difficulty understanding and communicating with one another?

CHAPTER four
Mysteries Past and Present

What is the force that determines human destiny? Is it luck, divine providence, or simply "blind" chance? First you read what mathematicians who deal with probability theory think about this question in relation to coincidences. Then, one of the classic puzzle stories of the English language focuses on the complex motivations of the human heart. The final selection examines how the legendary dragon helped modern Chinese scholars unravel an important mystery of their past.

SELECTION one

Against All Odds

Before You Read
Anticipating the Reading

Have you ever experienced what seemed to be an amazing coincidence? Perhaps you were thinking of a friend whom you had not seen in ten years and just at that moment the phone rang—and it was a call from that same person! Or perhaps you were traveling in a foreign country and entered a café, only to find out through conversation that the owner is a relative of your former teacher!

In the space below, describe the most amazing coincidence that you know of from your own personal experience or from that of a friend.

_____

_____

_____

_____

Can you think of any rational way to explain the coincidence you described in Exercise 1? Compare your story with those of your classmates. As a class, decide which coincidence seems the most "mysterious." Then see if the following article makes it seem less mysterious.

Matching Key Words to Definitions

exercise 3

Match these key words from the article to their correct definitions. As often happens in tests, there is one extra definition given in an attempt to trick you. If you are unsure about a word, scan for it and look for clues in the context.

1. vagrant   _____ a repetition, exact copy

2. statistical
3. likelihood   _____ a truth that seems unbelievable and contradictory

4. random   _____ amazing, astonishing

5. duplication
6. astounding   _____ based on statistics

7. paradox
8. hermit   _____ a person who lives alone and away from others

    _____ a substance containing two or more elements

    _____ a homeless person who wanders from place to place

    _____ unplanned, happening by chance

    _____ a probability, something likely to happen

The dictionary defines a coincidence as "an accidental and remarkable occurrence of events in a way that suggests that one caused the other." By their very nature, coincidences seem rather mysterious. What causes them? Are they controlled by providence, fate, or destiny? Are some of them caused by ESP (extrasensory perception, the power of sending messages by thought)? Or do these events simply happen by chance? The following article from *Games Magazine* tells us what mathematicians say about coincidences and also offers some less conventional explanations.

Against All Odds

Just how coincidental is a coincidence? Scientists still don't know.

Several years ago, a Connecticut businessman named George D. Bryson was traveling by train from St. Louis to New York when he decided to make an unscheduled stop in Louisville, since he was in no hurry and had never seen that city. At the Louisville train station, he asked for the name of the leading hotel and, accordingly, went to the Brown, where he was assigned room 307. After registering, he stepped over to the mail desk and inquired, just for fun, whether there was any mail waiting for him. The clerk handed over a letter addressed to "Mr. George D. Bryson, room 307."

By coincidence, it turned out the previous resident of the room had been another George D. Bryson, from Montreal, and the letter was for him.

An equally strange event happened to a Chester, Pennsylvania, man named John McCafferty, who was arrested in June 1949 as a vagrant. McCafferty insisted the police were wrong, claiming he had a home—at 714 McElvane Street. Tell it to the judge, the police said. McCafferty duly came before magistrate R. Robinson Lowry, who asked him, "Where did you get that address?"

"It's just an address," McCafferty replied.

"I'll say it is," responded the judge. "That's where I live. Ninety days."

Similarly fascinating coincidences have intrigued scientists and nonscientists alike for many years. They come in all sizes and degrees of significance, and have been attributed to everything from chance, fate, acts of God, and ESP to simple mathematics and the hidden order of the universe.

For the mathematician, coincidences aren't mysterious at all and can be explained by known laws of statistical probability. Such laws provide a way to estimate the chance that any event might occur, from the odds of a certain order of finish in a horse race to the likelihood that the second and third U.S. presidents (John Adams and Thomas Jefferson) would die on the same day—and that the day would be July 4, 1826, the fiftieth anniversary of the signing of the Declaration of Independence. ("No language can exaggerate it—no reason account for it," mused a Washington, D.C., magazine at the time.)

Suppose, for example, you were at a party with twenty-two strangers and, while talking with one, discovered that you have the same birthday. A remarkable coincidence? Hardly. The odds are better than fifty-fifty that among a group of twenty-three people chosen at random at least two will have identical birthdays.

In his book *Lady Luck,* the late Warren Weaver—who also related the George D. Bryson story—recalled mentioning these odds at a dinner meeting of high-ranking military officers. Many of the officers found it hard to believe. Noticing that there were twenty-two people at the table, one proposed a test. In turn, each person stated his birthday: There was no duplication. Then the waitress spoke up. "Excuse me," she said, "but I'm the twenty-third person in the room and my birthday is May 17, just like the general's over there."

Much more astounding is the so-called small-world paradox. We all have experienced the effects of this phenomenon, which can involve the most improbable-seeming chance encounters. While vacationing in Nepal, for instance, you might meet Joe Green from Dubuque who, it turns out, is married to the younger sister of your good friend Gertrude from Los Angeles. "Small world, isn't it?" you exclaim. Actually, sociologist Ithiel de Sola Pool of MIT has demonstrated that the chances are

"Well, against the odds, here we are—Fran, her ex, me, my ex, Dick, my ex's new, Phil, Fran's ex's new, Pearl, Fran's ex's ex, David, Fran's ex's ex's new. CHEERS!"

ninety-nine in a hundred that any randomly selected American adult can be linked to any other randomly selected American adult by only two intermediates. Thus, if Smith and Jones are two persons in the United States picked at random, the chances are almost certain that Smith will know someone who knows someone who knows Jones. This finding is based on the assumption that the "average" American knows about a thousand people well enough to recognize them on the street and greet them by name. But Pool has also shown that two hermits can be linked by seven intermediates at most, merely by assuming that each hermit knows one storekeeper (even hermits have to buy food).

The point, the mathematicians seem to be saying, is that even if the laws of probability show an event to be statistically *improbable,* that does not make it *impossible.* There's always that small chance.

Even if probability theory does account for unlikely coincidences, it does nothing to decrease the profound sense of wonder experienced by someone involved in such events. Moreover, certain coincidences depend on so many peculiar variables that the chances of their occurring cannot be calculated.

Some coincidences have given rise to original theories on the part of scientists who believe that probability can't explain everything. The pioneer in this field was Carl Jung, who was fascinated by the subject and who collected examples of rare coincidences all his life. Jung claimed in a 1952 essay that coincidences occur much more frequently than probability theories would predict, and that many coincidences must therefore be the work of an unknown force seeking to impose universal order.

Jung acknowledged that his theory might seem wildly illogical. But he suggested that the fault may lie with our concept of logic rather than with the theory.

Another theory about coincidences comes from research in crystallog-raphy. British plant physiologist Rupert Sheldrake has proposed a new hypothesis about the mystery of why compounds that are at first difficult to crystallize somehow become easier to crystallize in laboratories all over the world after the first successful crystallization is accomplished. The usual explanation is that very small pieces of the first crystals are carried from laboratory to laboratory on the hair and clothing of scientists, serving as "seeds" that start the crystallization process in the new laboratory. Not so, says Sheldrake. He believes that crystals—and, indeed, all objects—transmit invisible forces that create what he calls morpho-genetic fields, comparable to radio transmissions. The field created by the first crystal, in his view, serves as a code or pattern that influences the form and character of all later crystals of that type. Sheldrake suggests that people are no exception to this scheme. If true, each of us may transmit a field through which we unknowingly communicate knowledge and information to others, present and future, worldwide.

Of course, it's a long leap from such theories to real proof that coincidences are more than random occurrences. Still, they offer stimulus for the belief that there are, indeed, "more things in heaven and earth, Horatio, than are dreamt of in your philosophy." And as the scientific debate goes on, so the coincidences continue to occur, providing puzzles to delight everyone.

Richard Blodgett

After You Read
Recalling Information

Choose the best way of finishing each statement, based on what you have just read.

1. When George D. Bryson went to the mail desk of a Louisville hotel he had entered at random, he received:
   a. a letter from his wife
   b. a letter for a different George D. Bryson
   c. nothing at all

2. When a Pennsylvania man named McCafferty invented a false address in court, it turned out to be the address of:
   a. the judge
   b. his brother
   c. the mayor of the city

3. The amazing coincidence involving the second and third presidents of the United States is that they both:
   a. had the same name
   b. died on the same day
   c. signed the American Declaration of Independence

4. In general, mathematicians believe that coincidences can be explained by:
   a. the will of God
   b. mysterious unknown forces
   c. the laws of statistics

5. The odds that at a party of twenty-three strangers, two of them will have the same birthday are about:
   a. 1 in 365
   b. 1 in 100
   c. 1 in 2

6. The fact that Mr. Smith from California and Mr. Jones from New York meet on a trip and discover that Smith's doctor is a friend of Jones' aunt is:
   a. an amazing coincidence
   b. quite improbable
   c. not surprising

7. A pioneer in the field of explaining coincidences in nonmathematical ways was:
   a. William Shakespeare
   b. Carl Jung
   c. Ithiel de Sola Pool

8. The hypothesis that Sheldrake proposed to explain a mystery among crystallographers is that:
   a. tiny pieces of crystals are carried from laboratory to laboratory
   b. the laws of probability increase once a crystallization has been successful
   c. crystals and all objects transmit forces that create invisible fields

Understanding Abbreviations

The abbreviation ESP is used in the article. Do you remember what it means? (If not, refer to the introduction.) Do you know the following abbreviations or can you guess them from context?

1. Someone tells you he has seen a mysterious UFO. _____

   _____

   _____

   _____

2. In Canada, robbers and other evildoers run when they hear that the RCMP are coming. _____

   _____

   _____

   _____

3. You are asked to hand in an assignment ASAP. _____

   _____

   _____

   _____

4. A friend invites you to a party but tells you it is BYO. _____

   _____

   _____

Using Prefixes That Mean *Not*

The prefixes *un-* and *in-* are common ways to make English adjectives and adverbs mean the opposite. However, the prefix *in-* often changes its second letter. Look at the examples. Then find words from the article for the following.

examples: not remarkable, not significant — unremarkable, insignificant

not responsible, not literate — irresponsible, illiterate

1. not scheduled _____

2. not probable _____

3. not possible _____

4. not logical _____

5. not known _____

6. not likely _____

7. not visible _____

8. not knowingly _____

Talking It Over

In small groups, discuss the following questions.

1. Do you believe in ESP? Why or why not?

2. In your opinion, are most coincidences caused simply by chance, by fate, or by divine providence? Explain.

3. Do you think that Sheldrake's theory is a real possibility or just a crazy idea? Why?

4. The last paragraph contains a quotation from one of Shakespeare's most famous plays, *Hamlet*. Even if you do not know the play, what can you tell from the context of the paragraph about the meaning of the quotation?

5. The famous French biologist Louis Pasteur once said, "Chance favors the prepared mind." What do you think he meant by that?

Reading Critically: Applying What You've Read

In 1963 the world was stunned when the president of the United States, John Fitzgerald Kennedy, was killed by an assassin's bullet. Later, many people pointed out what seemed to be mysterious similarities between his death and that of a former American president, Abraham Lincoln. Is there really some strange force of circumstance that unites the two men? After reading the article on coincidences, you probably have a better idea about which combinations of events can really be considered improbable. Read the following description of these "astonishing parallels." Decide which ones you consider to be really astonishing and which ones you think are simply ordinary coincidences and explain why.

LINCOLN AND KENNEDY

Two of the most tragic and dramatic deaths in American history, the assassinations of Presidents Abraham Lincoln and John Fitzgerald Kennedy, involve the following astonishing parallels:

1. Lincoln was elected president in 1860. Exactly one hundred years later, in 1960, Kennedy was elected president.
2. Both men were deeply involved in civil rights for blacks.
3. Both men were assassinated on a Friday, in the presence of their wives.
4. Each wife had lost a son while living in the White House.
5. Both men were killed by a bullet that entered the head from behind.
6. Lincoln was killed in Ford's Theater. Kennedy met his death while riding in a Lincoln convertible made by the Ford Motor Company.
7. Both men were succeeded by vice-presidents named Johnson who were southern Democrats and former senators.
8. Andrew Johnson (Lincoln's vice-president) was born in 1808. Lyndon Johnson was born in 1908, exactly one hundred years later.
9. The first name of Lincoln's private secretary was John; the last name of Kennedy's private secretary was Lincoln.
10. John Wilkes Booth (Lincoln's assassin) was born in 1839 (according to some sources). Lee Harvey Oswald (Kennedy's assassin) was born in 1939, one hundred years later.
11. Both assassins were Southerners who held extremist views.
12. Both assassins were murdered before they could be brought to trial.
13. Booth shot Lincoln in a theater and fled to a barn. Oswald shot Kennedy from a warehouse and fled to a theater.
14. The names Lincoln and Kennedy each have seven letters.

Your opinion: _____

_____

_____

_____

_____

_____

_____

_____

_____

_____

_____

_____

The dollar bill in the illustration, issued in Dallas only two weeks before JFK was killed there, is now known as the Kennedy assassination bill. Since Dallas is the location of the eleventh of the twelve Federal Reserve Bank districts, the bill bears the letter *K*, the eleventh letter of the alphabet, and the number 11 appears in each corner. The serial number begins with *K* and ends with *A*, standing for Kennedy Assassination. Eleven also stands for November, the eleventh month of the year; two 11s equal 22, the date of the tragedy. And the series number is 1963, the year the assassination occurred.

SELECTION **two**

The Lady or the Tiger?

Before You Read

Skimming

Since this story has a surprise ending, you will probably enjoy it more if you don't skim the whole selection in advance. Just look at the title and skim the first half; then answer the following questions about the three key narrative elements of *setting*, *character*, and *plot*.

1. What do you find out about the *setting* (the where and when) from the first paragraph?_____

_____

2. Which of the *characters* is presented first?

_____

Since the tone is playful and ironic, you might have to read over the first three paragraphs several times to understand the description of this character. Do you think he is kind or cruel? Humble or arrogant? What other qualities does he have?_____

_____

_____

3. It is obvious that in this story the setting and characterization are given first and the *plot* (action) comes later. By skimming over the first part and looking at the title, what can you guess about the plot?_____

_____

_____

_____

_____

Analyzing Words and Phrases

exercise **2**

One skill that can help you guess the meanings of words better is analyzing: breaking the words down into smaller parts. Practice this skill by writing definitions for the italicized words in the following sentences taken from the reading. Use the hints and the context to help you.

1. "In the very olden time, there lived a *semibarbaric* king, who was a man of exuberant fancy and of an authority so irresistible that, at his will, he turned his varied fancies into facts." (lines 1–3) (*Hint:* What does the prefix *semi-* mean? If you know that *barbarous* and *barbaric* mean "not civilized, wild, rough," you should be able to combine these to get the meaning.)

semibarbaric: _____

2. "He was greatly given to *self-communing,* and when he and himself agreed upon anything, the thing was done." (lines 3–5) (*Hint:* Maybe you don't know *communing,* but what common word does it look like at the beginning?)

self-communing: _____

3. "This vast amphitheater, with its encircling galleries, . . . was an agent of poetic justice in which crime was punished, or virtue rewarded, by the decrees of an *impartial* and *incorruptible* chance." (lines 12–16) (*Hint:* Both words begin with prefixes that mean the same thing; both have smaller words—*partial* or *part* and *corrupt*—in them.)

impartial: _____

incorruptible: _____

4. "He was subject to no guidance or influence but that of the *aforementioned* impartial and incorruptible chance." (lines 27–28)

aforementioned: _____

5. "The moment that the case of the criminal was thus decided, . . . great wails went up from the hired mourners posted on the outer rim of the arena, and the vast audience, with bowed heads and *downcast* hearts, wended slowly their *homeward* way, mourning greatly. . . ." (lines 31–35)

downcast: _____

homeward: _____

6. "As is usual in such cases, she was the *apple of his eye* and was loved by him above all humanity." (lines 70–72) (*Hint:* Here it is a phrase, not a word, you must break into smaller parts. When you do that, the phrase doesn't make any literal sense, but can you guess the meaning from the latter part of the sentence?)

apple of his eye: _____

7. "In *afteryears* such things became *commonplace* enough, but then they were, in no slight degree, novel and startling." (lines 85–86)

afteryears: _____

commonplace: _____

The following story, written by the American writer Frank Stockton (1834–1902), has been considered a classic "brainteaser" ever since it first appeared. Perhaps this is because it builds up to an intensely dramatic moment, a moment during which a single act will decide between life and death, between the most exquisite pleasure and the most horrifying pain. The story is presented as it was originally written, with no adaptation. The vocabulary is difficult, so you should not try to understand every word. Read for the main story line only.

The Lady or the Tiger?

In the very olden time, there lived a semibarbaric king, who was a man of exuberant fancy and of an authority so irresistible that, at his will, he turned his varied fancies into facts. He was greatly given to self-communing, and when he and himself agreed upon anything, the thing was done. When everything moved smoothly, his nature was bland and genial; but whenever there was a little hitch, he was blander and more genial still, for nothing pleased him so much as to make the crooked straight, and crush down uneven places.

Among his borrowed notions was that of the public arena, in which, by exhibitions of manly and beastly valor, the minds of his subjects were refined and cultured.

But even here the exuberant and barbaric fancy asserted itself. This vast amphitheater, with its encircling galleries, its mysterious vault, and its unseen passages, was an agent of poetic justice in which crime was

15 punished, or virtue rewarded, by the decrees of an impartial and incorruptible chance.

When a subject was accused of a crime of sufficient importance to interest the king, public notice was given that on an appointed day the fate of the accused person would be decided in the king's arena.

20 When all the people had assembled in the galleries, and the king, surrounded by his court, sat high up on his throne of royal state on one side of the arena, he gave a signal, a door beneath him opened, and the accused subject stepped out into the amphitheater. Directly opposite him, on the other side of the enclosed space, were two doors, exactly alike and

25 side by side. It was the duty and the privilege of the person on trial to walk directly to these doors and open one of them. He could open either door he pleased. He was subject to no guidance or influence but that of the aforementioned impartial and incorruptible chance. If he opened the one, there came out of it a hungry tiger, the fiercest and most cruel that could

30 be procured, which immediately sprang upon him and tore him to pieces as a punishment for his guilt. The moment that the case of the criminal was thus decided, doleful iron bells were clanged, great wails went up from the hired mourners posted on the outer rim of the arena, and the vast audience, with bowed heads and downcast hearts, wended slowly their

35 homeward way, mourning greatly that one so young and fair, or so old and respected, should have merited so dire a fate.

But if the accused person opened the other door, there came forth from it a lady, the most suitable to his years and station that His Majesty could

select among his fair subjects; and to this lady he was immediately married, as a reward of his innocence. It mattered not that he might already possess a wife and family, or that his affections might be engaged upon an object of his own selection. The king allowed no such arrangements to interfere with his great scheme of punishment and reward. The exercises, as in the other instance, took place immediately, and in the arena. Another door opened beneath the king, and a priest, followed by a band of choristers, and dancing maidens blowing joyous airs on golden horns, advanced to where the pair stood side by side, and the wedding was promptly and cheerily solemnized. Then the gay brass bells rang forth their merry peals, and the people shouted glad hurrahs, and the innocent man, preceded by children strewing flowers on his path, led his bride to his home.

This was the king's semibarbaric method of administering justice. Its perfect fairness is obvious. The criminal could not know out of which door would come the lady. He opened either he pleased, without having the slightest ideas whether, in the next instant, he was to be devoured or married. On some occasions the tiger came out of one door, and on some, out of the other. The decisions were not only fair—they were positively decisive. The accused person was instantly punished if he found himself guilty, and if innocent, he was rewarded on the spot, whether he liked it or not. There was no escape from the judgments of the king's arena.

The institution was a very popular one. When the people gathered together on one of the great trial days, they never knew whether they were to witness a bloody slaughter or a hilarious wedding. This element of uncertainty lent an interest to the occasion which it could not otherwise have attained. Thus the masses were entertained and pleased, and the thinking part of the community could bring no charge of unfairness against his plan; for did not the accused person have the whole matter in his own hands?

The semibarbaric king had a daughter as blooming as his most rosy fancies, and with a soul as fervent and imperious as his own. As is usual in such cases, she was the apple of his eye and was loved by him above all humanity. Among his courtiers was a young man of that fineness of blood and lowness of station common to the heroes of romance who love royal maidens. This royal maiden was well satisfied with her lover, for he was handsome and brave to a degree unsurpassed in all this kingdom, and she loved him with an ardor that had enough of barbarism in it to make it exceedingly warm and strong. This love affair moved on happily for many months, until one day, the king happened to discover its existence. He did not hesitate or waver in regard to his duty. The youth was immediately cast into prison, and a day was appointed for his trial in the king's arena. This, of course, was an especially important occasion, and His Majesty, as well as all the people, was greatly interested in the workings and development of this trial. Never before had such a case occurred—never before had a subject dared to love the daughter of a king. In afteryears such things became commonplace enough, but then they were, in no slight degree, novel and startling.

The tiger cages of the kingdom were searched for the most savage and relentless beasts, from which the fiercest monster might be selected for the arena, and the ranks of maiden youth and beauty throughout the land were carefully surveyed by competent judges, in order that the young man might have a fitting bride in case fate did not determine for him a different destiny. Of course, everybody knew that the deed with which the accused was charged had been done. He had loved the princess, and neither he, she, nor anyone else thought of denying the fact. But the king would not think of allowing any fact of this kind to interfere with the workings of the court of judgment, in which he took such great delight and satisfaction. No matter how the affair turned out, the youth would be disposed of, and the king would take pleasure in watching the course of events which would determine whether or not the young man had done wrong in allowing himself to love the princess.

The appointed day arrived. From far and near the people gathered and thronged the great galleries of the arena, while crowds, unable to gain admittance, massed themselves against its outside walls. The king and his court were in their places, opposite the twin doors—those fateful portals, so terrible in their similarity!

All was ready. The signal was given. A door beneath the royal party opened, and the lover of the princess walked into the arena. Tall, beautiful, fair, his appearance was greeted with a low hum of admiration and anxiety. Half the audience had not known so grand a youth had lived among them. No wonder the princess loved him! What a terrible thing for him to be there!

As the youth advanced into the arena, he turned, as the custom was, to bow to the king. But he did not think at all of that royal personage; his eyes were fixed upon the princess, who sat to the right of her father. Had it not been for the barbarism in her nature, it is probable that lady would not have been there. But her intense and fervid soul would not allow her to be absent on an occasion in which she was so terribly interested. From the moment that the decree had gone forth that her lover would decide his fate in the king's arena, she had thought of nothing, night or day, but this great event and the various subjects connected with it. Possessed of more power, influence, and force of character than anyone who had ever before been interested in such a case, she had done what no other person had done—she had possessed herself of the secret of the doors. She knew in which of the two rooms behind those doors stood the cage of the tiger, with its open front, and in which waited the lady. Through these thick doors, heavily curtained with skins on the inside, it was impossible that any noise or suggestion should come from within to the person who should approach to raise the latch of one of them. But gold and the power of a woman's will had brought the secret to the princess.

Not only did she know in which room stood the lady, ready to emerge, all blushing and radiant, should her door be opened, but she knew who the lady was. It was one of the fairest and loveliest of the damsels of the court who had been selected as the reward if the accused youth should be proved innocent of the crime of aspiring to one so far above him; and the princess hated her. Often had she seen, or imagined that she had seen, this fair creature throwing glances of admiration upon the person of her lover, and sometimes she thought these glances were perceived and even returned. Now and then she had seen them talking together. It was but for a moment or two, but much can be said in a brief space. It may have been on most unimportant topics, but how could she know that? The girl was lovely, but she had dared to raise her eyes to the loved one of the princess, and, with all the intensity of the savage blood transmitted to her through long lines of wholly barbaric ancestors, she hated the woman who blushed and trembled behind the silent door.

When her lover turned and looked at her, his eye met hers as she sat there paler and whiter than anyone in the vast ocean of anxious faces about her, he saw, by that power of quick perception which is given to those whose souls are one, that she knew behind which door crouched the tiger, and behind which stood the lady. He had expected her to know it. He understood her nature, and his soul was assuredly that she would never rest until she had made plain to herself this thing, hidden to all other lookers-on, even to the king. The only hope for the youth in which there was any element of certainty was based upon the success of the princess in discovering the mystery, and the moment he looked upon her he saw she had succeeded.

Then it was that his quick and anxious glance asked the question, "Which?" It was as plain to her as if he shouted it from where he stood. There was not an instant to be lost. The question was asked in a flash; it must be answered in another.

Her right arm lay on the cushioned parapet before her. She raised her hand, and made a slight, quick movement toward the right. No one but her lover saw her. Every eye but his was fixed on the man in the arena.

He turned, and with a firm and rapid step he walked across the empty space. Every heart stopped beating, every breath was held, every eye was fixed immovably upon that man. Without the slightest hesitation, he went to the door on the right and opened it.

Now, the point of the story is this: Did the tiger come out of that door, or did the lady?

The more we reflect upon this question, the harder it is to answer. It involves a study of the human heart which leads us through roundabout pathways of passion, out of which it is difficult to find our way. Think of it, fair reader, not as if the decision of the question depended upon yourself, but upon that hot-blooded, semibarbaric princess, her soul at a white heat beneath the combined fires of despair and jealousy. She had lost him, but who should have him?

How often, in her waking hours and in her dreams, had she started in wild horror and covered her face with her hands as she thought of her lover opening the door on the other side of which waited the cruel fangs of the tiger!

But how much oftener had she seen him at the other door! How in her grievous reveries had she gnashed her teeth and torn her hair when she saw his start of rapturous delight as he opened the door of the lady! How her soul had burned in agony when she had seen him rush to meet that woman, with her flushing cheek and sparkling eye of triumph; when she had seen him lead her forth, his whole frame kindled with the joy of recovered life; when she had heard the glad shouts from the multitude, and the wild ringing of the happy bells; when she had seen the priest, with his joyous followers, advance to the couple, and make them man and wife before her very eyes; and when she had seen them walk away together upon their path of flowers, followed by the tremendous shouts of the hilarious multitude, in which her one despairing shriek was lost and drowned!

Would it not be better for him to die at once, and go to wait for her in the blessed regions of semibarbaric futurity?

195

And yet, that awful tiger, those shrieks, that blood!

Her decision had been indicated in an instant, but it had been made after days and nights of anguished deliberation. She had known she would be asked, she had decided what she would answer, and without the slightest hesitation, she had moved her hand to the right.

200

The question of her decision is one not to be lightly considered, and it is not for me to presume to set up myself as the one person able to answer it. So I leave it with all of you: Which came out of the opened door—the lady or the tiger?

Frank R. Stockton

After You Read
Talking It Over

activity 1

GROUP ACTIVITY

In small groups, discuss the following questions.

1. What do you think of the king's method of administering justice? The author states that by it the minds of the people were "refined and cultured" and that "its perfect fairness is obvious." Does he really mean this or is he being ironic? Explain.
2. In your opinion, are there some advantages to living in a kingdom like the one described? Do you think that most of the king's subjects probably lead fairly happy lives or not? Why?
3. Do any leaders in the world today have characters and governments similar to this king's? Explain.
4. How would you describe the character of the princess? Is she like her father or not?

Identifying Support for Hypotheses

exercise

What do you think was behind the door—the lady or the tiger? Why? Some parts of the story (certain words, phrases) support one hypothesis and some support the other.

Check either "lady" or "tiger" for each of the following statements to show which hypothesis it supports. Be prepared to explain your choice. (If you think a statement supports neither or both, put a 0 in front of each or check both.)

1. "The semibarbaric king had a daughter as blooming as his most rosy fancies, *and with a soul as fervent and imperious as his own.*"

_____ lady   _____ tiger

2. "This royal maiden *was well satisfied with her lover,* for he was handsome and brave to a degree unsurpassed in all this kingdom, and *she loved him with an ardor that had enough of barbarism in it to make it exceedingly warm and strong.*"

_____ lady   _____ tiger

3. "It was one of the *fairest and loveliest* of damsels of the court who had been selected as the reward of the accused youth, . . . *and the princess hated her.*"

_____ lady   _____ tiger

4. *"Often had she seen,* or imagined that she had seen, *this fair creature throwing glances of admiration upon the person of her lover, and sometimes* she thought *these glances were perceived and even returned.*"

_____ lady   _____ tiger

5. "When her lover turned and looked at her, his eye met hers as she sat there *paler and whiter* than anyone in the vast ocean of anxious faces . . ."

_____ lady   _____ tiger

6. *"He understood her nature, and his soul was assured that she would never rest until she had made plain to herself this thing, hidden to all other lookers-on. . . ."*

_____ lady   _____ tiger

7. "*Without the slightest hesitation,* he went to the door on the right and opened it."

_____ lady   _____ tiger

8. "But *how much oftener* had she seen him at the other door! How in her grievous reveries had she *gnashed her teeth and torn her hair when she saw his start of rapturous delight* as he opened the door of the lady!"

_____ lady   _____ tiger

Formulating a Line of Argument: The Lady or the Tiger?

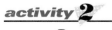

In small groups, discuss the central question of the story and try to reach a unanimous decision (one agreed on by everybody) about whether the princess chose the lady or the tiger. Use quotations from the preceding exercise or find others to support your position. After five to ten minutes, one member of each group should report the decision to the class and present the main argument(s) or reason(s) for the choice. If the decision was not unanimous, the statistics should also be presented (for example, tiger: 3 to 2, or lady: 4 to 1). After the reports from all the groups, determine which way the class as a whole answered the question.

If you do not have time for a class discussion, your teacher may ask you to give your opinion in writing on the central question of the story. For giving a brief written opinion and supporting it with arguments, you can follow this plan:

First (topic) sentence:

I believe that the princess in Frank Stockton's story chose the (lady/tiger).

Three to eight sentences:

Give at least two reasons, writing one or two sentences for each reason. You can use the author's descriptions of the princess's character, for example, and try to analyze her thoughts or feelings. You can quote briefly from the story to support your arguments.

Last sentence (conclusion):

Therefore, it is probable that the princess pointed to the door that concealed the (lady/tiger). You can use this sentence or write your own conclusion, summarizing briefly your previous ideas.

SELECTION three

It All Started with Dragon Bones

Before You Read

Scanning for Synonyms

Practice your scanning skill and learn key vocabulary by finding synonyms in the reading for the italicized words.

1. The beginning of this century was a *discouraging* time for Chinese intellectuals.

_____

2. They doubted the abilities of their own people and feared they were *basically* incapable of operating foreign machines.

_____

3. There was a general mood of *discontent* with the wisdom of the past.

_____

4. Many Chinese historians were looking for proof of their traditions to meet *Western* scientific standards.

_____

5. Old records described the *reigning periods* of the Yin and Chou families.

_____

6. According to Chinese religion, dragons were powerful cosmic forces that would *light up* people's minds and inspire them with *wonder.*

_____

7. Could anyone *decode* the mysterious marks *engraved* on the so-called dragon bones?

_____

8. One man was about to make a *clear soup* from some old bones when he saw *picture writing symbols* on them.

_____

9. Ancient rulers had employed *fortune tellers* who used these bones to *predict* the weather or the sex of unborn children.

_____

Does anybody believe in dragons? We think of them as mythical, fire-breathing beasts that exist only in the pages of storybooks. But even though they don't really exist, can they affect us? Can they influence our knowledge and our history? The title of the selection suggests that something important began with the bones of these legendary reptiles. Read to find out how myths can influence history.

It All Started with Dragon Bones

The beginning of the twentieth century was a low point in Chinese history. Drought, famine, and disease troubled the common people. Opium addiction spread, and the government was powerless to stop it, for British guns protected the drug importers. Because of economic

5 dominance, China was forced to bow before the superior weaponry and technology of countries it had once considered inferior.

Even worse, a cultural tradition three thousand years old was falling apart beneath the impact of Western scientific thought, further demoralizing Chinese intellectuals. Chinese writers published articles claiming

10 that their own people were inherently incapable of operating foreign machines, let alone inventing new ones. A mood of self-doubt, of dissatisfaction with old wisdom, extended into every branch of study.

Mountains in Guilin, China

Pushed by Occidental standards for scientific proof, Chinese historians studied their ancient records with increased skepticism. Were the stirring histories of the earliest dynasties Yin and Chou only legends? Were there enough hard facts to prove that Confucius really lived? Some Western scholars even cast doubt on the foundation stone of Chinese culture, its written language, by suggesting that Chinese characters had been imported from the Middle East in ages long past.

Then something happened to restore confidence in ancient tradition. A small coincidence struck a spark that would later become a light brilliant enough to illuminate the dim reaches of Chinese history. Here, then, is the story of this coincidence.

The farmers around the village of Hsiao T'un in northern Hunan Province sometimes earned extra money from a most unusual crop: pieces of bone turned up by the plow or by heavy rain. It was well known then that a dragon sheds its bones as a snake sheds its skin. Dragons have always played a starring role in Chinese folklore, religion, and philosophy.

To the common mind, dragons are generally good creatures (unlike the Western dragon, which is pictured as an evil monster in league with the devil) associated with rain, rivers, and mists, and with the emperor. Taoism, a native Chinese religion, later developed a complex mythology featuring the dragon as a mythical force of cosmic power who appears for

a moment to fill man with awe, then disappears into the mist. The
Buddhist sect called Ch'an in China and better known in the West by its
Japanese name, Zen, elevates the dragon to a philosophical symbol for
the flash of Truth that comes to enlighten the thinker. Traditional healers
believed that ground-up dragon bones could cure women's diseases,
dysentery, and malaria, as well as a number of other maladies.

The farmers of Hsiao T'un could not be sure the bones they found
came from dragons. Some had strange symbols scratched on them.
Crosses and straight and curved lines could be deciphered, and even
sketchy pictures. Might dragon bones carry these marks? Probably not.
But the pharmacies in Peking wanted dragon bones, and the farmers
needed money, so they scraped off the peculiar markings and sent the
bones to Peking.

Fortunately, one farmer did not scrape well, and a piece of marked
bone was sold by a Peking pharmacist to a scholar who was ill. Imagine
the sick man's astonishment when he recognized, on an object he was
about to grind up for medicinal broth, a written message from China's
mythical past!

The year was 1899. Tantalized by the mysterious "dragon bone" hieroglyphics, a small group of Chinese scholars collected quantities of
inscribed bones from the fields around Hsiao T'un. Five years passed
before enough symbols could be deciphered to reveal the true nature of
the "dragon bones."

Archeological dig in China

They were a record of a people who called themselves Shang, and ruled lands in the area some four thousand years ago. Here was objective proof for the existence of a dynasty called "Yin" (about 1766–1122 B.C.) by its Chou conquerors, part of a heroic epoch of Chinese history, described until then only in semilegendary histories.

60

The objects embedded in the fields of Hsiao T'un came not from dragons but from turtles and cattle. Shang kings sought to learn the future through their diviners, who inscribed royal questions on a carefully scraped and polished bone. The inscribed oracle shells and bones were partially drilled in prescribed patterns. Heat was applied, and the course of the resulting cracks, determined by ancestral spirits, indicated answers to their questions.

65

Shang oracle bones provide intriguing glimpses of life in China four thousand years ago. Kings then yearned to know the results of military campaigns and hunting expeditions. They asked spirits to forecast the weather, the sex of unborn children, the outcome of diseases bothering the royal family. Yet Shang oracle bones raise more questions than they answer. Like a tiny flashlight played over a dark room filled with unknown objects, they give us a fragmented understanding of the Shang people.

70

75

Raymond Chang and Margaret Scrogin Chang

After You Read

focus on testing

Improving Your Chances on True/False Exams

True or false is a common format on objective exams. You can use the following exercise to practice your strategy for this type of test. Do the exercise without looking back at the reading, as if it were an exam. Here are some tips to help you.

1. There is usually a time limit during a test, so first quickly look through the whole exercise and do the items you are sure of.
2. Next, *if there is no penalty for guessing,* take a guess at the remaining ones. Usually more answers are true. The exceptionally long statements tend to be false. If you cannot decide the correct answer, mark either *true* or *false,* and answer all remaining questions with the same choice.

3. Afterward, go back to the reading, scan for the answers, and correct your work.

exercise Write T (true) or F (false) in front of each statement. Correct false statements to make them true.

1. _____ At the beginning of the twentieth century, China found itself humiliated and controlled militarily and economically by cultures it had once considered unimportant.

2. _____ Chinese writers and intellectuals of this time paid no attention to Western scientific thought and maintained that the ancient wisdom of their culture was superior.

3. _____ Some Western scholars even suggested that the Chinese written language had been invented by the British.

4. _____ Just as in Western tradition, the Chinese dragon has always been portrayed as an evil monster in league with the devil.

5. _____ In the Chinese Buddhist sect called Ch'an (known as Zen in Japan), the dragon was a symbol for the flash of Truth that enlightens a person.

6. _____ The farmers from the village of Hsiao T'un used to scrape off the strange symbols from the bones because they didn't want people to know the origins of the Chinese language.

7. _____ Fortunately, a scholar in Peking bought a bone for medicine and recognized a symbol that had not been scraped off.

8. _____ The bones provided proof that the Chinese language was about a thousand years old.

9. _____ In reality, the "dragon bones" were from cattle and turtles.

10. _____ These bones had been used in ages past in special rituals for the purpose of answering questions about the future.

Talking It Over

In small groups, discuss the following questions below and on the next page.

1. In lines 21–22, the authors mention "a small coincidence" that was eventually to provide an important key to Chinese history. What is this coincidence?

2. Do you think that the origins of the Chinese language would have been discovered some day even without this coincidence? Why or why not? Do you believe that this coincidence occurred simply by chance?
3. Have you heard of any other legends or mysteries from the past that people used to laugh at but that were later discovered to be true?
4. Do North Americans have the same attitude toward tradition and history as the people in your culture? Explain.

Summarizing an Article

Write a summary of the selection "It All Started with Dragon Bones," using these guidelines.

1. Write a one-sentence thesis statement describing the main point of the article. To do this, mention the problem described at the beginning and the resolution to it.
2. Go back to the middle of the article and tell the story that supports the author's thesis in three to five sentences.
3. Finish with a brief concluding sentence. One way of doing this is to start out *In conclusion* (or *Thus, Therefore,* or *In this way*) and then repeat the main point in different words and shorter form.

Stories Behind Words: Words with Origins in Mythology

The article describes some Chinese scholars as being "*tantalized* by the mysterious dragon bone hieroglyphics." *Tantalized* is one of many English words that have their origins in myths and legends of the past (in this case, Greek and Roman ones). The meaning of the verb *tantalize* is a very particular one: "to promise or show something desirable to a person and then take it away; to tease by arousing hope." Many (but not all) English dictionaries give you a brief indication of a word's origins in brackets before or after the explanation of the meaning. For *tantalize* the following explanation is given: [>Tantalus]. This means that you should look up the name *Tantalus* to find out the word's origins, and if you do, you will find out that in Greek mythology, Tantalus was a king who was punished in the lower world with eternal hunger and thirst; he was put up to his chin in water that always moved away when he tried to drink it and with fruit on branches above him placed just a little bit out of his reach. Can you see why his name was changed into a verb meaning "to tease or torment by arousing desire"?

Another example is the word *siren,* familiar to us as the mechanical device that makes such an alarming sound when police cars, ambulances, or fire engines approach. This word also has its origins in Greek mythology. The traveler Odysseus (Ulysses to the Romans) made his men plug their ears so that they wouldn't hear the dangerous voices of the *sirens,* creatures who were half bird and half woman and who lured sailors to their deaths on sharp rocks. So the word came to be associated both with a loud sound and with danger! Of course, it also has another meaning when referring to a woman, and this one is also related to the legend. Similarly, when someone speaks of a "*jovial* mood" or a "*herculean*

In Greek mythology, Tantalus was punished by having to suffer eternal hunger and thirst while food and water were in sight.

effort," he or she is using words with origins in mythology. Look these words up to find their meaning and relationship to myths.

Many common words, such as the names for the days of the week and the months of the year, also come from mythology. *Wednesday* derives from the ancient Norse king of the gods, Woden, and *Thursday* was originally *Thor's day,* in honor of Thor, the god of thunder. Do you know which of the days of the week was named in honor of a Roman god? There is also a planet named for him. Another one of the planets is named for the Roman god of war because it is red, and one of the months is named for him too. Can you guess which one? In fact, all the planets, except the one we live on, bear names that come from Roman mythology, including the planet that is farthest away from the sun and for that reason was called after the Roman god of the dead. This god has also given his name to one of the chemical elements. Do you know what his name is? Several other elements have names that come from mythology, too.

It seems that myths and legends live on in the English language.

Talking It Over

In small groups, discuss the following questions.

1. What are the days of the week called in the language of your culture? Do their names relate to any myths or legends?
2. What about the names of the months, the planets, and the chemical elements?
3. Can you think of any ways that your language and culture preserve the ancient beliefs of your ancestors? Explain.

Finding Out More About Mysterious Phenomena

In small groups, prepare a brief report about one of the following unsolved mysteries. Each person should use a different source (book or magazine article). You should discuss in class beforehand how to find the information in the library. The first person will explain what the phenomenon is; then the others will read in turn a small section about it from their book or article.

1. the Yeti, or Abominable Snowman
2. UFOs
3. the Loch Ness monster
4. werewolves
5. the Lost Continent of Atlantis
6. ESP
7. the Bermuda Triangle
8. Count Dracula
9. The *Llorona* of Mexico
10. black holes

Answering Riddles

A riddle is a minimystery or little puzzle in the form of a question asked in such a way that it requires some cleverness to answer it. Often you must look at the whole question in a manner that is not at first obvious. Riddles are popular in most cultures and are often humorous. Some are silly and some are sophisticated, but they can all be fun if you are in the mood to relax and play with words and ideas. Read the following riddles. They all refer to letters of the alphabet and to the dictionary. The answer is given for the first one; the answers to the others are listed on the bottom of the next page. Tell which answer corresponds to each of the riddles.

example: I occur once in every minute, twice in every moment, but not once in a hundred thousand years. What am I?

The letter *m*.

RIDDLES

1. Why is the letter *e* lazy?

2. What is the end of everything?

3. What begins with a *t*, ends with a *t*, and has *t* in it?

4. Why is an island like the letter *t*?

5. What four letters frighten a thief?

6. Which is easier to spell, seventeen or eighteen?

7. Why is *smiles* the longest word in the dictionary?

8. Where does Thursday come before Wednesday?

9. What's the definition of *minimum*?

Answers

Tell which of the following is the answer to each of the riddles.

a. Because it is in the middle of *water*.
b. In the dictionary.
c. Because it is always in *bed*.
d. A teapot.
e. Because there is a *mile* in between its first and last letter.
f. "A small mother."
g. The letter "g."
h. 17 (Seventeen) because it is spelled with more "ease" (*e*'s).
i. O-I-C-U!

Solutions are on page 342.

WHAT DO YOU THINK?

The Secret of Firewalking

The firewalkers of Fiji, Hawaii, and the Cook Islands walk over blazing hot coals without flinching. When they come out of the fire, there is no sign of burns or blisters on their feet. Yet this is not always the case. One firewalker in the 1940s who had not prepared properly "spiritually and mentally" was so badly injured that both legs had to be amputated. What do you think is the secret of firewalking? What do you think is the "proper" preparation? What do people gain by accomplishing something like this? Have you heard of similar things in other cultures?

Firewalking is said to be a self-empowering experience.

CHAPTER five

Transitions

in this chapter

Human life is a series of transitions, both ordinary and extraordinary. The first selection in this chapter deals with the normal stages of life—childhood, youth, maturity, old age—and how individuals can adjust and prepare financially for each stage. The second selection shows how confronting the modern urban environment for the first time causes changes in some people in developing countries. Finally, you can read the story of Inna, a Russian immigrant to Canada who left her family, native land, and culture years ago and now eagerly awaits a visit from her only brother.

Life Cycle Planning

Before You Read

Relating Vocabulary to an Idea

activity

Words and expressions relating to money are important in the following selection. Working in groups, discuss the meaning of these words and expressions and arrange them in order from those indicating the *largest amount of money* to those indicating the *smallest*. (In some cases the exact order may be a matter of opinion.) After you understand the financial terms in the box, read the selection to see how they fit into the different stages of the life cycle.

taking on debt, going into debt	**Most $$**	_____
affluence		_____
the Great Depression of the 1930s		_____
the economic boom		_____
being prosperous		_____
struggling to make ends meet		_____
buying on credit		_____
making investments	**Least $$**	_____

In *The Lifetime Book of Money Management,* author Grace Weinstein writes about the financial aspects of the life cycle. She offers real-life examples of different attitudes toward money and practical tips on how to plan financially for life's transitions, such as the transition from childhood to adolescence, or from adulthood to middle age. In your opinion, what is the most important rule about handling money? Do you think your parents have the same belief?

Life Cycle Planning

- Ed is 22, a senior in college, and worried about what comes next. As a freshman, he saw recruiters flock to campus and graduating seniors choosing among multiple job offers. But times have changed. Many of last year's seniors are still unemployed, and Ed is thinking about graduate school or the Peace Corps as a temporary alternative. One problem, however, is the debt he took on to attend

5

college in the first place; it will be postponed, but not forgiven, if he remains in school. But what then? Will jobs be any easier to find in a few years?

- Sherry, Ed's sister, is 28 and engaged to be married. Raised in a society shaped by affluence and molded by ever-present inflation, Sherry has everything figured out: She'll start married life in an apartment, but she'll have a home of her own, because that's what people do. She'll go into debt to buy that home and to acquire other possessions as well, because that's also what people do. She'll keep working after children are born, so money will never be a problem. Her optimism is as intense as Ed's pessimism.

- Rob is their father. At 53, he is doing well with his own accounting firm. His early years were shaped by his parents' experience of the Depression, but his own youth was lived in the economic boom that followed World War II. He thinks his parents' frugality excessive, can't quite accept the free-spending ways of his daughter's generation, and is worried about what the future holds for both his children. Rob is, in fact, somewhat concerned about his own approaching retirement. He's afraid continually rising prices will make it increasingly difficult to live on a limited income.

- Fred is 82 and recently retired from the consulting work he took on after his first retirement at age 70. He married and became a father during the Great Depression of the 1930s, at a time when he was grateful for a Civil Service desk job instead of the law school he had always wanted but could not afford. His whole life has been shaped by the memories of those years: of his father losing a prosperous business, of neighbors out of work, of his own struggles to make ends meet and raise a growing family. The children are long since grown, and Fred and his wife, Trudy, have been financially comfortable for quite a few years. But old memories are hard to shed. Fred is still reluctant to buy on credit, still scrupulous in keeping track of expenditures. He suspects it's simply too late to change.

- Fred's older brother, Al, is facing a new set of problems. At 86, his health is failing and his wife has developed Alzheimer's disease. Al saved and scrimped all his life, but still isn't sure how he'll pay for the care his wife will need, first at home and then, probably, in a nursing home. And, if he depletes the family's savings on her care, what will happen to him?

The traditional life sequence—school, job, marriage, child-rearing, back to being a couple as children leave the nest, back to being alone as one spouse dies—has its counterpart in monetary terms: Income typically rises gradually from young adulthood through the child-rearing years, remains relatively stable from the middle years until retirement, then stays fixed or actually declines after retirement and in widowhood. Outgo, in the same sequence, starts low, rises for the setting-up-housekeeping expenses of early marriage, declines briefly, rises sharply with the arrival of children and still more sharply with the college years, and falls off abruptly as children leave the nest. The ascending lines, if this pattern were to be graphed, would be roughly parallel—except that the peak of outgo, associated with the growing family, frequently occurs ten full years earlier than the peak of income, which is attained in the middle years.

But this neat sequence is no longer universal. Young adults marry later, or not at all. Married couples often defer parenthood; many do not have children at all. Half of all marriages dissolve long before widowhood. The divorced remarry, form new families, and face the expenses of those new families against the backdrop of continuing expense for the existing family. All of these demographic changes reshape the face of society. They also affect the financial planning of the people involved.

Youngsters start a money-making business at an early age.

Wherever you are in the life cycle, whether you're following a traditional sequence or charting a new path, you can make your money work for you. Whatever your temperament, too, you can manage your money well. Look at the following sequence in terms of the financial tasks you face at different ages.

Financial Planning Throughout the Life Cycle

AGES 13–18

- Learn to budget through handling an allowance.
- Start to save toward future goals.
- Develop financial understanding by working for pay.
- Open a bank account.
- Begin to think about future career options.

AGES 19–24

- Begin to live independently.
- Identify long-range goals.
- Train for career.
- Attain financial independence.
- Build savings toward long-term goals.
- Establish a credit identity.
- Begin to invest.
- Protect belongings with insurance.
- Develop a financial record-keeping system.

AGES 25–40

- Provide for childbearing and child-rearing costs.
- Provide for expanding housing needs.
- Manage increased need for credit.
- Invest for capital growth.
- Expand career goals.
- Build an education fund.
- Add to property insurance to protect possessions.
- Purchase life insurance to provide for a growing family.
- Write a will; name guardian for children.
- Involve every member of the household in financial management.

AGES 41–54

- Continue career development, possibly consider a career change.
- Diversify investments.
- Provide greater income for growing needs.
- Continue to build education funds, provide education for children.
- Consider moving to a larger house, possibly buying a vacation home.
- Begin to develop estate plan.
- Explore retirement goals.
- Review and revise will as necessary.

AGES 55–64

- Evaluate and update retirement plans.
- Shift a portion of assets toward income-producing investments.
- Consider dropping life insurance if no longer needed.
- Think about providing for long-term health care through insurance or savings.
- Decide where to live in the first stage of retirement.
- Meet responsibilities for aging parents.
- Review estate plan.

AGES 65–74

- Reevaluate budget to meet retirement needs.
- Continue investing for growth as well as income.
- Investigate part-time employment and/or volunteer work for retirement.
- Be sure health insurance is in place to supplement Medicare.
- Review will.
- Write a letter of instructions to accompany will.

AGES 75 AND OVER

- Shift most or all investments from growth to income.
- Consider a living will, a health care proxy, and a durable power of attorney for financial affairs.
- Think about ways to reduce taxable estate.
- Consider places to live for the remainder of retirement.
- Share financial management and household management tasks with spouse; tell trusted children about your affairs.

Grace W. Weinstein

After You Read
Comparing Attitudes and Causes

exercise 1

Fill in the blanks to complete the comparison of the five different attitudes toward money given as examples. In the first blank, put the name and age of the appropriate person, and in the second, a cause of his or her attitude. Then answer this question: Which of the five people has an attitude similar to your own?

Ed, 22

Sherry, 28

Rob, 53

Fred, 82

Al, 86

1. _____ is very frugal and reluctant to buy on credit. In part, this attitude is due to memories of_____

2. _____ is worried about carrying a large debt for education that will be postponed but not forgiven. This person worries about the future because_____

3. _____ always scrimped and saved but now is afraid that there will not be enough money to solve a new set of problems due to_____

4. _____ has everything figured out and feels no reluctance about going into debt. One cause for this optimism is a childhood shaped by

   _____

5. _____ is a moderate who can't accept the frugality of the previous generation nor the free-spending ways of the following generation. One reason for this dual attitude is a clear memory of both _____ and_____

Sequencing and Evaluating Tasks

exercise **2**   Put the following financial planning tasks into correct chronological order (time sequence) for accomplishment, with 1 for the youngest age, and 10 for the oldest. Check your sequence with the outline at the end of the article.

A. _____ Explore retirement goals.

B. _____ Establish a credit identity.

C. _____ Write a will.

D. _____ Share financial management and household management tasks with a spouse; tell trusted children about your affairs.

E. _____ Build savings toward long-term goals.

F. _____ Develop financial understanding by working for pay.

G. _____ Decide where to live in the first stage of retirement.

H. _____ Build an education fund.

I. _____ Begin to develop an estate plan.

J. _____ Begin to live independently.

Avoiding "Traps" in Standardized Vocabulary Tests

Many vocabulary tests are similar to the following exercise. Each item is a sentence with a word in bold type, and this is followed by four choices. You must choose the best synonym or definition for the word in bold. Here are some tips to help you avoid the "traps" that often accompany this test design.

1. The choices may include a word that sounds and looks like the word in bold and begins with the same letter. It is usually (but not always) wrong. Remember: Do not choose a word because of its similar sound or appearance. Choose it because its meaning is similar. Three items in the exercise below have a word like this among the choices. Which numbers are they? ____ ____ ____

2. The choices may include an antonym of the word in bold. Because we learn by association, it is easy to fall into this trap and choose a word that means exactly the opposite of the correct one. Five of the items in the exercise below have antonyms among the choices. Which numbers are they? ____ ____ ____ ____ ____

3. The answer key may be in another section or on a different page. Be careful to fill in the correct circle. Sometimes it helps to "say the letter in your mind" until you have filled it in.

exercise: Choose the word or phrase that best explains the meaning of the word in bold type and darken its letter in the answer column. Scan for the word in the article, if necessary, to see it in another context. Words are given in order of appearance.

1. The **recruiters** were looking for applicants with skills in dealing with people.
   a. new employees
   b. members of the board
   c. people who hire others for jobs
   d. people who fire others from jobs

   Answer
   (a) (b) (c) (d)

2. **Inflation** was so high that many felt it wasn't worthwhile to save their money.
   a. the drop in prices
   b. the rise in prices
   c. the change in the stock market
   d. the high expectation of receiving cash

   Answer
   (a) (b) (c) (d)

3. Older people often speak of **frugality** as the greatest virtue when dealing with money.
   a. excess
   b. finality
   c. restraint
   d. generosity

   Answer
   (a) (b) (c) (d)

4. They were **reluctant** to accept the offer without knowing all the details.
   a. anxious
   b. hesitant
   c. interested
   d. relegated

   Answer
   (a) (b) (c) (d)

5. The accountant is **scrupulous** in recording expenses.
   a. careful
   b. reckless
   c. obstinate
   d. disheartened

   Answer
   (a) (b) (c) (d)

6. The manager often talks with her **counterpart** in the branch office in Europe.
   a. one who acts as a rival or enemy
   b. one who substitutes for another
   c. person or thing closely resembling another
   d. person or thing related to accounting programs

   Answer
   (a) (b) (c) (d)

7. The Watsons decided to **defer** their plans for a vacation.
   a. transfer
   b. regret
   c. relish
   d. postpone

   Answer
   (a) (b) (c) (d)

8. The **sequence** of events was different from what we expected.
   a. sequel
   b. meaning
   c. understanding
   d. order

   Answer
   (a) (b) (c) (d)

Vocabulary Analysis: The Suffix *-hood*

Several words ending in *-hood* are used for different stages of the life cycle: *motherhood, fatherhood, childhood,* for example. By thinking about the meaning of these words, what can you infer about the meaning of the suffix *-hood*? Scan the article for three other words ending in *-hood,* write them down, and explain their meanings. Then guess at the meanings of the two other words listed as 4 and 5 and use each one in a sentence.

1. _____ meaning:_____

2. _____ meaning:_____

3. _____ meaning:_____

4. *manhood* sentence:_____

5. *sisterhood* sentence:_____

Talking It Over

In small groups, discuss the following questions.

1. According to the selection, what is the traditional life sequence of North Americans? How does this relate to income and expenditures?
2. What does the author mean when she says that children "leave the nest"? How does this affect the household's finances?
3. Is the life sequence in your culture similar or different? Explain.
4. What are some of the recent changes in life sequence that are reshaping "the face of society"? Are these changes occurring in your culture too? Why or why not?

Attitudes can often be inferred by looking at possessions. What can you infer about someone's attitude toward money by looking at his or her car?

Conversations in Malaysia

Before You Read
Taking Note of the Change of Speakers

exercise

Although the title uses the word *conversations*, the following selection is really an *interview*. In what way is an interview different from a conversation? While reading, it is important to take note of which person is speaking in each section. How can you tell when the speaker changes? Sometimes the author tells you directly. Sometimes you get clues from the punctuation, the paragraph divisions, or simply the context. Sometimes the people speaking have different styles of speech. V. S. Naipaul speaks perfect English, for example, while Shafi makes certain grammar mistakes.

Skim the selection and note each time the speaker changes. Be prepared to explain how you know in each case. Then complete this statement by circling the correct number: In "Conversations in Malaysia," the number of "paragraphs" spoken by Shafi is 9   14   18   25.

The following selection is taken from the book *Among the Believers: An Islamic Journey* by V. S. Naipaul, one of the most renowned writers of English of our times. It is his interview of Shafi, a young Muslim man in Kuala Lumpur, the capital city of Malaysia. Shafi used to live in a village and finds that life in the big city is very different. Think for a moment about what it would be like to move from a very small village to a modern city. What aspects of the urban lifestyle do you imagine would appeal to him? Which aspects would disturb him or cause him trouble? As you read, try to understand Shafi's point of view. At the same time, notice what elements in his background would give him this point of view.

Conversations in Malaysia

Shafi worked for the Muslim cause. He didn't wear Arab clothes. But he understood the young men who did. Shafi had come to Kuala Lumpur from a village in the north. The disturbance of the move was still with him.

Shafi said: "When I was in the village the atmosphere is entirely
5   different. You come out of the village. You see all the bright lights, you begin to sense the materialistic civilization around you. And I forgot about my religion and my commitments—in the sense that you had to pray. But not to the extent of going out and doing nasty things like taking girls and drinking and gambling and drugs. I didn't lose my faith. I simply forgot to
10   pray, forgot responsibilities. Just losing myself. I got nothing firm in my framework. I just floating around and didn't know my direction."

I said, "Where did you live when you came to Kuala Lumpur?"

He didn't give a straight answer. At this early stage in our conversation concreteness didn't come easily to him. He said, "I was living in a suburb where I am exposed to materialistic civilization to which I had never been exposed before. Boys and girls can go out together. You are free from family control. You are free from society who normally criticize you in a village when you do something bad. You take a goat, a cow, a buffalo—somewhere where the goat is being tied up all the time—and you release that goat in a bunch of other animals: The goat would just roam anywhere he want to go without any strings."

"Is that bad for the goat?"

"I think the goat would be very happy to roam free. But for me I don't think that would be good. If goat had brains, I would want to say, 'Why do you want to roam about when you are tied and being fed by your master and looked after? Why do you want to roam about?'"

I said, "But I want to roam about."

"What do you mean by being free? Freedom for me is not something that you can roam anywhere you want. Freedom must be within the definition of a certain framework. Because I don't think we are able to run around and get everything. That freedom means nothing. You must really frame yourself where you want to go and what you want to do."

"But didn't you know what you wanted to do when you came to Kuala Lumpur?"

"The primary aim was education. That was a framework. But the conflict of this freedom and the primary aim is there, and I consider this is the problem I faced and many of my friends face."

"Other people in other countries face the same problem."

Shafi said, "Do they face the same restrictions of family life as I do?"

"What restrictions?"

"Religious restrictions. You have that frame with you. Religious tradition, family life, the society, the village community. Then you come into the city, where people are running, people are free. The values contradict.

"You see, in the village where I was brought up we have the bare minimum. We have rice to eat, house to live. We didn't go begging. In the city you can buy a lunch at ten dollars (Malaysian dollars, $2.20 to the American). Or in a stall you can have a lunch for fifty cents. That excess of nine-fifty which the city dwellers spend will be spent by us on other purposes. To us, with our framework and tradition and religion, that is excessiveness.

Rural Malyasia rice fields

"Sometimes my wife feels that we should go back to the village, and I also feel the same. Not running away from the modern world, but trying to live a simpler, more meaningful life than coming to the city, where you have lots of waste and lots of things that is not real probably. You are not honest to yourself if you can spend fifty cents and keep yourself from hunger, but instead spend ten dollars.

"I will tell you about waste. Recently the government built a skating rink. After three months they demolished it because a highway going to be built over it. They are building big roads and highways across the villages. And whose lorries are passing by to collect the produce of the poor and to dump the products that is manufactured by the rich at an exorbitant price—colour TVs, refrigerators, air conditioners, transistor radios?"

"Don't people want those things?"

"In the end they are going to use the colour TVs—which the people enjoy—to advertise products to draw people into wasteful living."

"Village life—wouldn't you say it is dull for most people?"

"The village? It's simple. It's devoid of—what shall I say?—waste-fulness. You shouldn't waste. You don't have to rush for things. My point about going back to the *kampong* is to stay with the community and not to run away from development. The society is well knit. If someone passed away there is an alarm in the *kampong,* where most of us would know who passed away and when he is going to be buried, what is the cause of death, and what happened to the next of kin—are they around? It's not polluted in the village. Physical pollution, mental, social."

"Social pollution?"

The capital city of Kuala Lampur, Malyasia

"Something that contradicts our customs and traditions. A man cannot walk with a woman who doesn't belong to his family in the *kampong*. It is
80 forbidden."

"Why is it wrong?"

"The very essence of human respect and dignity comes from an honourable relationship of man and woman. You must have a law to protect the unit of your society. You need your family to be protected.
85 When the girls come from the villages to Kuala Lumpur, they don't want to be protected by the law."

V. S. Naipaul

After You Read
Finding Support for Main Ideas

Check the statement in each group that expresses one of Shafi's ideas. (Remember: You are looking for Shafi's ideas, not those of the author.) Then find at least two examples in the reading that support or illustrate that idea.

1. _____ City life is better than village life because it gives more freedom.

_____ City life is not as good as village life because it lacks structure.

2. _____ People in the city are wasteful.

_____ People in the village are dull.

3. _____ The city offers many wonderful products—color TVs, refrigerators, and so on—that improve people's lives.

4. _____ The village (*kampong*) offers a sense of community that improves people's lives.

Paraphrasing What You've Read

exercise **2**   Explain the following opinions here and on the next page taken from the selection in a clear and concise manner and in your own words.

1. "He didn't give a straight answer. At this early stage in our conversation concreteness didn't come easily to him."

_____

_____

_____

_____

_____

2. "You take a goat, a cow, a buffalo—somewhere where the goat is being tied up all the time—and you release that goat in a bunch of other animals: The goat would just roam anywhere he want to go without any strings."

_____

_____

_____

_____

_____

3. "In the end they are going to use the colour TVs—which the people enjoy—to advertise products to draw people into wasteful living."

_____

_____

_____

_____

_____

4. "It's not polluted in the village. Physical pollution, mental, social."

_____

_____

_____

_____

Talking It Over

In small groups, discuss the following questions.

1. In your opinion, why does Shafi have problems adjusting to city life?
2. Do you agree with Shafi's ideas about the city and the village or not? In which place would you live more happily? Explain.
3. When Shafi gives an example of the excesses of city life, he talks about the difference between a lunch of ten dollars and one of fifty cents. He speaks as if the nine dollars and fifty cents were simply thrown away and would not benefit anyone in any way. What might an urban person argue in defense of the ten-dollar lunch?

Interviewing a Classmate

Select a partner and interview him or her about some important transition that you each have made (for example, a move from one country to another, a change of lifestyle, a change of job, a marriage). Before you start, decide on four or five questions. Try to focus on how the other person's point of view has changed or is changing because of the transition. Take notes and be prepared to hand them in or read them to the class.

Some Differences Between British and American English

Most people learn either the British or American form of English. Canadians speak in their own style, which contains some elements in common with each of the others. Could you tell which type was being used by the author and the young man he interviewed in Malaysia? Two words show us immediately that they are using the British form of English: _lorries_ in line 61 and _honourable_ in line 83. Americans do not use the word _lorry,_ and many of them would not even know what it means; instead they say _truck. Honourable_ would be spelled _honorable_—without the _u_—by an American.

exercise 3   How good are you at spotting differences in vocabulary and spelling between the two types of English? Do you know which of the two types has retained the longer, more old-fashioned way of spelling certain words and which one now spells them in a shorter way?

Test your skill at making this distinction by guessing which of the words in the following pairs is American and which is British.

VOCABULARY	SPELLING
1. subway/underground	1. programme/program
2. (electric) flex/cord	2. cheque/check
3. stove/cooker	3. color/colour
4. (car) hood/bonnet	4. catalogue/catalog
5. flashlight/torch	5. behavior/behaviour

WHAT DO YOU THINK?

The Refugee Problem

In 1975, there were 2.5 million refugees in the world. Today there are over 20 million. The war in the former Yugoslavia alone has left more than 3.7 million displaced persons. Whether it be for reasons of war, economics, political persecution, or changes in borders, the world is filled with mass migrations of refugees. In your opinion, what is the obligation of stable and prosperous countries toward these refugees? How many should be allowed to enter prosperous nations? Which refugees should be accepted and which ones turned away?

Bosnian Serb refugees expelled from their homes

Before You Read
Selecting Adjectives to Fit the Context

 Well-chosen adjectives bring the characters and setting of a story to life. Adjectives from the story are given in the list, along with their definitions. Fill in the blanks with the appropriate adjectives. If you cannot guess a word from its definition and context, scan the story for it.

ADJECTIVE	DEFINITION
exhausted	very, very tired, completely fatigued
exquisite	unusually beautiful and fine
herculean	very difficult (like the tasks of Hercules)
inebriated	drunk, intoxicated by alcohol or emotion
indefatigable	untiring, incapable of fatigue
mundane	ordinary, without special meaning
marshy	swampy, soft and wet like a swamp or marsh
prosaic	dull, unimaginative, like prose (instead of poetry)
rejuvenated	brought back to youth, made young again
shabby	worn out, poor, dilapidated

1. Grandma would put on her blue checkered apron and seem instantly
   _rejuvenated_____.

2. Their _____ , sooty kitchen suddenly became
   bright and cheerful.

3. The stove would become the airport in the "_____ forest."

4. There was an amber brooch, perfumes, books, wooden spoons, and a small
   _____ box from Boris.

5. Grisha was _____ by these bright photographs
   and looked at his sister with admiration.

6. Grisha took childish pleasure in everything and was very enthusiastic. He
   was _____ in his activity.

7. The mountain of goods on the living room floor grew . . . but the shopping list hardly got shorter. . . . It was a _____ task.

8. She had expected a very significant moment in her life—the family reunion—and it had turned out to be very _____, even _____.

9. Suddenly Inna felt _____.

Predicting the Action

As you read this story, try to think ahead of the plot by asking yourself, "What will happen next?" Predicting action helps comprehension. The text will be interrupted in a few places and you will be asked questions to guide your predictions. The story begins with a *flashback,* the description of a scene that happened earlier, before the time of the story. Skim lines 1–24. Then tell when the flashback occurred to Inna, the main character. Was it in her childhood, her youth, or her adulthood?

What is it like to leave your home and move to another country? Many people go through this transition. They often speak of being "uprooted," like a tree that has been transplanted into new ground.

The following story was written by a Russian who left her native country and immigrated to western Canada. It describes the visit to a Russian-Canadian woman from her brother Grisha at a time when goods and commodities were very difficult to obtain in Russia. The situation has changed and many Russians now say, "Back then we had money, but there was nothing to buy; today there is plenty to buy, but we have no money!" In either case, there is a great difference in the material standard of living between Russia and Canada. In your opinion, what problems can this cause between relatives living in the two countries? Read the story to see if this creates problems for Inna and her brother Grisha.

*Grisha Has Arrived**

Whenever Grisha was expected in the apartment on Novosibirskaya Street, Babushka made some pirozhki filled with meat and cabbage.[†] She would put on her blue checkered apron and seem instantly rejuvenated.

---

*The story has been shortened but not changed in any other way.
†Two Russian words are used in this sentence, *Babushka* (Grandmother) and *pirozhki* (meat pies), which many English speakers know and others would guess from the context. Later in the story, the Russian word *dacha* (country house) is used.

Little Inna would seal these pirozhki on a wooden board while Babushka presided over the boiling oil. Their shabby, sooty kitchen suddenly became bright and cheerful. In this way Grisha's arrival became forever linked to an expectation of joyful festivity.

He would rush in, thin and pale. At once the long hallway, dimly lit by a single electric bulb, was filled with lively bustle. They played in the kitchen. It was warmer there. Babushka covered the large stove with an oilcloth. The stove would become the airport in the "marshy forest." Grisha made paper airplanes and launched them skillfully from the stove towards the electric light. The small, white airplanes briefly shone against the soot-covered ceiling and fell into the dark space near the door.

Grisha would bring his tin soldiers. He was a guerrilla leader and little Inna was a doctor. They always played the same war game. Inna's military hospital was located in Babushka's room. Could Inna ever forget this narrow room with the fireplace and the photograph of a young woman on the dressing table? There, among various treasures with which Inna was not allowed to play, was a carved box with letters.

Later she would read these yellowed sheets which Babushka had preserved so carefully. They were letters from her mother who had died in a labour camp. Inna could not remember her parents. She had been raised by Babushka, while Grisha had been adopted by relatives of their father.

Memory is a strange thing! In its vast foggy valleys one's past is kept untouched. Now, when forty-two-year-old Inna was on the way to the airport to meet her brother coming from Moscow, the smell of the swamp grass suddenly released distant memories of frying pirozhki, of childhood, of bliss. . . .

> **Prediction**   A conflict does not always mean a problem. Sometimes it is just a change. In this case the conflict that begins the story is the arrival of Grisha. In the flashback, what do we learn of Inna and Grisha's family? Why is he especially important to Inna? What do you think she expects from his visit? Finish this statement to predict what happens next: *When Inna sees Grisha she will be (a) happy to see he has not changed at all (b) surprised to see he is dressed in shabby clothes   (c) sad to find he is very depressed.*

On the stairs of the airport Inna came face to face with Grisha, but did not recognize him at first. His hair had gone completely grey and he seemed shorter. She was struck at once by how badly he was dressed. He was wearing a brown raincoat fit only for picking mushrooms. His worn out shoes were of an indefinable colour. Grisha was carrying a small suitcase.

They embraced, kissed, and walked slowly to her car. Grisha was telling her excitedly about the flight across the ocean, about the last days before departure, how frightened he had been that he might fall ill and be unable to come.

Inna was listening to Grisha happily and distractedly. She realized that he must be tired from lack of sleep, but why this pathetic shabbiness? Why would Yelena have allowed him to leave home in this Godforsaken state? They had a marvellous apartment and dacha. Both were working, and Grisha earned substantial amounts from translations.

As though he had read her mind, Grisha said: "Do you know, all our acquaintances advised me to travel in my oldest clothes so that I could discard them without regret here. They said that you, my sister, anyway would clothe me and Yelena and our children."

Maybe it was because she had no family of her own that Inna was very attached to Grisha's children. She gave them expensive presents and spoiled them, especially his oldest daughter, Lyuba. Inna tolerated Yelena, no more than that. Her relationship with her brother's wife had gone wrong from the very beginning. Probably deep down Inna envied Yelena. . . .

They soon reached home. Inna put a bowl with fruit on the table and a bottle of French wine which she had bought yesterday to welcome Grisha.

Grisha opened his suitcase and brought out presents from himself and Yelena, from Lyuba and Yura who had already had families of their own,

Russian immigrants in conversation at an American Café

and from Inna's numerous friends and relatives. There was an amber brooch, perfumes, books, wooden spoons, and a small exquisite box from Boris. He had put a sheet of paper with comical verses for Inna's birthday into the box. How many years had passed since she had seen his familiar bold handwriting?

Inna had been a young girl in Moscow when she had become involved with Boris, who was much older. On various occasions he had left his wife to move in with Inna. At other times he had left her to return to his family. Inna had been his friend, his mistress, his graduate student, and eventually his co-worker in the laboratory. This pattern of life had continued up to the time of her leaving Moscow.

Brother and sister sat on the balcony, smoking and talking almost till dawn. From the twelfth floor there was a view over Edmonton and the dark river valley spanned by a bridge. Below them the street lights shone moistly.

> **Prediction**   Why did Grisha arrive in shabby clothing? What do we find out about Inna's relationship with Grisha's wife and children? What do we find out about Boris? Finish this statement to predict what happens next: *Grisha will show a great interest in his sister's* (a) *thoughts and feelings* (b) *work and ambitions* (c) *possessions and appliances.*

Grisha walked about the apartment inspecting Inna's habitation. For a while, he remained in the bedroom where, beside the bed, there was a large desk with a computer. On the chest of drawers, he found their mother's faded photograph in its walnut frame, that had stood in Babushka's room. In the kitchen, he wanted to know how the dishwasher worked and opened the door to the microwave oven.

Inna made a bed for Grisha on the living room sofa. The following morning she got up as early as usual. She was tired from lack of sleep and took two Tylenol tablets before going into the kitchen to prepare breakfast. Grisha was up already and was doing yoga exercises on the balcony.

After breakfast they went for a walk and then to the university. Inna showed Grisha her laboratory. As it was a holiday, the university campus was deserted. They ate in a small Chinese restaurant. The evening was spent sitting on the balcony. Inna brought out albums with photographs taken on various trips; one to France and Spain, another to the Scandinavian countries, still another to South America, and finally one to Indonesia and Hong Kong.

Grisha was inebriated by these bright photographs and looked at his sister with admiration.

They were drinking tea with cake when Grisha suddenly asked:

"How much does a Lada cost here?"

"I don't know, perhaps around five thousand or maybe seven. Why do you want to know?" Inna was very surprised.

"You see, it can be paid for here, and Yura would be able to get it in Moscow. Many people buy them in this way for their relatives."

"Really? They buy a whole car?"

"Of course, they can't buy it in pieces, can they?" Grisha started laughing.

The magnitude of his expectations and naive faith in her financial prowess struck Inna like a splash of cold water. All her achievements, of which she had been so proud only yesterday, were reduced to rubble and lost their significance.

The woman in the rocking chair was suddenly middle-aged and lonely.

"For myself, I bought a secondhand car and that was almost seven years ago."

Inna cut herself short. In the depth of Grisha's eyes as in two dark mirrors she saw herself as she must have appeared to him—a rich world traveller.

Prediction   What do we learn about Inna's work and lifestyle? What impresses Grisha? Why does Inna suddenly feel old and lonely? Finish this statement to predict what happens next: *Inna and her brother will spend a lot of their time*   (a) *talking*   (b) *travelling*   (c) *shopping*.

Every morning Grisha got up early and did yoga exercises frantically. Then he went to the swimming pool. The highrise building in which Inna lived had a sauna and whirlpool in the basement. Grisha took childish pleasure in everything and was very enthusiastic. He was indefatigable. Inna took a vacation in order to devote herself completely to her brother.

She showed him the sports complex which belonged to the university. They pushed a shopping cart around the superstore which was the size of an airplane hangar. They bought groceries and Grisha had his picture taken against a backdrop of mountains of fruits and vegetables and colourful cans of cat food.

They spent a whole day at West Edmonton Mall, the world-famous shopping centre. They wandered through the shops, inspected Fantasyland, and, while there, took a trip in a submarine. They had lunch in a French café.

The mountain of goods on the livingroom floor grew and threatened to become Mt. Everest, but the shopping list hardly got shorter. A sheepskin coat for Lyuba, high winter boots for Yura's wife, a waterproof coat for Yelena, a videotape recorder, some kind of rings for the camera of the sister of Lyuba's husband, a Japanese walkman radio for Yura and a mouthpiece for a trumpet belonging to some person unknown to her. It was a herculean task.

Grisha had excellent taste and an unfailing sense for what was beautiful and very expensive. He said to Inna: "We must buy this blouse for Lyuba." The blouse was certainly unusually pretty. Inna would have bought it for herself if it had been on sale.

Goodness, how she had waited for him, her only brother! She would have liked to complain to him of her loneliness, the fact that her job was only a temporary five-year contract, and that her future looked extremely uncertain. After all was said and done, the trips that she had taken to conferences and seminars were all that she possessed.

His visit lasted over two weeks and, not counting the first evening, when they had sat on the balcony and smoked, there had not been a free moment when they could have had a heart-to-heart talk. She wondered if such a talk was even possible. She had expected a very significant moment in her life—the family reunion—and it had turned out to be very prosaic, even mundane.

The gap between brother and sister was widening at an alarming rate. His trip gradually became transformed into a giant shopping expedition to North America. Each day spent wandering through stores moved them further apart into mutual incomprehension.

Once Inna took Grisha to dinner with Lyova who (amazing coincidence!) had been Grisha's fellow pupil in the eighth grade of Moscow school #214. Inna's and Grisha's arrival was eagerly awaited in the elegant two-storey house overlooking the ravine. Other guests were drinking cocktails on the wooden veranda surrounded by creepers. Later on, there was a barbecue on the lawn. Grisha was enthusiastic about the barbecued meat, which he had never tasted before. For dessert, Lyova's wife brought out a basket carved out of a pineapple filled with large, fresh strawberries.

Grisha soaked up all this like a sponge. He committed it to memory, imagining how he would relate every minute detail in Moscow. To Grisha, Inna's new life must seem just such a fragrant pineapple-strawberry basket, which only lacked immortality to be perfect.

Suddenly Inna felt exhausted. She felt that she was participating in some sort of farce, that she was on stage and Grisha was viewing her from the back of a hall without being able to hear her. The loneliness became unbearable.

> **Prediction** How do Inna and Grisha spend their time together? Do you think they are enjoying themselves at Lyova's party? Why or why not? Finish this statement to predict what happens next: *Before Grisha leaves, Inna will* (a) *have a heart-to-heart talk with him about her situation* (b) *get angry with him about his selfishness* (c) *remain silent about her true feelings.*

170
People were laughing on the veranda. In the house Lyova demonstrated his new stereo system with the compact disk player to Grisha. Through the open window Inna could see Grisha's forced smile and the sweat droplets on his forehead. She felt sorry for him and wanted more than anything for him to leave as soon as possible.

175
She went down from the veranda and walked along the path to the ravine. The air smelt fresh and moist. From that angle her friend's brightly lit house seemed even grander.

"I wonder how Boris would have behaved?" she thought. "Was it possible that he, too . . . ?"

"Experience determines consciousness." Inna remembered the long-forgotten Marxist formula.

180
During the last days before leaving, Grisha could talk only of the customs inspection in Moscow. He flew off on July 15th.

"Next time I will bring Yelena," Grisha promised when leaving.

From the airport, Inna drove straight to work. She was sad and felt like crying. The small white airplane of her childhood vanished in the empty

185
blue sky.

Tanya Filanovsky

After You Read
Talking It Over

In small groups, discuss the questions here and on the next page.

1. What went wrong with Grisha's visit to his sister Inna?
2. Do you think that Inna should buy a car for Grisha's son Yura? Why or why not?

3. What quotation of Karl Marx does Inna remember at the end of the story? Why does it seem important to her? What do you think of it?
4. The story begins and ends with the image of an airplane. What does the airplane represent in Inna's memory of childhood? What does the airplane represent at the end?
5. Which is more important to you: family feeling or material success? In your opinion, why are these two aspects of life often in conflict?

Noticing Canadian and American Spelling Differences

Look at the differences described on page 127 between American and British spelling. Americans would write *labor camp, color, center, colorful*. How are these words spelled in Tanya Filanovsky's story that was translated by a Canadian?

1. labor camp _____
2. gray _____
3. color _____

4. center _____
5. colorful _____

Summarizing the Story

Write a summary (from six to nine sentences) of the story "Grisha Has Arrived," following these guidelines.

1. Identify the two main characters and setting, and state the conflict.* (1–2 sentences)
2. Describe the complication, in this case involving Grisha's actions and Inna's needs and feelings. (2–3 sentences)
3. Describe the climax that occurs at Lyova's party and brings a new insight (way of thinking) to Inna. (1–2 sentences)
4. State the resolution at the end. (1–2 sentences)

An Imaginary Interview with Grisha

Work with a partner. One of you plays the role of Grisha, who is visiting your city. The other one plays the role of a radio commentator interviewing Grisha with the following questions. After you finish, the radio commentator may be asked to tell the class about Grisha's impressions.

1. How are things with your wife and children in Russia now?
2. Why have you come here to visit?
3. What has impressed you most about our city?
4. What is your greatest wish?

_____

*To review the meanings of *setting, conflict, complication, climax,* and *resolution,* see page 36.

CHAPTER SIX

The Mind

in this chapter

Many scientists speak of the mind as the "new frontier," the most dynamic area of research. The first selection discusses some amazing results of psychologists who have been studying people with an extraordinary ability to remember or memorize. Next, you explore the actual physical repository of the mind, the human brain. Some electrical and chemical aspects of the brain's functions are described. Then Edgar Allan Poe provides an inside look at the disordered and diseased mind of a madman. Finally, there is a timed reading about a very unusual American man.

SELECTION **one**
A Memory for All Seasonings

Before You Read
Anticipating the Reading

Before beginning to read an article, it's helpful to try to anticipate what it will be about and determine what associations you have with the topic.

1. When you think of a person with an extraordinary memory, what is the first question that comes to your mind?

   _____

   _____

2. Is there something practical you might learn from this reading?

   _____

   _____

3. What is the earliest distinct event in your life that you can remember?

   _____

   _____

   _____

4. Approximately how old were you when it occurred?

   _____

   _____

Compare your first memory (described in Exercise 1) with those of your class-mates. When you read the article, you will find out how these memories compare with the earliest memory of John Conrad, a young man with an extraordinary memory. You may also learn the answers to your questions about memory.

Memory is one of the most important functions of the mind. Without our memories, we would have no identity. The following article is about a *mnemonist,* a person with an extraordinary power to remember. The title includes a *pun,* a form of humor based on a play on words. The usual phrase to describe something constant and dependable is "for all seasons"; here the phrase is changed to "for all *seasonings.*" (*Seasonings* is another word for spices, such as salt, pepper, and curry.) What hint does this give you about the mnemonist? (Early in the article you will find out.)

A Memory for All Seasonings

One evening two years ago, Peter Polson, a member of the psychology department at the University of Colorado, took his son and daughter to dinner at Bananas, a fashionable restaurant in Boulder. When the waiter took their orders, Polson noticed that the young man didn't write anything down. He just listened, made small talk, told them that his name was John Conrad, and left. Polson didn't think this was exceptional: There were, after all, only three of them at the table. Yet he found himself watching Conrad closely when he returned to take the orders at a nearby table of eight. Again the waiter listened, chatted, and wrote nothing down. When he brought Polson and his children their dinners, the professor couldn't resist introducing himself and telling Conrad that he'd been observing him.

The young man was pleased. He wanted customers to notice that, unlike other waiters, he didn't use a pen and paper. Sometimes, when they did notice, they left him quite a large tip. He had once handled a table of nineteen complete dinner orders without a single error. At Bananas, a party of nineteen (a bill of roughly $200) would normally leave the waiter a $35 tip. They had left Conrad $85.

Polson was impressed enough to ask the waiter whether he would like to come to the university's psychology lab and let them run some tests on him. Anders Ericsson, a young Swedish psychologist recently involved in memory research, would be joining the university faculty soon, and

Waiters who don't have John Conrad's wonderful memory skills have to use pencil and paper.

Polson thought that he would be interested in exploring memory methods with the waiter. Conrad said he would be glad to cooperate. He was always on the lookout for ways to increase his income, and Polson told him he would receive $5 an hour to be a guinea pig.

Conrad, of course, was not the first person with an extraordinary memory to attract attention from researchers. Alexander R. Luria, the distinguished Soviet psychologist, studied a Russian newspaper reporter named Shereshevskii for many years and wrote about him in *The Mind of a Mnemonist* (Basic Books, 1968). Luria says that Shereshevskii was able to hear a series of fifty words spoken once and recite them back in perfect order fifteen years later. Another famous example of extraordinary memory, the conductor Arturo Toscanini, was known to have memorized every note for every instrument in 250 symphonies and 100 operas.

For decades the common belief among psychologists was that memory was a fixed quantity; an exceptional memory, or a poor one, was something with which a person was born.

This point of view has come under attack in recent years; expert memory is no longer universally considered the exclusive gift of the genius, or the abnormal. "People with astonishing memory for pictures, musical scores, chess positions, business transactions, dramatic scripts, or faces are by no means unique," wrote Cornell psychologist Ulric Neisser in *Memory Observed* (1981). "They may not even be very rare." Some university researchers, including Polson and Ericsson, go a step further than Neisser. They believe that there are no physiological differences at all between the memory of a Shereshevskii or a Toscanini and that of the average person. The only real difference, they believe, is that Toscanini trained his memory, exercised it regularly, and wanted to improve it.

Like many people with his capacity to remember, Toscanini may also have used memory tricks called mnemonics. Shereshevskii, for example, employed a technique known as *loci*. As soon as he heard a series of words, he mentally "distributed" them along Gorky Street in Moscow. If one of the words was "orange," he might visualize a man stepping on an orange at a precise location on the familiar street. Later, in order to retrieve "orange," he would take an imaginary walk down Gorky Street and see the image from which it could easily be recalled. Did the waiter at Bananas have such a system? What was his secret?

John Conrad would be the subject of Anders Ericsson's second in-depth study of the machinations of memory. As a research associate at Carnegie-Mellon University in Pittsburgh, Ericsson had spent the previous three years working with William Chase on an extensive study of Steve

"Memorize this, it's your New Year's resolutions.

Faloon, an undergraduate whose memory and intellectual skills were considered average. When Ericsson and Chase began testing Faloon, he could remember no more than seven random digits after hearing them spoken once. According to generally accepted research, almost everyone is capable of storing five to nine random digits in short-term memory. After twenty months of working with Chase and Ericsson, Faloon could memorize and retrieve eighty digits.

"The important thing about our testing Faloon is that researchers usually study experts," Chase says. "We studied a novice and watched him grow into an expert. Initially, we were just running tests to see whether his digit span could be expanded. For four days he could not go beyond seven digits. On the fifth day he discovered his mnemonic system and then began to improve rapidly."

Faloon's intellectual abilities didn't change, the researchers say. Nor did the storage capacity of his short-term memory. Chase and Ericsson believe that short-term memory is a more or less fixed quantity. It reaches saturation quickly, and to overcome its limitations one must learn to link new data with material that is permanently stored in long-term memory. Once the associations have been made, the short-term memory is free to absorb new information. Shereshevskii transferred material from short-term to long-term memory by placing words along Gorky Street in Moscow. Faloon's hobby was long-distance running, and he discovered that he could break down a spoken list of eighty digits into units of three or four and associate most of these with running times.

To Faloon, a series like 4, 0, 1, 2 would translate as four minutes, one and two-tenths seconds, or "near a four-minute mile"; 2, 1, 4, 7 would be encoded as two hours fourteen minutes seven seconds, or "an excellent marathon time." When running didn't provide the link to his long-term memory, ages and dates did; 1, 9, 4, 4 is not relevant to running, but it is "near the end of World War II."

Chase and Ericsson see individual differences in memory performance as resulting from previous experience and mental training. "In sum," they write, "adult memory performance can be adequately described by a single model of memory."

Not every student of psychology agrees with Chase and Ericsson, of course. "I'm very suspicious of saying that everyone has the same kind of memory," says Matthew Erdelyi, a psychologist at Brooklyn College. "In my research," he says, "I find that people have very different memory levels. They can all improve, but some levels remain high and some remain low. There are dramatic individual differences."

It is unlikely that there will be any agreement among psychologists on the conclusions that they have thus far drawn from their research. The debate about exceptional memory will continue. But in the meantime it is interesting to look deeper into the mind of a contemporary mnemonist.

Ericsson and Polson, both of whom have tested Conrad over the past two years, believe that there is nothing intellectually outstanding about him. When they began testing Conrad's memory, his digit scan was normal: about seven numbers. His grades in college were average.

Conrad himself says that he is unexceptional mentally, but he has compared his earliest memories with others' and has found that he can recall things that many people can't. His first distinct memory is of lying on his back and raising his legs so that his mother could change his diapers. As a high school student he didn't take notes in class—he says he preferred watching the girls take notes—and he has never made a list in his life. "By never writing down a list of things to do, and letting it think for me," he says, "I've forced my memory to improve."

Conrad does believe that his powers of observation, including his ability to listen, are keener than most people's. Memory, he says, is just one part of the whole process of observation. "I'm not extraordinary, but sometimes people make me feel that way. I watch them and realize how many of them have disorganized minds and memories and that makes me feel unusual. A good memory is nothing more than an organized one."

One of the first things Conrad observed at Bananas was that the headwaiter, his boss, was "a very unpleasant woman." He disliked being her subordinate, and he wanted her job. The only way he could get it was by being a superior waiter. He stayed up nights trying to figure out how to do this; the idea of memorizing orders eventually came to him. Within a year he was the headwaiter.

"One of the most interesting things we've found," says Ericsson, "is that just trying to memorize things does not insure that your memory will improve. It's the active decision to get better and the number of hours you push yourself to improve that make the difference. Motivation is much more important than innate ability."

Conrad began his memory training by trying to memorize the orders for a table of two, then progressed to memorizing larger orders.

He starts by associating the entree with the customer's face. He might see a large, heavy-set man and hear "I'd like a big Boulder Steak." Sometimes, Peter Polson says, "John thinks a person looks like a turkey and that customer orders a turkey sandwich. Then it's easy."

In memorizing how long meat should be cooked, the different salad dressings, and starches, Conrad relies on patterns of repetition and variation. "John breaks things up into chunks of four," Ericsson says. "If he hears 'rare, rare, medium, well-done,' he instantly sees a pattern in their relationship. Sometimes he makes a mental graph. An easy progression—rare, medium-rare, medium, well-done—would take the shape of a steadily ascending line on his graph. A more difficult order—medium, well-done, rare, medium—would resemble a mountain range."

The simplest part of Conrad's system is his encoding of salad dressings. He uses letters: *B* for blue cheese; *H* for the house dressing; *O* for oil and vinegar; *F* for French; *T* for Thousand Island. A series of orders, always arranged according to entree, might spell a word, like *B-O-O-T,* or a near-word, like *B-O-O-F,* or make a phonetic pattern: *F-O-F-O.* As Ericsson says, Conrad remembers orders, regardless of their size, in chunks of four. This is similar to the way Faloon stores digits, and it seems to support Chase and Ericsson's contention that short-term memory is limited and that people are most comfortable working with small units of information.

One of the most intriguing things about Conrad is the number of ways he can associate material. Another is the speed with which he is able to call it up from memory. Ericsson and Polson have also tested him with animals, units of time, flowers, and metals. At first, his recall was slow and uncertain. But with relatively little practice, he could retrieve these "orders" almost as quickly as he could food.

"The difference between someone like John, who has a trained memory, and the average person," says Ericsson, "is that he can encode material in his memory fast and effortlessly. It's similar to the way you can understand English when you hear it spoken. In our tests in the lab, he just gets better and faster." "What John Conrad has," says Polson, "is not unlike an athletic skill. With two or three hundred hours of practice, you can develop these skills in the same way you can learn to play tennis."

Stephen Singular

After You Read
Study Skills: Underlining and Marginal Glossing

John Conrad spoke of the importance of having an organized mind for developing one's memory. In this textbook, three skills will be presented to help you organize materials for study: underlining, marginal glossing, and study mapping. This section will deal with underlining and marginal glossing.

Underlining

Before underlining, read the material once. Then skim the reading, underlining key words and phrases that relate to main ideas and important statistics or examples that support them. Underline only about 20 to 30 percent of the material. Many students underline with felt pens, often using one color for main concepts and a different color for statistics and examples.

Another effective method is to underline main ideas and circle or draw rectangles around names, terms, or statistics you want to remember. Supporting ideas can be underlined with broken lines. Practice underlining a few different ways until you find a method you like.

Marginal Glossing

Marginal glossing is another way to organize material for study. A marginal gloss is a note in the margin of your book summarizing the material next to it. When you study, these notes stand out and remind you of other points as well. This saves time because you do not reread everything, only the brief notes. You can also try to think of questions that might be asked on a test and write these questions in the margins.

Here are the first eight paragraphs from a "Memory for All Seasonings" with underlining and marginal glosses done for the first four paragraphs. Look over the four paragraphs that have been marked. Then finish the remaining paragraphs by underlining and glossing them yourself. Afterward, compare with your classmates. You should find that the first part of the comprehension quiz is quite easy after this preparation.

A Memory for All Seasonings

One evening two years ago, (Peter Polson,) a member of the psychology department at the University of Colorado, took his son and daughter to dinner at Bananas, a fashionable restaurant in Boulder. When the waiter took their orders, Polson noticed that the young man didn't write anything down. He just listened, made small talk, told them that his name was (John Conrad,) and left. Polson didn't think this was exceptional: There were, after all, only three of them at the table. Yet he found himself watching Conrad closely when he returned to take the orders at a nearby table of eight. Again the waiter listened, chatted, and wrote nothing down. When he brought Polson and his children their dinners, the professor couldn't resist introducing himself and telling Conrad that he'd been observing him.

The young man was pleased. He wanted customers to notice that, unlike other waiters, he didn't use a pen and paper. Sometimes, when they did notice, they left him quite a large tip. He had once handled a table of nineteen complete dinner orders without a single error. At Bananas, a party of nineteen (a bill of roughly $200) would normally leave the waiter a $35 tip. They had left Conrad $85.

Polson was impressed enough to ask the waiter whether he would like to come to the university's psychology lab and let them run some tests on him. (Anders Ericsson,) a young Swedish psychologist recently involved in memory research, would be joining the university faculty soon, and Polson thought that he would be interested in exploring memory methods with the waiter. Conrad said he would be glad to cooperate. He was always on the lookout for ways to increase his income, and Polson told him he would receive $5 an hour to be a guinea pig.

Marginal glosses:

Peter Polson, from University Colo. Psy. Dept., saw a waiter at Bananas Restaurant with an amazing memory. The waiter was John Conrad.

Conrad did not write his orders. He memorized all of them.

Polson invited Conrad to the lab for further memory study for $5 an hour.

Line numbers: 5, 10, 15, 20, 25

Other people
with amazing
memories
include a
Russian
reporter
named
Shereshevskii
and the
conductor
Arturo
Toscanini.

30

35

Conrad, of course, was not the first person with an extraordinary memory to attract attention from researchers. Alexander R. Luria, the distinguished Soviet psychologist, studied a Russian newspaper reporter named Shereshevskii for many years and wrote about him in *The Mind of a Mnemonist* (Basic Books, 1968). Luria says that Shereshevskii was able to hear a series of fifty words spoken once and recite them back in perfect order fifteen years later. Another famous example of extraordinary memory, the conductor Arturo Toscanini, was known to have memorized every note for every instrument in 250 symphonies and 100 operas.

For decades the common belief among psychologists was that memory was a fixed quantity; an exceptional memory, or a poor one, was something with which a person was born.

40

45

50

55

This point of view has come under attack in recent years; expert memory is no longer universally considered the exclusive gift of the genius, or the abnormal. "People with astonishing memory for pictures, musical scores, chess positions, business transactions, dramatic scripts, or faces are by no means unique," wrote Cornell psychologist Ulric Neisser in *Memory Observed* (1981). "They may not even be very rare." Some university researchers, including Polson and Ericsson, go a step further than Neisser. They believe that there are no physiological differences at all between the memory of a Shereshevskii or a Toscanini and that of the average person. The only real difference, they believe, is that Toscanini trained his memory, exercised it regularly, and wanted to improve it.

Like many people with his capacity to remember, Toscanini may also have used memory tricks called mnemonics. Shereshevskii, for example, employed a technique known as *loci*. As soon as he heard a series of words, he mentally "distributed" them along Gorky Street in Moscow. If one of the words was "orange," he might visualize a man stepping on an orange at a precise location on the familiar street. Later, in order to retrieve "orange," he would take an imaginary walk down Gorky Street and see the image from which it could easily be recalled. Did the waiter at Bananas have such a system? What was his secret?

60　　John Conrad would be the subject of Anders Ericsson's second in-depth study of the machinations of memory. As a research associate at Carnegie-Mellon University in Pittsburgh, Ericsson had spent the previous three years working with William Chase on an extensive study of Steve Faloon, an undergraduate whose memory and intellectual skills were
65　considered average. When Ericsson and Chase began testing Faloon, he could remember no more than seven random digits after hearing them spoken once. According to generally accepted research, almost everyone is capable of storing five to nine random digits in short-term memory. After twenty months of working with Chase and Ericsson, Faloon could
70　memorize and retrieve eighty digits.

Comprehension Quiz

Choose the best way of finishing each statement, based on what you have just read.

1. The psychology professor discovered John Conrad's incredible ability to memorize:
   a. in school
   b. on a test
   c. in a restaurant

2. Conrad agreed to let the professor study his memory because:
   a. Conrad was interested in psychology
   b. Conrad wanted to increase his income
   c. Conrad needed to improve his memory

3. The famous Russian mnemonist Shereshevskii used a memory trick called *loci* to remember objects by:
   a. associating them with events in Russian history
   b. imagining them placed along a street in Moscow
   c. picturing each one in his mind in a different color

4. The memory trick used by Steve Faloon was the association of certain numbers with:
   a. running times
   b. important dates
   c. both of the above
   d. none of the above

5. Conrad had been
   a. a gifted student
   b. a below-average student
   c. an average student

6. Part of Conrad's motivation for developing memory tricks to aid him as a waiter was
   a. his desire to get his boss's job
   b. his great admiration for the headwaiter
   c. his fear of not finding any work

7. Imagine that four customers have requested that their steaks be cooked in the following way: well-done, medium, medium-rare, rare. According to John Conrad's "mental graph" technique, this order would be remembered as
   a. a steadily ascending line
   b. a steadily descending line
   c. a mountain range

8. From this article a careful reader should infer that
   a. everyone has about the same memory capacity and can develop a superior memory through practice and motivation
   b. a good or bad memory is an ability that a person is born with and cannot change to any great degree
   c. there is still no conclusive evidence as to whether outstanding memories are inborn or developed

Applying Concepts from the Reading

activity 1

Several different mnemonic systems (memory tricks) are described in the reading. Working in small groups, show that you have understood these tricks by applying them to the following situations. (A list of the systems with line references is given in case you want to review them.)

MNEMONIC SYSTEMS MENTIONED IN ARTICLE

a. *loci* (imagining objects in a familiar place), used by Shereshevskii, lines 52–58
b. number association, used by Steve Faloon, lines 85–93
c. physical appearance association, used by John Conrad, lines 139–142
d. mental graph or picture, used by Conrad, lines 143–150
e. word or sound pattern association, used by Conrad, lines 151–155

Situation 1 You want to remember the names of all the psychologists mentioned in this article: Polson, Ericsson, Luria, Neisser, Chase. How would you do this using word or sound pattern association?

Situation 2   You want to remember to buy the following items at the grocery store: apples, milk, rice, pepper, salad dressing, and olives. How would you do this, using *loci*? How would you do it using word or sound pattern association? Which system would be better for you?

Situation 3   You have just a minute or two to look at the alphabetical list of exam grades and want to remember the grades of seven of your friends. What kind of mental graph would you picture in your mind to remember them in the following order: A, D, A, D, B, C, B?

Situation 4   You want to remember the combinations for the locks you use for your bicycle, your school locker, and your gym locker: 0915, 1220, 1492. How could you do this, using number association? Can you think of any other way of doing it?

Situation 5   You are at a dinner party and want to remember the names of the four other guests: a very tall lady named Mrs. Stemski; a large, heavy-set man named Mr. Barnes; a cheerful young woman with a big smile named Miss Rich; and a sad-looking young man named Mr. Winter. How could you use physical appearance association to remember their names?

Talking It Over

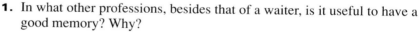

In small groups, discuss the following questions.

1. In what other professions, besides that of a waiter, is it useful to have a good memory? Why?
2. Do you know or have you heard of any people (besides those mentioned in the article) who have extraordinary memories?
3. What techniques, other than those mentioned in the preceding exercise, are sometimes used to aid memory?
4. Are there some situations in life when it is important to develop the ability to forget rather than to remember? If so, how can this be done? Explain.

Finding Support for or Against a Hypothesis

As the article points out, some psychologists today believe that extraordinary memories are simply the result of development through hard work and the application of a system. According to them, an average person could achieve a superior memory if he or she tried hard enough. Find evidence from the article to support this hypothesis. Then find evidence from the article that goes against this hypothesis. What is your opinion of this controversial question?

SELECTION **two**

Under the Skull

Before You Read
Anticipating the Reading

Thinking ahead about the contents of an article can help you focus on the important points. What do you already know about the human brain? Fill out the following description as well as you can, using the drawings on page 154 to help you. Then, as you read the excerpt from Calder's book, see what new information you can learn about these aspects of the brain.

Color: _____ *Weight:* _____

Consistency: _____

Major sections: _____

_____

Number and types of cells: _____

_____

Method of transmitting its messages: _____

_____

While psychologists are learning a great deal about memory and other functions of the human mind through clinical studies, biologists and neurophysiologists are using experiments, dissection, and high technology to penetrate its mysteries. Did you know that a particular section of the brain controls laughing? This was discovered by accident in 1955 during an operation. When one part of his brain was touched, the patient immediately broke out into wild laughter, completely amazing the doctor, who had certainly not expected his surgery to be so entertaining!

Scientists have discovered a great deal about our mental functioning, but they still have a long way to go. Nigel Calder, a noted British scientist and writer, presents some basic facts about the brain in this excerpt from his book *The Mind of Man.*

Under the Skull

*T*he "face barrier" is a perpetual problem for anyone to overcome who tries to imagine the brain at work. The brain seems almost like an abstract theory, even though it lies only a few millimetres behind the eyebrows. Yet it is the more durable embodiment of human and individual nature, while the face is just a kind of cinema screen across which flicker the projections of the brain's activities.

Even when exposed, the human brain is not very impressive to look at. Greyish in colour and with the consistency of soft cheese, it fits snugly inside the top of the skull. It weighs about as much as a dictionary of moderate size. But this lump of tissue, your brain or mine, is the most intricate and powerful of all the works of nature known to us. It is a machine millions of times more complex than the mightiest computers now built; furthermore, it is a machine that is conscious of its own existence. Here, and nowhere else, we presume, are generated the thoughts and feelings, dreams and creative actions that are the essence of human life; it is the organ of the mind of man.

Like all other parts of the body, and all plants and animals, the brain consists of cells, little units of life normally visible only under the microscope. There are many billions of cells in the brain. The ones most directly involved in mental and other processes are the neurons, nervelike cells that come in many shapes and sizes and have vast numbers of connections. The others are glia, or "flue" cells. If the cells were as big as grains of sand, they would fill a large truck. This great mass of cells is bewildering for those who try to trace its organisation and connections, but it is certainly not without pattern. The cells are arranged neatly in layers, which plainly has something to say about how the brain operates. Furthermore, the overall sculpture of the brain is far from meaningless.

The most obvious part of the human brain consists of the two cerebral hemispheres on the top. The hemispheres are separated by a fissure running from front to back, but they are reconnected by thick cables of fibres lying towards the centre of the brain. Message-carrying fibres also fill much of the volume of the hemispheres, leaving most of the work of the brain to be done in the outermost three millimetres. This is the cerebral cortex, to which I shall refer as "the roof of the brain." It is very crumpled; if it were ironed flat, it would form a sheet about half a metre square.

The upper components of the brain grow outwards from a stem. The central part of the brain, closest to the top of the brain stem, is the hub of communications for the whole brain, with busy traffic of information flowing in all directions. It also has a specialised role in the expression of drives and emotions. The brain stem itself runs down to connect with the cables of the spinal cord, from which radiates the tracery of nerves that carry signals to and from all parts of the body. The important sense organs, including those of sight, hearing, and smell, have more direct access to the higher parts of the brain. At the back of the brain there is an

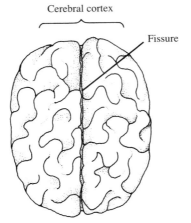

Cerebral cortex

Fissure

Left hemisphere   Right hemisphere

View from the top. The wrinkled surface of the two cerebral hemispheres, the cortex, is much greater than the cortex of any comparable animal brain.

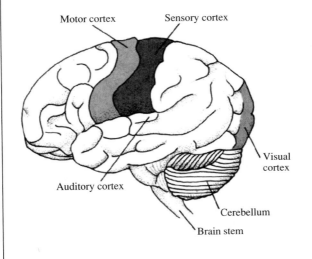

Motor cortex   Sensory cortex

Visual cortex

Auditory cortex

Cerebellum

Brain stem

Left hemisphere. This hemisphere, in the great majority of cases, is responsible for language. It also contains regions responsible for vision, the senses, and movement on the right side of the body.

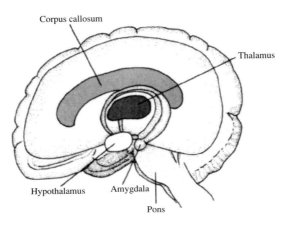

Corpus callosum

Thalamus

Hypothalamus   Amygdala

Pons

Right hemisphere. The connection between the hemispheres is the *corpus callosom*. The *thalamus* and *hypothalamus* both contain many nuclei dealing with specific functions of body and brain (such as emotions, regulation of body temperature, and secretions of the pituitary glands).

additional component, the cerebellum, or "little brain," which is dedicated to learning and reconstructing skilled movements.

The brain is an electrical machine. That much is evident from the EEG [electroencephalograph] recorded at its outer surface, and disturbances due to epilepsy and other malfunctions appear in the wavy traces of the pen recorders. The technique was pioneered in the 1920s by Hans Berger of the University of Jena. Apart from other obvious uses in studies of sleeping, waking, and excitement, the EEG recorded at the scalp remains rather disappointing. After half a century, it still tells us little about how the normal human brain works, although, with modern techniques, it is possible to detect the arrival of signals in particular regions of the brain.

The intricate electric business of the brain is transacted by impulses within individual brain cells which "fire" intermittently. These can be detected only with very fine probes, or microelectrodes, inserted right into the brain. An understanding of the ever-changing patterns of electrical

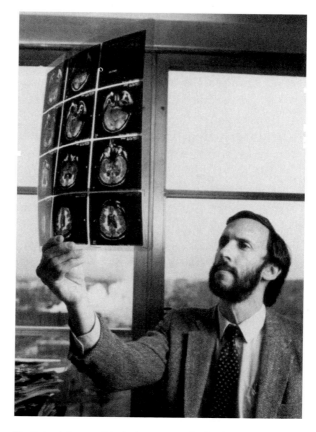

Radiologists are able to better see the intricacies of the brain with a machine called the CAT scanner.

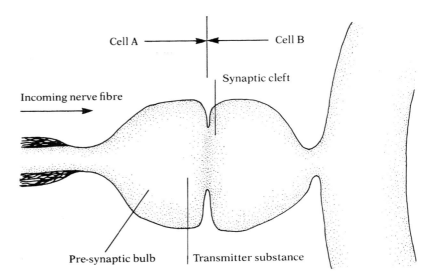

Cell A ———→ ←——— Cell B

Synaptic cleft

Incoming nerve fibre

Pre-synaptic bulb | Transmitter substance

The link, or synapse, between one brain cell and another. A signal travels from left to right by the release of a transmitter substance.

activity comes with the simultaneous tracing of connections and influences involving many individual cells, but in very few parts of the brain has this tracing been done thoroughly.

The brain is also a chemical machine. The discovery that chemicals are involved in nerve action outside the brain was made at about the same time as that of the EEG. In 1921 Otto Loewi of the University of Graz showed that material produced when a nerve stopped the action of one frog's heart could be used to stop the heart of another frog. The identification of chemical agents within the brain has been a slow business. But it is now abundantly clear that one brain cell influences the action of another not by direct electrical connection but by releasing a "transmitter" substance into a narrow gap that separates them.

Different cells use different transmitters with fairly awkward names: Noradrenalin, serotonin, dopamine, GABA, and acetylcholine are all now thought to figure as brain transmitters. One recent benefit of the studies of transmitters has been the introduction of dopa, a drug related to dopamine, as a treatment for many cases of Parkinson's disease. This brain disorder, which causes loss of muscular control and was known to our forefathers as the shaking palsy, is found sometimes to involve shortages of dopamine in an important mass of cells deep in the brain.

Nigel Calder

After You Read
Study Skills: Study Mapping

In the first section of this chapter, you were instructed to underline and gloss the important points in part of an article to help you review it. Another way to organize information for study is to make a study map.

Study mapping is a method of taking notes. It is unique in that an entire article or even a chapter of a textbook is mapped on just one page. To make a map, you must select the major and minor points of the article or chapter. Then arrange them in graph form. Students who enjoy drafting, charts, or symbols tend to like mapping. No exact method of map making is standard. Figures or shapes, lines, and arrows can be used. Some students prefer treelike designs for their maps; others use circles, octagons, or squares.

Like underlining, mapping should be done after the first reading. A study map of the preceding paragraph appears below.

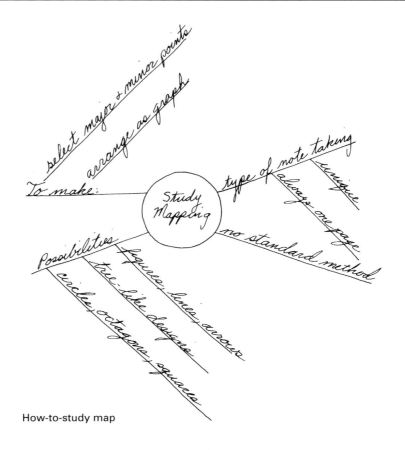

How-to-study map

Look at the incomplete study map for "Under the Skull" shown below. Working in small groups, finish the map. Compare your work afterward with your classmates'. Did you add too much information? Too little? Refer to your map if you need help as you work on the comprehension quiz.

How-to-study map for "Under the Skull"

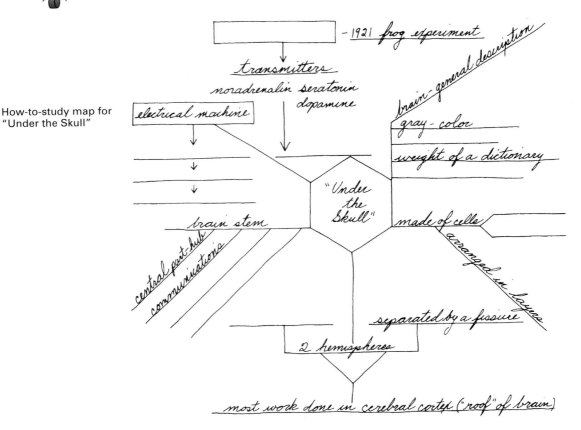

- 1921 *frog experiment*

transmitters
noradrenalin seratonin dopamine

electrical machine

brain - general description

gray - color

weight of a dictionary

"*Under the Skull*"

brain stem

central part-hub communications

made of cells

arranged in layers

separated by a fissure

2 hemispheres

most work done in cerebral cortex ("roof" of brain)

Comprehension Quiz

Choose the best way of finishing each statement, based on what you have just read.

1. The brain has the consistency of:
   a. soft cheese
   b. hard wood
   c. dry cotton

2. The cells of the brain most directly involved in mental processes are:
   a. glia
   b. "flue" cells
   c. neurons

3. The two large hemispheres of the brain are separated by
   a. thick cables of fibres
   b. a fissure running between them
   c. the crumpled cerebral cortex

4. The cerebellum, or "little brain," specializes in
   a. the expression of drives and emotions
   b. sending signals to and from all parts of the body
   c. learning and reconstructing skilled movements

5. The EEG demonstrates that the brain is an electrical machine by
   a. measuring intelligence with electrical energy
   b. drawing a map of the mind's functions
   c. recording disturbances with a wavy line

6. In 1921, Otto Loewi stopped the heart of a frog with a substance produced
   in a different frog when a nerve had stopped its heart. This experiment was
   important because it showed that
   a. one brain cell influences the action of another by direct electrical
      connection
   b. the brain is a chemical machine and depends in part on chemicals to
      send its messages
   c. the impulses that "fire" within individual cells can be detected by very
      fine probes

7. Transmitters such as noradrenalin and dopamine are substances that
   a. cure many diseases, such as measles and the common cold
   b. act as a bridge to carry messages from one cell to another
   c. are related to the brain's action in a way that is still not understood

Paraphrasing Complex Ideas

 Show that you have understood the following excerpts here and on the next page
from the article by rephrasing the ideas in simpler words.

1. "The 'face barrier' is a perpetual problem for anyone to overcome who
   tries to imagine the brain at work."

   _____

   _____

   _____

2. "The cells are arranged neatly in layers, which plainly has something to
   say about how the brain operates."

   _____

   _____

   _____

3. "The central part of the brain, closest to the top of the brain stem, is the hub of communications for the whole brain, with busy traffic of information flowing in all directions."

_____

_____

_____

Talking It Over

activity **2**

In small groups, discuss the following questions.

1. What examples can you give from the article to show that research into the brain has benefited humanity?

2. What is one new fact you learned about the human brain from the article?

3. Do you think there is any danger in scientists' continued research into the brain's functions? Why or why not?

4. There are many common expressions related to the brain in English. Would you rather that someone called you _brainy_ or _scatterbrained_? Why? What does it mean if someone says that he or she has just had a _brainstorm_? If someone complains about the _brain drain_ that is affecting certain countries?

Some Small Differences Between British and North American English

> Calder states that there are "many billions of cells in the brain." Exactly what does this author mean by the word _billion:_ 1,000,000,000 or 1,000,000,000,000? Here we see a difference between usage in Great Britain and in the United States and Canada. Nigel Calder is British, and so he actually means a million millions (the second figure), whereas a North American means a thousand millions (the first figure) when he or she says a _billion._

exercise **3**

All languages that have spread over a large geographic area show differences from one region to another, but in written English, these are surprisingly small. Examples of these are in the spelling of the following words taken from the selection. How would an American spell them?

1. organisation _____

2. specialised _____

3. fibre _____

4. metre _____

5. colour _____

The Tell-Tale Heart

Before You Read

Reading Nineteenth-Century English

Some words and expressions in the following story are now archaic (no longer used in modern English). Most English-speaking readers would not be familiar with them. However, they would have little trouble following the story because the context provides many clues.

Many great American and English writers lived in the nineteenth century; to read nineteenth-century English, skip words or expressions you do not understand and then go back and reread after you see more of the context. Practice this technique in the following exercise. Read the sentences from Edgar Allan Poe's story here and on the next page, and select the modern word or expression that best fits the context to replace the old-fashioned one in italics.

1. "How, then, am I mad? *Hearken!* and observe how healthily—how calmly I can tell you the whole story." (lines 5–6)
   a. Speak!
   b. Listen!
   c. Go away!

2. "It is impossible to say how first the idea entered my brain, but once conceived, it haunted me day and night. *Object* there was none. Passion there was none. . . . For his gold I had no desire." (lines 7–10)
   a. fear
   b. purpose
   c. argument

3. "Now this is the point. You *fancy* me mad. Madmen know nothing. But you should have seen <u>me.</u>" (lines 15–16)
   a. like
   b. imagine
   c. offend

4. "Presently I heard a slight groan, and I knew it was the groan of mortal terror. It was not a groan of pain or of grief—oh, no!—it was the low stifled sound that arises from the bottom of the soul. . . . I knew the sound well. Many a night . . . it has welled up from my own *bosom.* . . ." (lines 56–60)
   a. house
   b. chest
   c. table

5. "I knew what the old man felt, and pitied him. . . . His fears had been ever since growing upon him. . . . He had been saying to himself—'It is nothing but the wind in the chimney. . . .' Yes, he had been trying to comfort himself with these suppositions: but he had found all *in vain. All in vain;* because Death . . . had stalked with his black shadow before him, and enveloped the victim." (lines 61–69)
   a. useless
   b. successful
   c. harmful

6. "But, for many minutes, the heart beat on with a muffled sound. This, however, did not *vex* me; it would not be heard through the wall. *At length* it ceased. The old man was dead." (lines 103–105)

   vex: a. delight
              b. confuse
              c. irritate

   at length: a. soon
              b. finally
              c. in a moment

7. "I took my visitors all over the house. I *bade* them search—search well." (lines 129–130)
   a. finished
   b. requested
   c. refused

8. "They sat, and while I answered cheerily, they chatted of familiar things. But, *ere long,* I felt myself getting pale and wished them gone." (lines 137–139)
   a. after many hours
   b. in a short while
   c. with too much time

It is not only science that brings us a better understanding of the human mind: Throughout the ages writers of fiction have examined the mind also. The famous American poet and short-story writer Edgar Allan Poe was born in Boston, Massachusetts, in 1809. He died forty years later after a stormy but productive life that included wild sprees of drinking and gambling and numerous love affairs as well as a great deal of serious writing in journalism and literature. His works are still popular today, and several have served as the basis for modern plays and movies. He is best known for his tales of horror, such as "The Tell-Tale Heart."

The story is told from the point of view of a madman who commits a terrible crime. Many psychologists and criminologists have felt that Poe describes with great accuracy the inner workings of a severely disordered mind. What do you know, from reading or from personal contact, about madness (insanity)? What are some of the characteristics of the thinking, perception, or speech of a person that show he or she is insane? Watch for examples of these characteristics in the story.

The Tell-Tale Heart

True—nervous—very, very dreadfully nervous I had been and am; but why *will* you say that I am mad? The disease had sharpened my senses—not destroyed—not dulled them. Above all was the sense of hearing acute. I heard all things in the heaven and in the earth. I heard many things in hell. How, then, am I mad? Hearken! and observe how healthily—how calmly I can tell you the whole story.

It is impossible to say how first the idea entered my brain; but once conceived, it haunted me day and night. Object there was none. Passion there was none. I loved the old man. He had never wronged me. He had never given me insult. For his gold I had no desire. I think it was his eye! Yes, it was this! He had the eye of a vulture—a pale blue eye, with a film over it. Whenever it fell upon me, my blood ran cold; and so by degrees—very gradually—I made up my mind to take the life of the old man, and thus rid myself of the eye forever.

Now this is the point. You fancy me mad. Madmen know nothing. But you should have seen *me.* You should have seen how wisely I proceeded—with what caution—with what foresight—with what dissimulation I went to work! I was never kinder to the old man than during the whole week before I killed him. And every night, about midnight, I turned the latch of his door and opened it—oh, so gently! And then, when I had made an opening sufficient for my head, I put in a dark lantern, all closed, closed, so that no light shone out, and then I thrust in my head. Oh, you would have laughed to see how cunningly I thrust it in! I moved it slowly—very slowly, so that I might not disturb the old man's sleep. It took

Edgar Allan Poe

Scene from the animated version of "The Tell-Tale Heart" based on the short story by Edgar Allan Poe

me an hour to place my whole head within the opening so far that I could see him as he lay upon his bed. Ha!—would a madman have been so wise as this? And then, when my head was well in the room, I undid the lantern cautiously—oh so cautiously—cautiously (for the hinges creaked)—I undid it just so much that a single thin ray fell upon the vulture eye. And this I did for seven long nights—every night just at midnight—but I found the eye always closed; and so it was impossible to do the work; for it was not the old man who vexed me, but his Evil Eye. And every morning, when the day broke, I went boldly into the chamber, and spoke coura- geously to him, calling him by name in a hearty tone, and inquiring how he had passed the night. So you see he would have been a very profound old man, indeed, to suspect that every night, just at twelve, I looked in upon him while he slept.

Upon the eighth night I was more than usually cautious in opening the door. A watch's minute hand moves more quickly than did mine. Never before that night, had I *felt* the extent of my own powers—of my sagacity. I could scarcely contain my feelings of triumph. To think that there I was, opening the door, little by little, and he not even to dream of my secret deeds or thoughts. I fairly chuckled at the idea; and perhaps he heard me; for he moved on the bed suddenly, as if startled. Now you may think that I drew back—but no. His room was as black as pitch with the thick darkness (for the shutters were close fastened, through fear of robbers), and so I knew that he could not see the opening of the door, and I kept pushing it on steadily, steadily.

I had my head in, and was about to open the lantern, when my thumb slipped upon the tin fastening, and the old man sprang up in bed, crying out—"Who's there?"

I kept quite still and said nothing. For a whole hour I did not move a muscle, and in the meantime I did not hear him lie down. He was still sitting up in the bed listening;—just as I have done, night after night, hearkening to the death watches in the wall.

Presently I heard a slight groan, and I knew it was the groan of mortal terror. It was not a groan of pain or of grief—oh, no!—it was the low stifled sound that arises from the bottom of the soul. I knew the sound well. Many a night, just at midnight, when all the world slept, it has welled up from my own bosom, deepening, with its dreadful echo, the terrors that distracted me. I say I knew it well. I knew what the old man felt, and pitied him, although I chuckled at heart. I knew that he had been lying awake ever since the first slight noise, when he had turned in the bed. His fears had been ever since growing upon him. He had been trying to fancy them causeless, but could not. He had been saying to himself—"It is nothing but the wind in the chimney—it is only a mouse crossing the floor." Yes, he had been trying to comfort himself with these suppositions: but he had found all in vain. *All in vain;* because Death, in approaching him had stalked with his black shadow before him, and enveloped the victim. And it was the mournful influence of the unperceived shadow that caused him to feel—although he neither saw nor heard—to *feel* the presence of my head within the room.

When I had waited a long time, very patiently, without hearing him lie down, I resolved to open a little—a very, very little crevice in the lantern. So I opened it—you cannot imagine how stealthily, stealthily—until, at length a single dim ray, like the thread of the spider, shot from out the crevice and fell full upon the vulture eye.

It was open—wide, wide open—and I grew furious as I gazed upon it. I saw it with perfect distinctness—all a dull blue with a hideous veil over it that chilled the very marrow in my bones; but I could see nothing else of the old man's face or person: for I had directed the ray, as if by instinct, precisely upon the damned spot.

And have I not told you that what you mistake for madness is but overacuteness of the senses?—now, I say, there came to my ears a low, dull, quick sound, such as a watch makes when enveloped in cotton. I knew *that* sound well, too. It was the beating of the old man's heart. It increased my fury, as the beating of a drum stimulates the soldier into courage.

But even yet I refrained and kept still. I scarcely breathed. I held the lantern motionless. I tried how steadily I could maintain the ray upon the eye. Meantime the hellish tattoo of the heart increased. It grew quicker and quicker, and louder and louder every instant. The old man's terror *must* have been extreme! It grew louder, I say, louder every moment—do you mark me well? I have told you that I am nervous: so I am. And now at the dead hour of the night, amid the dreadful silence of that old house, so strange a noise as this excited me to uncontrollable terror. Yet, for some minutes longer I refrained and stood still. But the beating grew louder, louder! I thought the heart must burst. And now a new anxiety seized me—the sound would be heard by a neighbor! The old man's hour had come! With a loud yell, I threw open the lantern and leaped into the room. He shrieked once—once only. In an instant I dragged him to the floor, and pulled the heavy bed over him. I then smiled gaily, to find the deed so far done. But, for many minutes, the heart beat on with a muffled sound. This, however, did not vex me; it would not be heard through the wall. At length it ceased. The old man was dead. I removed the bed and examined the corpse. Yes, he was stone, stone dead. I placed my hand upon the heart and held it there many minutes. There was no pulsation. He was stone dead. His eye would trouble me no more.

If you still think me mad, you will think so no longer when I describe the wise precautions I took for the concealment of the body. The night waned, and I worked hastily, but in silence. First of all I dismembered the corpse. I cut off the head and the arms and the legs.

I then took up three planks from the flooring of the chamber, and deposited all between the scantlings. I then replaced the boards so cleverly, so cunningly, that no human eye—not even *his*—could have detected anything wrong. There was nothing to wash out—no stain of any kind—no blood-spot whatever. I had been too wary for that. A tub had caught all—ha! ha!

When I had made an end of these labors, it was four o'clock—still dark as midnight. As the bell sounded the hour, there came a knocking at the street door. I went down to open it with a light heart,—for what had I *now* to fear? There entered three men, who introduced themselves, with perfect suavity, as officers of the police. A shriek had been heard by a neighbor during the night; suspicion of foul play had been aroused; information had been lodged at the police office, and they (the officers) had been deputed to search the premises.

I smiled,—for *what* had I to fear? I bade the gentlemen welcome. The shriek, I said, was my own in a dream. The old man, I mentioned, was absent in the country. I took my visitors all over the house. I bade them search—search *well*. I led them, at length, to *his* chamber. I showed them his treasures, secure, undisturbed. In the enthusiasm of my confidence, I brought chairs into the room, and desired them *here* to rest from their fatigues, while I myself, in the wild audacity of my perfect triumph, placed my own seat upon the very spot beneath which reposed the corpse of the victim.

The officers were satisfied. My *manner* had convinced them. I was singularly at ease. They sat, and while I answered cheerily, they chatted of familiar things. But, ere long, I felt myself getting pale and wished them gone. My head ached, and I fancied a ringing in my ears: but still they sat and still chatted. The ringing became more distinct:—it continued and became more distinct: I talked more freely to get rid of the feeling: but it continued and gained definiteness—until, at length, I found that the noise was *not* within my ears.

No doubt I now grew *very* pale;—but I talked more fluently, and with a heightened voice. Yet the sound increased—and what could I do? It was a *low, dull, quick sound—much such a sound as a watch makes when enveloped in cotton.* I gasped for breath—and yet the officers heard it not. I talked more quickly—more vehemently; but the noise steadily increased. I arose and argued about trifles, in a high key and with violent gesticulations; but the noise steadily increased. Why *would* they not be gone? I paced the floor to and fro with heavy strides, as if excited to fury by the observations of the men—but the noise steadily increased. Oh God! what *could* I do? I foamed—I raved—I swore! I swung the chair upon which I had been sitting, and grated it upon the boards, but the noise arose over all and continually increased. It grew louder—louder—*louder*! And still the men chatted pleasantly, and smiled. Was it possible they heard not? Almighty God!—no, no! They heard!—they suspected!—they *knew*!—they were making a mockery of my horror!—this I thought, and this I think. But anything was better than this agony! Anything was more tolerable than this derision! I could bear those hypocritical smiles no longer! I felt that I must scream or die! and now—again!—hark! louder! louder! louder! *louder!*

"Villains!" I shrieked, "dissemble no more! I admit the deed!—tear up the planks! here, here!—it is the beating of his hideous heart!"

Edgar Allan Poe

After You Read
Recalling Information

exercise 1

Choose the best way of finishing each statement, based on what you have just read.

1. The narrator believes that he suffers from acute nervousness that has:
   a. destroyed the power of his senses
   b. increased the power of his senses
   c. driven him mad

2. The motive for the murder was:
   a. a strong desire for the victim's money
   b. an intense hatred for the victim
   c. a dislike of the victim's eye

3. During the week before he killed him, the narrator's manner toward the old man was very:
   a. kind
   b. angry
   c. indifferent

4. Each night just at midnight, he thrust into the old man's room a:
   a. black cat
   b. chain
   c. lantern

5. On the eighth night, the old man awakened because of a noise and then:
   a. went right back to sleep
   b. began to shriek for help
   c. sat up waiting in terror

6. After a while, the murderer heard a sound that increased his fury and that he thought was:
   a. a watch enveloped in cotton
   b. the neighbors coming to enter the house
   c. the beating of his victim's heart

7. The murderer disposed of the old man's body by putting it:
   a. in the garden
   b. under the floor
   c. into the chimney

8. At four in the morning, three police officers arrived because neighbors had complained of:
   a. the lights
   b. some knocking
   c. a shriek

9. The officers found out the truth because:
   a. the murderer confessed
   b. they heard a strange sound
   c. there was a bloodstain on the floor

Talking It Over

In small groups, discuss the following questions.

1. Give three statements the narrator makes to prove he is sane. Then show how the author indicates to us that these claims are not true.
2. We are not told what relationship the murderer had to the old man or why they lived together. What did you imagine about this?
3. To whom do you think the murderer is telling this story and for what reason?
4. Have you heard of people who believe in the "evil eye"? According to this belief, you can suffer bad luck or illness if you are looked at by someone who has this power. What do you think is the origin of this belief? Why do you think the narrator of the story was so disturbed by the old man's eye?
5. Various interpretations have been given to explain the loud beating that the narrator hears during the police visit. Do you agree with any of the following interpretations?
   a. It is simply a clock or other normal sound that seems louder to him because of his guilt.
   b. It is really the beating of his *own* heart, which becomes stronger as he gets more and more nervous.
   c. It is the old man's ghost taking revenge on him.

   Or do you have some other interpretation? Explain.

Identifying Elements That Create a Feeling of Horror

Edgar Allan Poe is considered a master of the horror story. Have you ever read a horror story or seen a horror movie that really frightened you? Many people in North America seem to enjoy being frightened in this way. Are horror stories popular in your culture as well?

This story and several others by Poe have been recorded. If you can get one of these recordings, listen to it in class. If you cannot get a recording, your teacher and a few volunteers from the class should read aloud some sections. After listening to them, try to explain how tone of voice increases the feeling of terror.

Most horror stories include certain elements commonly used to provoke terror. Can you think of some of these? Listen to the story or look through it and make a list of these elements. Then compare your lists. Why do you think that these elements are frightening?

WHAT DO YOU THINK?

The Treatment of Mental Illness

Mental illness in many ways remains a mystery to us. Some scientists think that it is hereditary, passed down from parents to children in the genes. Others think it is caused by the environment, perhaps by some trauma in a person's experience or by brain damage at the time of birth. Today, most experts feel that mental illness is caused by a combination of these factors, but they do not agree on how to treat it. One method of treatment is to lock up mentally ill people in asylums and separate them from society. Another method is to place these people in *halfway houses* under the care of guardians who supervise them and allow them to mix with other people for some hours of the day. In some places mentally ill patients are given drugs, and in other places they receive many hours of counseling and talk therapy of the type pioneered by Sigmund Freud (1856–1939), the inventor of the study of psychiatry. What do you think is the cause of mental illness? How should it be treated? How is mental illness treated in your culture?

Making a Summary from a Different Point of View

What really happened when the three police officers came to search the narrator's house? What did he do or say to make them so suspicious that they stayed to chat with him? The events are presented from *his* point of view, but we must read "between the lines" in order to see what really happened. We must take into account his character and pinpoint the places in which he describes events incorrectly. Working in small groups, make a summary of what really occurred in the form of a brief police report from the point of view of the three officers.

focus on testing

Reading for Speed

Most tests have a time limit, so good reading speed can be a great asset. One way of reading a passage quickly is to fix in your mind what you want to know and then to skim for that information. Very fast readers often move their eyes down the middle of the page rather than reading every word.

exercise Try reading the following selection, "May's Boy," by moving your eyes down the center of the page to find out the answer to these two questions: (1) Who is May? (2) Who is Leslie Lemke, and why is he famous? Time yourself and see if you can read the article and correctly do the comprehension exercise that follows it in five minutes.

TIMED READING

May's Boy

Oshkosh, WI (AP)—It was only fitting that this concert be held in a church. After all, it had to do with miracles. Leslie Lemke, whose name has

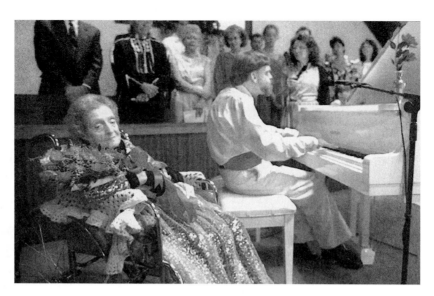

Leslie Lemke playing the piano while his mother, May, listens.

become synonymous with the savant syndrome,* meaning an "island of genius," has come to be even more associated with the term "miracle of love."

Blind, retarded, palsied, Leslie, who has to be led to the piano by his sister, Mary Parker, can play any piece of music he's ever heard.

Last Sunday, his genius came through more strongly than ever. This day he was playing for a special lady—his mother, May—who was celebrating her 93rd birthday and her last scheduled public appearance with him.

It was she who had taken him in and told her own children, "God has something special in mind for Leslie." But even she could not have known what "May's boy," as Leslie has come to be known, could accomplish.

Walter Cronkite used May and Leslie as his "Christmas miracle" years ago. Since then, Leslie has appeared on "That's Incredible," "Donahue," "60 Minutes," and finally, served as a prototype for the film *Rain Man*. He's played the piano for the King of Norway and appeared in Japan. Japanese television sent a crew to film Leslie for its Discovery program at the concert held both at the Seventh-Day Adventist Church in Neenah and St. John Lutheran Church in Oshkosh. "There Was a Lady May Who Prayed for a Miracle," a song written especially for May, was sung by

*The "savant syndrome" is the name given to the condition of certain people who are very retarded but have a special genius for one subject or skill, often for mathematics or music. Their general intelligence is usually so low that they cannot lead an independent life, but in their one area of genius, they show extraordinary aptitude that is far above the average.

Leslie as his mother, now suffering from Alzheimer's disease, was wheeled next to the piano.

25 "Day by day and year by year, she stuck by his side. Others thought it hopeless, but he never even cried," he sang in the presence of May's children, grandchildren, great-grandchildren, and even a few great-great-grandchildren.

A spark of recognition lit May's eyes as the song continued, and her
30 family came up to embrace her, though the years when she actually outtalked Donahue on the program are gone. All that is left is the loving glance she casts toward Leslie, as he plays the piece that has become his theme song, Tchaikovsky's Piano Concerto No. 1.

It was that piece May and Joe Lemke heard in the night a decade and a
35 half ago when they were awakened by beautiful music and discovered their profoundly handicapped boy at the piano. It was the miracle May had told her family would come. From that night on, Leslie has been researched, lauded, filmed.

His ability to hear any piece of music just once, imprint it in his brain,
40 and repeat it on the piano on command and in its entirety has brought him fame. No one knows how many pieces are forever locked in his memory. He can play and sing hundreds of songs at will—spirituals, ballads, arias, marches, ragtime, folksongs, and the classics. And yet, seconds before he appears before the crowd, he sits in a chair, head bowed, eyes shut, hand
45 gnarled, unaware of his surroundings, waiting for his sister, Mary, to come and take him to the piano.

As soon as he sits down at the piano bench and lifts his head heavenward, his palsied fingers spread across the keys and praise the Lord with "How Great Thou Art." In the front pew, May's own hands lift in
50 adoration.

Maya Penikis

Comprehension

1. May is Leslie Lemke's _____.
   a. teacher
   b. mother
   c. doctor

2. Leslie Lemke is _____.
   a. a retarded man with the ability to sing, dance, and play classical music on television and in the movies
   b. a piano player of very low intelligence who can play from memory any song he has ever heard
   c. a genius who has learned to play many different musical instruments with near perfection

Talking It Over

In small groups, discuss the following questions.

1. In your opinion, how important was May in Leslie's success?
2. What lesson can most people learn from the case of Leslie Lemke?
3. How many minutes did it take you to read this article?
4. When do you like to read fast? When and why do you like to read slowly?

CHAPTER seven

Working

Sometimes people complain that work is all they do. It's true. Most people spend a third of their lives working. Many factors determine whether work brings pleasure, compensation, and fulfillment, or boredom and frustration. First we explore business ethics. The second piece gives good advice to managers. The third selection talks about women in nontraditional jobs, and the timed reading gives advice on what not to do in job interviews.

Why Ethics?

Before You Read
Relating Vocabulary to Ideas

Because the following selection comes from a book often used in business seminars, the authors employ a number of colloquial and slang expressions. Some of these are listed below as Key Vocabulary. Discuss what each expression means. Then decide which of the three main ideas from the excerpt you think each expression is related to. Write down the appropriate number(s) after each one.

MAIN IDEAS FROM THE ARTICLE

1. Some types of unethical conduct
2. Punishment for getting caught
3. Reasons for unethical behavior

key vocabulary	main idea
confidence in one's anonymity	3
become the scapegoat	_____
public penance	_____
ethical naiveté	_____
reneging on contracts	_____
cheating	_____
careers that hit a dead end or go down the tubes	_____
trained to "think business"	_____

If you are still unsure about the meanings of some of the key vocabulary, watch for them as you read and try to figure out their meanings from context.

In the past five to ten years, a new course has appeared in the curriculum of most American business schools: Business Ethics. No one knows exactly why this change has taken place. Perhaps the chief reason is the growing conviction expressed in the title of a recent book on the subject by Robert C. Solomon and Kristine Hanson, *It's Good Business.* One of the goals stated on the book jacket is to show "how ethics is the key to improved performance in business—for your company and yourself." Before reading the following excerpt from the book, answer these questions: Do you think that ethics is important in business today? Why?

Why Ethics?

To err is human, perhaps, but to be caught lying, cheating, stealing, or reneging on contracts is not easily forgotten or forgiven in the business world. And for good reason: Such actions undermine the ethical foundation on which the business world thrives. Almost everyone can have compassion for someone caught in an ethical dilemma. No one can excuse immorality.

For every glaring case of known unethical conduct that goes unpunished, a dozen once-promising careers silently hit a dead end or quietly go down the tubes. On relatively rare occasions, an unhappy executive or employee is singled out and forced to pay public penance for conduct that everyone knows—he or she and the attorney will loudly protest—"goes on all the time." But much more often, unethical behavior, though unearthed, will go unannounced; indeed, the executive or employee in question will keep his or her job and may not even find out that he or she has been found out—may never even realize the unethical nature of his or her behavior. A career will just go nowhere. Responsibilities will remain routine, promotions elusive.

What makes such career calamities so pathetic is that they are not the product of greed or immorality or wickedness. They are the result of ethical naiveté.

- They happen because an employee unthinkingly "did what he was told to do"—and became the scapegoat as well.
- They happen because a casual public comment was ill-considered and had clearly unethical implications—though nothing of the kind may have been intended.
- They happen because a middle manager, pressed from above for results, tragically believed the adolescent cliches that pervade the mid-regions of the business world, such as, "In business, you do whatever you have to do to survive."
- They happen because upper management wasn't clear about standards, priorities, and limits, or wasn't reasonable in its expectations, or wasn't available for appeal at the critical moment.
- They happen because an anonymous employee or middle manager hidden in the complexity of a large organization foolishly believed that such safe anonymity would continue, whatever his or her behavior.
- They happen, most of all, because a person in business is typically trained and pressured to "think business," without regard for the larger context in which business decisions are made and legitimized.

Unethical thinking isn't just "bad business"; it is an invitation to disaster in business, however rarely (it might sometimes seem) unethical behavior is actually found out and punished.

Below are four ethical dilemmas that a person in the business world might encounter. Put yourself in the position of the person who is faced with the dilemma, and, keeping in mind your ethical responsibilities, see if you can resolve the problems:

1. You are in charge of new-product development at Company A in the midst of fierce competition for the development of a new and more efficient gizmo. The research department has come up with a workable model, and the engineering department is just now in the midst of "getting the bugs out." One of your main competitors, Company B, has obviously fallen behind and offers you a lucrative position, more than commensurate with your present duties and at almost double the salary. Your current employer insists that he cannot possibly match the offer but does give you a 20 percent raise, "to show our appreciation." Should you feel free to accept the competing offer from Company B? If you do accept it, should you feel free to develop for Company B the gizmo designed by Company A?

2. A worker in an automobile factory becomes convinced that the hood latch on the new-model Crocodiliac is insufficiently secure and may well pop open at high speeds in a small number of cars, probably causing an accident or, at the least, considerable damage to the car itself. He goes to his supervisor and insists that the latch be redesigned, but he is told that the production is too far under way; the cost would be formidable and the delay intolerable. The worker goes to the president of the firm and gets the same response. Is he justified in going to the news media?

These cars are unsafe!

3. Your company sells pharmaceutical products in a developing country, in which one of your products, Wellness Plus, promises to provide an effective cure for a common infantile illness. But you find, much to

your horror, that the product is being systematically misused, with sometimes serious medical consequences, by people who are mostly illiterate and have no medical supervision. At the same time, the product is selling like hotcakes. What should you do?

75   4. Your Fashion Jean Co. could save almost 30 percent on labor costs by moving your main manufacturing plant just across the border to a neighboring country where labor is much cheaper. Should you do so?

Robert C. Solomon and Kristine Hanson

After You Read
Making Inferences

Inferences are ideas or opinions that are not stated but that can be inferred or concluded from the information given. On the basis of what you have read, which of these statements is the best inference about the authors' views of unethical conduct in business? Check the statement and find specific parts of the selection to support your choice.

1. _____ Unethical behavior is quite rare in business and when it does occur, the person in question is almost always forced to pay public penance for his or her conduct.

2. _____ Unethical behavior is fairly common in business, but it is usually excused by management because everyone knows that it "goes on all the time."

3. _____ Unethical behavior is common in business and often results in negative consequences for the person in question without his or her finding out about it.

4. _____ No one knows how frequently unethical behavior occurs in business, but generally a scapegoat is found to pay the price for it in place of the person who is responsible.

Analyzing Sentence Structure

Answer the questions on the structure of these sentences from the selection.

1. "On relatively rare occasions, an unhappy executive or employee is singled out and forced to pay public penance for conduct that everyone knows—he or she and the attorney will loudly protest—'goes on all the time.'"

    Dashes usually signal an interruption in the main idea. How does the clause in between the dashes change the meaning of the main idea of this sentence?

    _____

    _____

    _____

2. "Responsibilities will remain routine, promotions elusive."

With two short parallel ideas like these, words can be omitted from the second without impeding understanding. What two words are omitted from the second part of the sentence?

_____   _____

Talking It Over

In small groups, discuss the following questions.

1. What are some kinds of unethical behavior that occur in business? Which do you think is the most serious?

2. According to the article, who is responsible for ethical misconduct? (Note that you can say "unethical conduct" or "ethical misconduct" and they mean the same thing.) In general, why does it happen?

3. What do you think of the saying that is quoted in the article: "In business, you do whatever you have to do to survive"? Do you think that in reality many people in business practice this?

4. Do you think that an employee who is underpaid and/or treated badly by his or her boss has the right to take home some work supplies or use the company phone for personal calls when no one is around? Why or why not?

Solving Problems Through Group Discussion

In small groups, select two of the problems given at the end of the article. First make a list of possible solutions to both problems. Second, discuss the good and bad points of each solution. Third, choose the best solution for each problem and write it down, telling what you would do in each case and why.

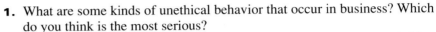

SELECTION **two**

A Lifetime of Learning to Manage Effectively

Before You Read

Understanding Idiomatic Phrases

Sometimes you recognize every word in a phrase but still do not understand the meaning of the whole phrase in the special (idiomatic) way it is being used. Usually, if you keep reading, you will find a clue to the meaning—an example, an explanation, or a contrasting phrase. All the following italicized phrases from the selection have these kinds of clues except the first one. Scan the article for each phrase and write a definition or explanation; then write the words that provided clues to the meaning. (Line references are given to make scanning faster.)

1. *raw brain power* (line 3)

definition: _____

_____

(In this case there are no clues. You have to think of the more common usage of *raw* when applied to foods and extend the meaning.)

2. *broad human beings* (line 19)

definition: _____

_____

clue: _____

_____

3. *sense of integrity* (line 27)

definition: _____

_____

clue: _____

_____

4. *cut corners* (line 38)

definition: _____

_____

clue: _____

_____

5. *in the short run* (line 39)

definition: _____

_____

_____

clue: _____

_____

6. *hard knocks* (line 67)

definition: _____

_____

clue: _____

_____

Have you ever worked for someone you really liked and admired? Have you had the opposite experience—working for someone you disliked and did not respect? If so, you know that a manager or boss can make a great difference in the quality of an employee's work. The following article is written by Ralph Z. Sorenson, president and chief executive officer (CEO) of Barry Wright Corporation, a manufacturer of computer accessories and other products. He gives his opinion on the kind of person who makes a good manager and explains how his views on this subject have changed over the years.

A Lifetime of Learning to Manage Effectively

Years ago, when I was a young assistant professor at the Harvard Business School, I thought that the key to developing managerial leadership lay in raw brain power. I thought the role of business schools was to develop future managers who knew all about the various functions of business—to teach them how to define problems succinctly, analyze these problems and identify alternatives in a clear, logical fashion, and, finally, to teach them to make an intelligent decision.

My thinking gradually became tempered by living and working outside the United States and by serving seven years as a college president. During my presidency of Babson College, I added several additional traits or skills that I felt a good manager must possess.

The first is the *ability to express oneself* in a clear, articulate fashion. Good oral and written communication skills are absolutely essential if one is to be an effective manager.

"These executive decisions are never easy."

Mosaic II • Reading

Second, one must possess that intangible set of qualities called *leadership skills.* To be a good leader one must understand and be sensitive to people and be able to inspire them toward the achievement of common goals.

Next I concluded that effective managers must be *broad human beings* who not only understand the world of business but also have a sense of the cultural, social, political, historical, and (particularly today) the international aspects of life and society. This suggests that exposure to the liberal arts and humanities should be part of every manager's education.

Finally, as I pondered the business and government-related scandals that have occupied the front pages of newspapers throughout the seventies and early eighties, it became clear that a good manager in today's world must have *courage and a strong sense of integrity.* He or she must know where to draw the line between right and wrong.

That can be agonizingly difficult. Drawing a line in a corporate setting sometimes involves having to make a choice between what appears to be conflicting "rights." For example, if one is faced with a decision whether or not to close an ailing factory, whose interests should prevail? Those of stockholders? Of employees? Of customers? Or those of the community in which the factory is located? It's a tough choice. And the typical manager faces many others.

Sometimes these choices involve simple questions of honesty or truthfulness. More often, they are more subtle and involve such issues as having to decide whether to "cut corners" and economize to meet profit objectives that may be beneficial in the short run but that are not in the best long-term interests of the various groups being served by one's company. Making the right choice in situations such as these clearly demands integrity and the courage to follow where one's integrity leads.

But now I have left behind the cap and gown of a college president and put on the hat of chief executive officer. As a result of my experience as a corporate CEO, my list of desirable managerial traits has become still longer.

It now seems to me that what matters most in the majority of organizations is to have reasonably intelligent, hard-working managers who have a sense of pride and loyalty toward their organization; who can get to the root of a problem and are inclined toward action; who are decent human beings with a natural empathy and concern for people; who possess humor, humility, and common sense; and who are able to couple drive with "stick-to-it-iveness" and patience in the accomplishment of a goal.

It is the *ability to make positive things happen* that most distinguishes the successful manager from the mediocre or unsuccessful one. It is far better to have dependable managers who can make the right things happen in a timely fashion than to have brilliant, sophisticated, highly educated executives who are excellent at planning and analyzing, but who are not so good at implementing. The most cherished manager is the one who says "I can do it," and then does.

Many business schools continue to focus almost exclusively on the development of analytical skills. As a result, these schools are continuing to graduate large numbers of MBAs and business majors who know a great deal about analyzing strategies, dissecting balance sheets, and using computers—but who still don't know how to manage!

As a practical matter, of course, schools can go only so far in teaching their students to manage. Only hard knocks and actual work experience will fully develop the kinds of managerial traits, skills, and virtues that I have discussed here.

Put another way: The best way to learn to manage is to manage. Companies such as mine that hire aspiring young managers can help the process along by:

- providing good role models and mentors
- setting clear standards and high expectations that emphasize the kind of broad leadership traits that are important to the organization, and then rewarding young managers accordingly
- letting young managers actually manage

Having thereby encouraged those who are not only "the best and the brightest" but *also* broad, sensitive human beings possessing all of the other traits and virtues essential for their managerial leadership to rise to the top, we just might be able to breathe a bit more easily about the future health of industry and society.

Ralph Z. Sorenson

A good manager listens to employees' suggestions and complaints.

After You Read

Reviewing Study Skills: Underlining and Marginal Glossing

 Use the preceding article to practice underlining and marginal glossing (discussed in Chapter Six). (You may want to make a photocopy of the article first.) Write your marginal gloss for lines 54–60.

_____

_____

_____

_____

_____

_____

 Compare your gloss from Exercise 1 with the glosses written by your classmates. Who wrote the best one? Why is it the best? Use your underlined and glossed copy to help you with the following exercises.

Recalling Information

exercise 3 Choose the best way of finishing each statement here and on the next page, based on what you have just read.

1. The author's work experience includes:
   a. college teaching and administration
   b. working outside the United States
   c. business management
   d. all of the above

2. Since he believes managers should be broad human beings, he would like to see their education focused on business and also on:
   a. the humanities and liberal arts
   b. computers and high technology
   c. accounting and finance

3. For him, a manager should have leadership skills; a good *leader* is one who:
   a. defines problems succinctly
   b. understands and inspires people
   c. expresses his or her ideas clearly
   d. none of the above

4. One of the experiences that convinced him of the need for a sense of integrity in managers was:
   a. a conversation with a high government official
   b. the discovery of dishonesty among students
   c. reading about scandals in the newspapers

5. According to Sorenson, when facing a decision about the possible closing of a factory that is not profitable, a manager should consider the interests of:
   a. the stockholders and customers
   b. the employees
   c. the community
   d. all the above

6. He thinks that managers should think not just of what is profitable in the short run but also of:
   a. how to "cut corners" to meet objectives
   b. the long-term interests of those involved
   c. the fastest way to make money for the company

7. In his view at present, the trait that distinguishes the successful manager from the mediocre is:
   a. high academic achievement
   b. the ability to get things done
   c. a critical and analytical mind

8. Companies that hire young managers ought to:
   a. let them manage right away
   b. put them under the authority of an older manager
   c. give them a training course

Applying Inferences to a Specific Situation

activity

Now that you have read Sorenson's article, imagine that he is looking for a new manager for a department of his company and has received the following descriptions of three candidates for the position. Based on what he says in the article, what can you infer about his reaction to these candidates? Working in small groups, decide which one he would probably hire and why. Support your opinion for or against each candidate with specific statements from the reading.

CANDIDATE A

- graduated with high honors from a top East Coast university
- majored in business, minored in computer science
- won two prizes for inventing new computer programs
- was chess champion of the university for two years
- received a medal for highest academic achievement in her senior year
- was described by her teachers as "brilliant, analytical, clear-thinking"

CANDIDATE B

- graduated with above-average marks from a large Midwestern state university
- majored in history, minored in business
- spent two summers traveling through Europe and the Orient
- won a national essay contest
- was secretary of a debate club
- was active in community activities—for example, neighborhood cleanup drive, fund-raising for new senior citizens' center
- worked part-time for three years as assistant manager of the school bookstore in order to finance his education
- was described by his teachers as "well-liked, honest, industrious"

CANDIDATE C

- graduated with honors from a well-known California university
- had a joint major in political science and business and a minor in economics
- is fluent in three languages
- spent his junior year at an international school in Switzerland
- was president of the music society and treasurer of the drama club
- was editor of the campus humor magazine
- organized and successfully ran (for two years) a small mail-order company that sold tapes and records of local singers
- was suspended from the university for six months for cheating on an accounting exam but was later reinstated without penalties
- was described by his teachers as "highly intelligent, ambitious, a natural leader"

Candidate most likely to be hired by Sorenson: _____

Reasons: _____

_____

"I had a terrible dream. Someone offered me a job."

Interpreting a Table

In small groups, look over the table titled "The Top Twenty Industrial Corporations in the United States" on the next page. Then answer the questions below. When working with a table like this one, follow these steps.

1. Note what pieces of information are given and where.
2. Read each question carefully until you understand exactly what is being asked for.
3. Locate the section of the table that gives this information and scan it until you find the information.
4. Write it down.

activity **2**

Working in small groups, answer the following questions.

1. Which of the top twenty U.S. companies earned the most profits in 1992?

_____

2. Which one had the highest sales in 1992? _____

_____

3. Which state has the largest number of companies in the top twenty? Which one comes in second? And third? _____

_____

4. Judging from this table, what types of business are the most profitable?

_____

5. Which companies had a rise in rank between 1991 and 1992? Which ones had drops? _____

_____

The Top Twenty Industrial Organizations in the United States*

1992	1991	company	headquarters	industry	sales ($ millions)	profits ($ millions)
1	2	Exxon	New York, NY	Fuel	104,217	5,600.0
2	3	Philip Morris	New York, NY	Consumer	48,064	3,927.0
3	4	General Electric	Fairfield, CT	Conglomerates	59,379	4,435.0
4	6	Wal-Mart Stores	Bentonville, AR	Retailing	43,887	1,608.5
5	5	Merck	Rahway, NJ	Health care	8,603	2,121.7
6	9	Coca-Cola	Atlanta, GA	Consumer	11,572	1,618.0
7	8	American Telephone & Telegraph	New York, NY	Telecomms.	44,651	522.0
8	1	International Business Machines	Armonk, NY	Office equipment	64,792	−564.0
9	7	Bristol-Myers Squibb	New York, NY	Health care	11,159	2,056.0
10	10	Procter & Gamble	Cincinnati, OH	Consumer	28,229	1,787.0
11	11	Johnson & Johnson	New Brunswick, NJ	Health care	12,447	1,461.0
12	16	Du Pont	Wilmington, DE	Chemicals	38,695	1,403.0
13	20	GTE	Stamford, CT	Telecomms.	19,621	1,529.0
14	23	Abbott Laboratories	Abbott Park, IL	Health care	6,877	1,088.7
15	15	Pepsico	Purchase, NY	Consumer	19,608	1,080.2
16	28	Pfizer	New York, NY	Health care	6,950	722.1
17	27	American Home Products	New York, NY	Health care	7,079	1,375.3
18	14	Mobil	New York, NY	Fuel	56,432	1,921.0
19	18	General Motors	Detroit, MI	Automotive	123,056	−4,992.0
20	17	Bellsouth	Atlanta, GA	Telecomms.	14,446	1,506.9

*Data from The 1992 Business Week 1000.

Barriers Fall for Women at Work

Before You Read

Inferring the Meaning of Key Words and Expressions

Scan the article for the following italicized words and expressions, and write your own definitions or explanations of what they mean. Use the hints to help you.

1. *go co-ed* (This phrase comes right at the beginning, but you may have to read a few paragraphs to get its meaning.)

   _____

2. *line technician* (The first three paragraphs give an example of this job.)

   _____

3. *blue-collar jobs* (These are usually contrasted with "white-collar jobs," and the reference is to male clothing.)

   _____

4. *barriers* (This word appears in the title and again in the fifth paragraph.)

   _____

5. *trade jobs* (This term is similar to "blue-collar jobs" above, but more specific; *trade jobs* are one kind of blue-collar jobs.)

   _____

6. *WOW* (This is a proper noun and an acronym. Tell what the letters stand for and what the group does.)

   _____

7. *make inroads* (This expression is used in the middle of the article.)

   _____

8. *discrimination lawsuits* (This occurs toward the end of the article.)

   _____

"A man, he works from sun to sun, but a woman's work is never done." This is an old saying, but what does it really mean? What is "woman's work"? Honestly, what jobs do you think are best done by men? Read the following newspaper article to find out how the idea of woman's work is changing in North America.

Barriers Fall for Women at Work

Nontraditional, Skilled-Trade Jobs Slowly Go Co-ed

Greenwich, Conn.—The telephone company worker throws a heavy belt laden with tools over a sweatshirt, then, oblivious to the gentle snowfall, quickly scales the 35-foot utility pole.

A common sight perhaps, but there's something different about this picture—a woman's soft curls frame the hard hat, a touch of makeup dusts the face.

For four years, Kim Callanan, 27, has driven her truck around this New York City suburb, fixing downed lines and restoring phone service, one of the handful of female Nynex Corp. workers to hold the job of line technician.

Slowly, very slowly, women are moving into higher-paying occupations they rarely had access to in the past—as welders, carpenters and truck drivers, among others.

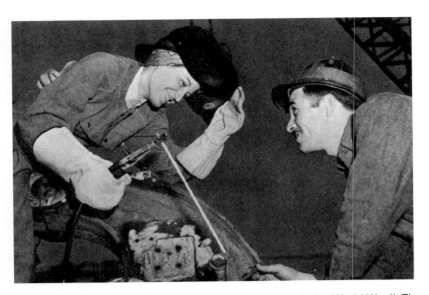

Rosie the Riveter was a picture shown on propaganda posters during World War II. The posters showed Rosie, a happy and attractive woman working with tools in a factory. This picture shows one of the real working women of the period.

15   Training programs nationwide are helping mostly poor, single mothers get skilled blue-collar or technical jobs that don't require a college degree. But there are still significant barriers to women in the so-called trade professions, with many facing opposition from employers, colleagues, friends and family.

20   Ability usually isn't the question. Rosie the Riveter came to symbolize the women who stepped in at factories and other work sites during World War II. They helped turn out tanks and ammunition.

    "The experience showed that when you pay women well and train them well, they perform," said Karen Nussbaum, director of the Women's Bureau, the entity within the Labor Department concerned with women's 25 employment issues.

    But when the men returned from war, women were expected to return to their homes and more traditional jobs as nurses, secretaries and teachers.

    Now, with almost 54 million women employed, only 6.6 percent of 30 women are in nontraditional jobs, according to Wider Opportunities for Women, or WOW, a Washington-based advocacy group. The Labor Department defines nontraditional jobs as those in which women make up less than 25 percent of the work force.

Women and nontraditional work

U.S. Department of Labor defines nontraditional occupations as jobs in which women make up less than 25% of the total number of workers in that occupation.

When women work in the same occupations as men they still do not earn equal pay.

Occupation	Women	Men	Wage gap
Printing machine operator	$308	$464	33%
Truck driver	$299	$421	29%
Police/Detective	$445	$552	19%
Freight, stock and material handler	$278	$314	12%

Over the past five years, the greatest increase of women working in nontraditional jobs has been in the professional occupations.

Occupation	1988	1992
Lawyer	19.3%	21.4%
Engineer	7.3%	8.5%
Physicist/Astronomer	7.1%	11.1%
Surveyor/Mapmaker	4.3%	6.7%

Even though most working women (73%) are in nonprofessional occupations, gains in those nontraditional jobs have been minimal or nonexistent over the past five years.

Occupation	1988	1992
Telephone installer	12.1%	10.5%
Truck driver	4.3%	4.6%
Electrician	1.4%	1.2%
Automobile mechanic	0.7%	0.8%

Indeed, three-quarters of working women have low-paying jobs with little security, few benefits and little room for advancement. At the same time, nearly half of all working women earn the family's primary income.

The "tough guy" occupations are those with higher salaries, benefits and greater potential for career advancement. The most skilled of the trade jobs pay between $23 and $27 an hour, while blue-collar women's work usually offers salaries in the $5-an-hour range.

Even without reaching the highest skill levels, women in nontraditional labor typically earn between 20 and 30 percent more than those in traditionally female blue-collar jobs, according to WOW.

"The challenge is getting the word out about these jobs," said Kristin Watkins of WOW. "Women don't grow up necessarily thinking that they want to be a carpenter. . . . they don't grow up tinkering on the car with dad."

And because they haven't seen other women working in trade jobs they can't imagine themselves on a construction crew, welding or driving a truck, Watkins said.

Women have made inroads into the professions requiring advanced degrees—in law, business and medicine—but have been less successful breaking into skilled blue-collar labor.

"This is the unfinished agenda of women entering jobs that were closed off to them before," Nussbaum said.

Encouraged by civil rights legislation and the women's movement, they began to advance about 20 years ago, often forcing their way in doors through discrimination lawsuits.

But progress has been slow. Between 1988 and 1992, the number of women in nontraditional jobs remained relatively unchanged at 3 percent of the total number of employed workers, according to WOW.

In 1991, President Bush signed the Nontraditional Employment for Women Act, requiring federal job training centers to increase training for women in nontraditional jobs.

The growing numbers of training programs for nontraditional labor is particularly important, experts say, as pressure builds in Congress to cut welfare payments to single mothers.

Still, federal guidelines call for contractors on government-subsidized jobs to hire women to perform at least 6.9 percent of total hours worked. But enforcement has never been strict.

"Where employers feel like they have to meet federal guidelines, they do, when they don't, they don't," Nussbaum said. "We need to make it clear to employers that this is the law and compliance is relatively easy."

Persuading employers to hire women for nontraditional jobs in rural Tulare County, Calif., is a challenge, said Kathy Johnson, who helps run a nontraditional training program through the county's Private Industry Council.

"Typically, employers say women can't do the job, that they are not strong enough, that they will cause problems, that they will distract the men."

Lisa Genasci

After You Read
Distinguishing Between the General and the Specific

exercise 1

Decide which of the following statements from the reading are general and which are specific. There are three of each. Then tell which general statement each specific statement supports.

1. "But there are still significant barriers to women in the so-called trade professions. . . ."

   _____ general   _____ specific

2. "For four years, Kim Callanan . . . has driven her truck around . . . , fixing downed lines and restoring phone service. . . ."

   _____ general   _____ specific

3. "Slowly . . . women are moving into higher-paying occupations they rarely had access to in the past. . . ."

   _____ general   _____ specific

4. "The most skilled of the trade jobs pay between $23 and $27 an hour, while blue-collar women's work usually offers salaries in the $5-an-hour range."

   _____ general   _____ specific

5. "'Typically, employers say women . . . are not strong enough, that they will cause problems, that they will distract the men.'"

   _____ general   _____ specific

6. "The 'tough guy' occupations are those with higher salaries. . . ."

   _____ general   _____ specific

Talking It Over

In small groups, discuss the following questions.

1. Who was Rosie the Riveter, and what did she symbolize?
2. What happened to the working women in North America at the end of World War II? Do you think this was necessary?
3. According to WOW, why aren't there more women in trade jobs? What other reasons are there for this lack?
4. What did the United States government do in 1991 to encourage women to take nontraditional jobs? Do you think this is a good idea?
5. What kinds of jobs do women do in your culture? Is their role changing now? Should it change?

Vocabulary: Finding Related Nouns and Verbs

Find nouns in the article "Barriers Fall for Women at Work" that are related to the following verbs. (Look at the examples. There are a number of different endings added to verbs to make nouns in English, so all the words will not be similar.)

examples: oppose   opposition _____

employ   employers, employment _____

1. advocate _____   5. discriminate _____

2. advance _____   6. pay _____

3. construct _____   7. enforce _____

4. legislate _____   8. comply _____

Relating the Reading to a New Perspective

Look at the illustration of Maslow's "Hierarchy of Human Needs." Working in small groups, discuss the following questions relating the reading and the illustration. Afterward, your teacher may call on you to share the ideas of your group with the class.

1. Which human needs do you think are fulfilled for men and women in our society?
2. Does the level of needs being fulfilled depend on the type of job? Explain.
3. In your opinion, are these needs fulfilled for men and women equally?

When people have their basic needs satisfied (food, water, shelter, sex), they can begin to think of other things to fulfill their life expectations. Well-known psychologist Abraham Maslow has developed a "Hierarchy of Human Needs" pyramid in which he categorizes the steps to "self-fulfillment." At which stages of the pyramid do working and job satisfaction fit in? What are the most important requirements for a job? Is self-esteem directly connected with the type of job one has or are other things in life more important?

Self-actualization
(self-fulfillment)

Esteem needs
(recognition, status)

Social needs
(place in family and community)

Safety needs
(security, stability, law and order)

Physiological needs
(food, water, shelter, sex)

Reading Charts on Tests

If you have a reading-comprehension test that includes a chart, don't panic. At first glance, a chart may seem incomprehensible, but it is usually not as difficult as it looks. Look again at the chart "Women and Nontraditional Work" on page 193 and follow these steps. Then do this exercise:

1. Ask yourself: What is the main point the chart wants to show? For example, what kind of information is given in the chart?

   _____

2. If the chart has different sections, look at them and decide how they are different. How many sections are there? _____ How are they

   different? _____

3. Work out the questions or items you have to do one at a time and check your answers with the chart. If there is one part you just don't understand, skip it and go to the next.

exercise Tell if the following statements are true (T), false (F), or not present (NP) according to the chart on page 193. (Mark a statement NP if the chart does not give you information about it.)

1. _____ Women printing-machine operators have a higher weekly income than men printing-machine operators.

2. _____ Women carpenters have a higher weekly income than men carpenters.

3. _____ Men police detectives make 19% more money than women police detectives.

4. _____ Men lawyers make more money than women lawyers.

5. _____ There are more men engineers than women engineers.

6. _____ Most working women are in the professional occupations.

7. _____ In the past five years, the number of women electricians has not increased.

8. _____ The percentage of women truck drivers is going up faster than the percentage of women physicists and astronomers.

9. _____ For every one of the professions listed on the chart, there are at least three men to every woman.

10. _____ Women who work in the same occupation as men always earn less than the men.

The Worst Recruiters Have Seen

What do you *not* want to do during a job interview? The following article from *The Wall Street Journal* describes the worst mistakes some recruiters have seen during job interviews. These are referred to as *faux pas,* a French phrase that literally means "false steps" and is often used in English to describe the small mistakes that make a bad impression.

Read the selection quickly to find out what mistakes were made and what the consequences were. Try to finish the reading and comprehension exercises in eight minutes.

The Worst Recruiters Have Seen

Let's face it: It's a jungle out there, and you can use all the help available to avoid the mistakes that can doom a promising job candidacy.

Perhaps you can draw some lessons from these fatal *faux pas*, gleaned from veteran corporate and executive recruiters. They consider them the
5 worst mistakes they've seen.

Red-Handed

During his interview with me, a candidate bit his fingernails and proceeded to bleed onto his tie. When I asked him if he wanted a Band-Aid, he said that he chewed his nails all the time and that he'd be fine. He continued to chew away.   *—Audrey W. Hellinger, Chicago office of Martin*
10 *H. Bauman Associates, New York*

Let's Be Buddies

In his first meeting with me, a candidate made himself a little too comfortable. Not only did he liberally pepper his conversation with profanities, he also pulled his chair right up to the edge of my desk and started picking up and examining papers and knickknacks.   *—Nina Proct,*
15 *Martin H. Bauman Associates, New York*

Deep Water

One of the top candidates for a senior vice presidency at a big consumer-products company was a young man under 35 who had grown up in a small town in the Midwest. As I frequently do, I asked about his years in

high school. He said he'd been a star swimmer—so good that he'd even won a gold medal in the Olympics. It hung in his high-school gymnasium. The client liked him very much and was preparing to make him an offer. But when I checked his references, I discovered he hadn't gone to the college he'd listed, and he had never even swum in the Olympics. — *John A. Coleman, Canny, Bowen Inc., New York*

Loser's Circle

I walked into the reception area to pick up my next applicant, Sarah B., a recent college graduate.

Once in my office, I glanced at her well-written resume and wondered how much time and money she had spent preparing it. She was obviously intelligent and articulate. How, I wondered, could she misjudge our corporate climate this way?

The sad fact was that I could never send her out to be interviewed by our administrators or physicians. They might forgive her sandals, her long billowy skirt and her white peasant blouse—but never, ever, the large gold ring through her nose. —*Janet Garber, Manager of Employment-Employee Relations, Cornell University Medical College, New York*

Bon Voyage

It was a million-dollar job, and he was a top-notch candidate. My client had decided to hire him, and he was having dinner with the chief executive officer. He asked the CEO, "How do we travel?" The response was: "We're being careful of costs these days. We travel business class internationally and back-of-the-bus domestically." Without thinking, the candidate said, "I'm used to traveling first class." —*Tony Lord, New York office of A. T. Kearney Executive Search, Chicago*

It's Not Always the Candidate

It isn't always the job candidate who's the disaster. Consider what happened to the top aspirant for a senior position at one of Richard Slayton's client companies. As related by the Chicago executive recruiter, the candidate was set for a full day of interviews with senior executives, including a final session over dinner with the CEO.

His first interview was with the general counsel, who arrived thirty minutes late because there had been a work stoppage. "His second session, with the executive vice president of marketing, also ran a half-hour late because he was on a conference call with the company's largest customer, who had just been acquired," says Mr. Slayton.

At lunch with the candidate, the senior vice president of human resources broke a bridge and lined up the pieces of broken teeth on a napkin in front of him. And, finally, the CEO was called away unexpectedly and never met with the candidate.

But, says Mr. Slayton, the day from hell had a happy ending. "My client said that if he could survive all that with good humor, he was worth serious consideration. He got the job."

The Wall Street Journal

Comprehension Quiz

Put an X in front of the mistakes made by the job applicants described in the article.

1. _____ acting too casual

2. _____ acting too formal

3. _____ arriving thirty minutes late for the appointment

4. _____ biting fingernails

5. _____ dropping papers and personal items on the floor

6. _____ forgetting the company's name

7. _____ not carrying a business card

8. _____ not leaving a tip

9. _____ showing a gold medal won in swimming class

10. _____ showing an unwillingness to economize

11. _____ telling lies

12. _____ using swear words and bad language

13. _____ wearing a nose ring

14. _____ wearing inappropriate clothing

15. _____ breaking his teeth

 *exercise* 2   Choose the best way of finishing each statement, based on what you have just read.

1. The job candidates described in the article are:
   a. all men
   b. all women
   c. mostly men
   d. mostly women

2. In the article there is only one job candidate who gets the job. He gets the job because
   a. his father works for the company
   b. he doesn't make any mistakes
   c. he acts like an old buddy
   d. he shows patience and humor

"You misspelled *graduate*."

WAISGLASS/COULTHART
Farcus © Farcus Cartoons. Dist.
by Universal Press Syndicate.
Reprinted with permission. All
rights reserved.

WHAT DO YOU THINK?

Home Offices

With modern inventions of instant communications such as fax and e-mail, many people have chosen to set up their work offices at home. Over 4 million Americans now have their main office at home. They work as consultants, writers, editors, and businesspeople. No more commuting; no more office hassle. Would you like to work from your home? What are the advantages of a home office? What are the disadvantages?

"I think it's great that you can work at home."

CHAPTER eight
Breakthroughs

Within the last twenty years, a number of "breakthroughs" have been made in the fields of technology, communications, and agriculture. Sometimes people are stunned by these new developments and wonder how to incorporate them into their lives. We explore a breakthrough in architecture with the huge new Denver International Airport (DIA). Then we look at the controversial "super plants," genetically engineered crops. Next we read about the pros and cons of promoting "breakthrough" scientific discoveries. Finally, a timed reading asks: Are computers alive?

SELECTION **one**
DIA's Best Feature

Before You Read
Making Background Inferences

Often an article is written in a way that assumes the reader knows about the background of a situation. If, in fact, you are not familiar with the situation, you have to make inferences from the clues given. Read the following statements. Then read carefully the first three paragraphs of the first reading selection. Write *C* in front of correct inferences and *I* in front of incorrect ones.

1. _____ The baggage system at DIA is the biggest passenger convenience.

2. _____ The baggage system at DIA has made the airport the largest and most modern in the nation.

3. _____ The baggage system at DIA has had some well-known problems.

4. _____ Stapleton International Airport has more space than DIA.

5. _____ Stapleton International Airport has less space than DIA.

6. _____ Stapleton International Airport has as much landing and departure capacity as DIA.

7. _____ Before the construction of DIA, Denver had a good reputation for air traffic.

8. _____ Before the construction of DIA, Denver had a bad reputation for air traffic.

Denver International
Airport

LANDING SYSTEMS

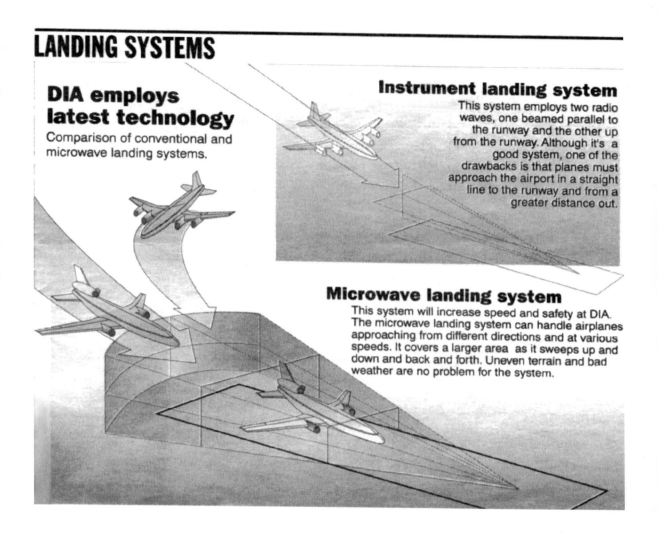

DIA employs latest technology
Comparison of conventional and microwave landing systems.

Instrument landing system
This system employs two radio waves, one beamed parallel to the runway and the other up from the runway. Although it's a good system, one of the drawbacks is that planes must approach the airport in a straight line to the runway and from a greater distance out.

Microwave landing system
This system will increase speed and safety at DIA. The microwave landing system can handle airplanes approaching from different directions and at various speeds. It covers a larger area as it sweeps up and down and back and forth. Uneven terrain and bad weather are no problem for the system.

It's not just in the fields of medicine and science where life-saving discoveries are made. Sometimes a design can be a breakthrough with important consequences. Read the following article from the *Rocky Mountain News* about the revolutionary design of the DIA (Denver International Airport) built in the mid-1990s.

DIA's Best Feature

Top-Flight Runway Design

All the attention on the troubled baggage system has overshadowed the biggest passenger convenience at Denver International Airport—the nation's largest and most modern airfield.

Two baggage systems will serve DIA on opening day. The automated system will

BAE'S AUTOMATED SYSTEM

After you check your bag at the curb or ticket counter, a bar-coded tag is attached. Laser scanners read the tag while the bag travels on conveyor belts.

Bag is transferred from conveyor belt to a cart, which moves up to 20 mph on a network of tracks. Each cart carries one bag, loaded on the move. Computer uses information from the tag to direct the cart through a series of switches to the proper destination. A radio transponder on the cart signals its location to the computer during transit.

RAPISTAN'S BACKUP SYSTEM

After you check your bag at the curb or ticket counter, a bar-coded tag is attached. Conveyor takes bag to the third level of the parking garages.

Bag passes through laser scanner that reads the tag and directs the bag to a carousel. Worker grabs the bag off the carousel and loads it on a cart. Drivers haul the carts through tunnels built for the automated system, as much as a mile, to the three concourses.

THE BAGGAGE SYSTEM

Two baggage systems will serve DIA on opening day. The automated system will serve outbound and some inbound United baggage, the Rapistan system all others.

Unlike Stapleton International Airport and other airports with space constraints, DIA has plenty of room: 54 square miles. The new airport has five runways that radiate in all directions from the terminal. The airfield's design dramatically increases the landing and departure capacity over Stapleton's.

"Denver will no longer be the choke point in the national air traffic system," predicted Larry Parrent, air traffic manager for the Federal Aviation Administration at DIA.

Snowstorms, thunderstorms, fog and heavy crosswinds often slow Stapleton flights and trigger a ripple effect at other airports.

During bad weather, air traffic at Stapleton is funneled to one runway because its two north-south runways are too close together to permit simultaneous landings. And only one runway has the instrument-landing system required for low-visibility approaches.

At DIA, all the runways have instrument capacity and are spaced at least a mile apart. That allows more airlines to land at DIA in bad weather than can land at Stapleton in good weather.

und and some inbound United baggage, the Rapistan system all others.

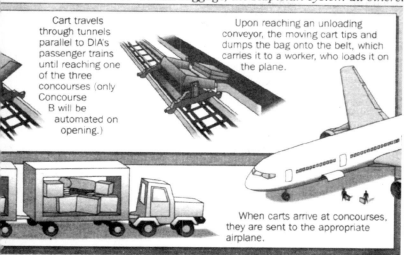

Cart travels through tunnels parallel to DIA's passenger trains until reaching one of the three concourses (only Concourse B will be automated on opening.)

Upon reaching an unloading conveyor, the moving cart tips and dumps the bag onto the belt, which carries it to a worker, who loads it on the plane.

When carts arrive at concourses, they are sent to the appropriate airplane.

"DIA is the only airport in the world that can land three aircraft on three runways simultaneously in bad weather," Parrent said.

Weather delays, however, will not be eliminated. The city has roughly the same snow-removal equipment at DIA as it has had at Stapleton, and takeoffs and landings during snowstorms will be dictated more by runway cleanup and plane deicing than by the capacity of the airfield.

"No matter how you set up an airport, severe snow conditions are going to affect operations," said FAA procedures specialist Larry Bell.

The airfield was built with the future in mind. The site, which Denver annexed from Adams County in a 1988 election, will allow up to 12 runways to be built.

FAA officials won't predict when air traffic will grow to a level that requires more runways. A sixth runway originally was planned to be built this year, but the city and the federal government delayed that project because of cost concerns.

Christopher Broderick

After You Read
Finding the Visual Metaphors

Scan the article and diagrams for the visually suggestive words that can replace the direct words in italics.

1. All the attention on the troubled baggage system has *taken attention away from* the . . . convenience . . . <u>overshadowed</u>

2. The new airport has five runways that *go out from the center* in all directions . . . _____

3. Denver will no longer be the *place where air traffic slows down* in the national . . . system. _____

4. During bad weather, air traffic at Stapleton is *directed* to one runway . . . _____

5. Snowstorms . . . often slow Stapleton flights and *set off a chain reaction of problems* at other airports. _____

6. This system employs two radio waves, one *projected* parallel to the runway . . . _____ (diagram, page 205)

7. It covers a larger area as it *moves* up and down . . . _____

Summarizing the Main Point

Write a one-sentence summary of the article about DIA. Be sure to include the *two* main improvements of the new airport from this list: baggage system, more space, increased air traffic, better landing system, superior snow removal equipment, simultaneous delays.

_____

_____

Talking It Over

In small groups, discuss the following questions.

1. Why will there still be weather delays at DIA?
2. How do you feel about flying in bad weather? About flying in general?
3. Which is your favorite airport? Why?

4. Can you think of any other examples of excellent design in buildings or facilities?

5. Look at the diagram of the two baggage systems at Denver International Airport on pages 206 and 207. Compare the two systems. Which one do you think is faster? Which do you think is more efficient? Which do you think is more trouble free?

Telling Travel Stories

Work with a classmate. Each of you tells the other about a funny, frightening, or unusual travel incident. The other person takes notes and asks questions. Your teacher may ask you to write or speak about what you hear.

CITY AIRPORT

RUNWAY

RUNWAY

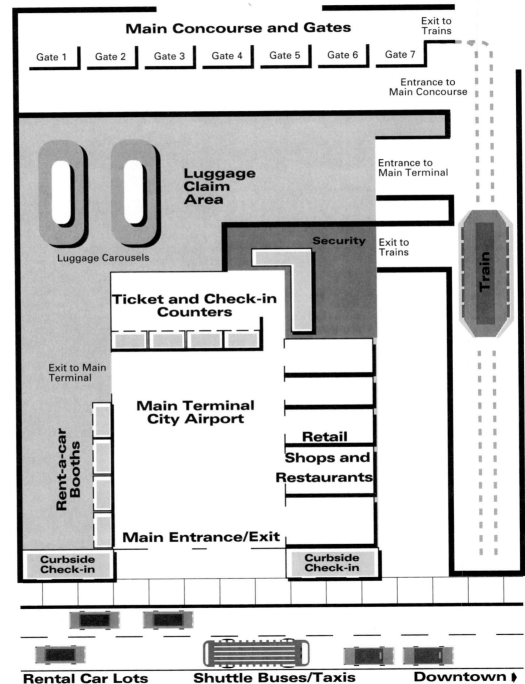

Main Concourse and Gates

Gate 1　Gate 2　Gate 3　Gate 4　Gate 5　Gate 6　Gate 7

Exit to Trains

Entrance to Main Concourse

Entrance to Main Terminal

Luggage Claim Area

Security

Exit to Trains

Train

Luggage Carousels

Ticket and Check-in Counters

Exit to Main Terminal

Rent-a-car Booths

Main Terminal City Airport

Retail

Shops and Restaurants

Main Entrance/Exit

Curbside Check-in

Curbside Check-in

Rental Car Lots　　**Shuttle Buses/Taxis**　　**Downtown ▶**

Reading Diagrams on Tests

If you find a diagram on a test, stay calm. It is not necessary to be an engineer to understand it. Information on a diagram generally shows a relationship between items—often a time, space, or size relationship. Look at the City Airport diagram and follow these steps. Then do the exercise that follows.

1. Define the question. What exactly are you being asked to do?
2. Define the relationship(s) shown on the diagram.
3. Read the information in the correct order, following the sequences.
4. Answer the question(s) briefly or do the exercise.

exercise Sequence the following steps in time order, with *1* as the first, according to the information on the City Airport diagram. Then, if you wish, take a pencil and make a line on the diagram following the steps for arrival and departure at City Airport.

STEPS FOR ARRIVING AT CITY AIRPORT

a. _____ Exit train and go to baggage-claim area.

b. _____ Make arrangements to rent the car.

c. _____ Get on a train and take it to the main terminal.

d. _____ Get off your plane at one of the gates.

e. _____ Get luggage from assigned carousel.

f. _____ Exit through main doors to catch a shuttle or a taxi, or pick up your car at the rental car lots.

STEPS FOR DEPARTURE FROM CITY AIRPORT

a. _____ Board train for concourse and gates.

b. _____ Check in at gate and wait for plane.

c. _____ Go through security.

d. _____ Buy last minute gifts at shops.

e. _____ Check luggage and ticket at curbside or at ticket counter.

f. _____ Arrive at airport.

g. _____ Exit train and go up to concourse and gate.

SELECTION **two**

Sowing the Seeds of Super Plants

Before You Read

Anticipating the Reading

 *exercise* **1**

Answer the following questions.

1. What do you imagine when you think of the words *super plant*? What traits or characteristics should it have?

_____

_____

Compare your ideas with the artist's concept on page 215.

2. What are some problems in the world today that could be solved if botanists were able to produce made-to-order plants in their laboratories? Do you think there would also be dangers?

_____

_____

Identifying the Meaning of Technical Terms from Context

 *exercise* **2**

Many new scientific terms have passed into common usage through reports in newspapers and magazines. Key scientific terms from the article are used in the following two paragraphs. Read the paragraphs. Then match each of the italicized terms with its definition, given after the paragraphs. Write the correct term in the blank after each definition.

GENETIC ENGINEERING AND PUBLIC FEARS

People used to think that hereditary traits, such as brown eyes, tallness, red hair, and so forth, were passed from parents to children in the blood. Terms such as "bad blood" and "blood brothers," though incorrect, are still used. Modern science has shown that these traits are passed in the *genes* from the parents' cells, which recombine during reproduction. The actual chemical in the gene responsible for this transmission is *deoxyribonucleic acid,* usually referred to as *DNA.* In the last two decades scientists have managed to isolate the genes that cause particular traits in some organisms and plants. In certain cases they can

10 even use the techniques of *recombinant* DNA or *gene splicing* to insert a fragment of a gene from one animal or plant directly into the genes of another, usually by splicing it to a chemical. From these advances the new field of *genetic engineering* was born.

Reactions to announcements of this latest scientific progress in the 15 1970s were mixed. Some people foresaw the curing of inherited diseases and the improvement of agriculture. Other sectors of the press and the public responded with fear and loathing. Were human beings trying to play God? What if scientists were to create a new *bacterium* that would escape from the lab and infect the world with a terrible disease? Concern 20 grew with the announcement of *cloning:* the production from a single cell of one or many identical individuals, or *clones.* Science fiction writers imagined armies of cloned soldiers. Philosophers worried about the loss of individual identity. Were these techniques stopped? Or was it shown that the dangers had been greatly exaggerated? The answer is given in the 25 following article.

DEFINITIONS

1. any one of a type of microscopic organism, some of which cause disease:

_____

2. the technique of putting pieces of the genes from one organism into the genes of another:

_____

3. an acid found in the nucleus of cells, responsible for the transmission of hereditary characteristics:

_____

4. a group of identical organisms derived from a single individual:

_____

5. the units of heredity that transmit traits from one generation to another:

_____

6. referring to the uniting or joining together of different things:

_____

7. a new branch of biochemistry in which genes are altered to change or improve the traits of plants or animals:

_____

8. the growing of genetically identical plants or animals from a single cell:

_____

Read the following article to find out more about what science is doing in the quest for perfect plants.

Sowing the Seeds of Super Plants

Somewhere deep in the mountains of Peru, plant geneticist Jon Fobes is collecting samples of a very special tomato. This tomato will never win a prize at a county fair; it is remarkably ugly—a green, berrylike fruit that is not good to eat. But to Fobes it has a winning quality. It is twice as meaty as an ordinary tomato. Other exotic tomatoes that Fobes is gathering can grow at very cold altitudes or in salty soil, or they are remarkably resistant to drought, insects, and disease. Fobes's goal: to bring them back to his laboratory at the research division of the Atlantic Richfield Company in California and isolate and identify the genes that give them such strong characteristics, so that someday they can be genetically engineered into commercial tomatoes.

Fobes is just one of the many scientists who are searching the wilderness to find plants with genes that may eventually be used to create a whole new garden of super plants. Until recently there was little incentive for such quests. Although molecular biologists were making rapid progress in the genetic engineering of bacteria to produce human proteins such as insulin, botanists faced a set of problems that apparently could not be solved by the same recombinant DNA techniques. Recently, however, they have overcome some of the barriers that nature placed in the way of the genetic engineering of plants. Items:

- Biologists John Kemp and Timothy Hall, University of Wisconsin professors who do research for Agrigenetics, a private company, announced the first transfer of a functioning gene from one plant to another—from a bean plant into a sunflower plant.
- Jeff Schell, of the State University of Ghent in Belgium, announced an important step toward the regulation of transplanted genes. His research team introduced into tobacco cells artificial genes that were activated in light but not in darkness.
- Researchers at the Cetus Madison Corporation of Madison, Wisconsin, won approval from the recombinant DNA advisory committee of the NIH (National Institutes of Health, a government agency) to field test plants genetically engineered to resist certain diseases.

Not everyone is delighted. Within days after the Cetus announcement, Jeremy Rifkin, a publicity-seeking author of a poorly received book about genetic engineering, attacked the NIH committee for hearing the Cetus

proposal at a session closed to the public. He also asked for an investigation by the NIH of possible conflict of interest because a scientist at
Cetus is a former member of the committee, and a leading scientist from
another genetics engineering firm is a member now.

Earlier in the month, Rifkin had filed suit in a general district court in
Washington to block the field testing of a bacterium genetically
engineered at the University of California at Berkeley to protect plants
from frost. He claimed that the NIH committee had not adequately
examined the field testing for possible environmental hazards. Although
the suit seemed to lack merit, it had an effect. Complaining that the suit
had delayed their experiment, which was dependent on weather conditions, the Berkeley scientists postponed the test.

The sudden hubub over gene splicing was similar to the controversy
over use of the newly developed recombinant DNA techniques in the
1970s. That uproar occurred after the scientists themselves had recommended strict testing guidelines to prevent engineered organisms from
escaping from the laboratory, and the NIH put them into effect. Later it
became apparent that the techniques were not dangerous, the rules were
relaxed, and the protests died out. The latest NIH decision that allows field
testing of genetically engineered plants reflected a general confidence
among scientists that proper precautions were being taken and that the
work was safe.

Some plant scientists found a touch of the absurd in Rifkin's
harassment. Plant breeders have been introducing new genes into plants
for thousands of years. They have used techniques such as cross-polli-
nation, inserting pollen from one group of plants into another group, to
produce hybrid plants that are hardier, more attractive, more nutritious, or

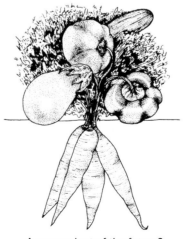

A super plant of the future?

tastier than nature's own. Still, these traditional methods have their limitations. Crossbreeding is useful only in plants of the same or similar species. It also takes time, sometimes hundreds of crosses over many years, to breed a plant with even a single new trait.

Genetic engineering provides a dramatic new shortcut. Eventually, it could allow scientists to insert a wider variety of beneficial genes into plants in a few days. The potential seems enormous. Crops that now need expensive fertilizer could be changed so that they could extract nitrogen (the most important element in fertilizer) from the air; they could be engineered to produce toxins to protect themselves from insects, grow in salty soils, live for weeks without water, and use the sun's energy more efficiently. Plants with engineered characteristics could one day be the basis for a new "green revolution" that would provide enough food for the world's hungry people.

The genetic engineering of plants owes much of its recent success to an ingenious solution to an old problem: the lack of an effective way to transplant foreign genes into the DNA of plant cells. The solution came from bacteria—in the form of a plasmid (a tiny piece of DNA engineered to carry genes) from the bacterium *Agrobacterium tumefaciens.* The bacterium is not ordinarily a benefactor of humanity. It causes small brown tumors to form on such important plants as tobacco and grapes. But in the laboratory it is proving to be extraordinarily useful. After foreign genes are spliced into its plasmid, the plasmid can carry them into more than 10,000 different plants, where they find their way into the DNA. To assist these genes in entering plant cells, scientists mix them with tiny fatty bubbles called liposomes. (See the diagram "How to Move a Plant Gene.")

How to Move a Plant Gene

In their efforts to create new plants by transferring genes, scientists have not overlooked another problem: how to produce the new plants in quantity. This will require better methods of cloning than are now available. Cloning now works only with a very limited variety of plants. Carrots, petunias, and tobacco, for example, can be cloned with ease, but the important cereal grains respond poorly—if at all—to cloning.

Scientists are still seeking the biological key to the regeneration of plants, trying to learn why a lone plant cell will sometimes sprout into an entire new plant and at other times will simply refuse to divide and multiply. Once they are able to combine cloning and genetic engineering, the payoffs, both scientifically and commercially, could be dazzling.

Sana Siwolop

HOW TO MOVE A PLANT GENE

1. Donor plant with desired gene   2. Gene after removal   3. Gene is inserted into an Agrobacterium plasmid   4. Plasmids are mixed with liposomes   5. Plasmid-liposome packages enter a plant cell   6. Cells are cultured   7. New plant carries the desired gene

After You Read

Recalling Information

exercise 1   Choose the best way of finishing each statement here and on the next page, based on what you have just read.

1. The exciting news about genetic engineering in plants is that scientists have just recently managed to
   a. find some plants in Peru with hardy characteristics
   b. transfer a functioning gene from one plant to another
   c. create and clone a whole new species of super plants

2. The field testing of genetically engineered plants is
   a. an unusual and frightening occurrence
   b. a serious concern to most plant biologists
   c. probably not dangerous

3. The great fear in the 1970s caused by the newly developed recombinant DNA technique turned out to be
   a. almost groundless
   b. highly beneficial
   c. completely justified

4. If scientists master the techniques of genetic engineering, they could eventually produce crops that
   a. could live for weeks without any water
   b. grow without the need for fertilizer
   c. produce their own poisons against insects
   d. all the above and more

Scientists at the University of Wisconsin have recently developed a potato plant that poisons destructive beetles.

5. The big problem of what to use to carry genes from one plant into another seems to be solved now by the use of
   a. a small piece of specially made plastic
   b. a plasmid carried by a bacterium
   c. a slime mold found on tomatoes in Peru

6. At the moment, the best way to describe the cloning of plants in the laboratory is that
   a. it's only successful with cereal grains
   b. it simply cannot be done
   c. sometimes it works and sometimes it doesn't

Using Information to Disprove False Opinions

The eighteenth-century English poet Alexander Pope once wrote, "A little knowledge is a dangerous thing." Many people express strong opinions on certain subjects about which they know very little. The following false opinions are examples of this. Find information from the article to disprove each one.

1. A state senator hears that plant geneticist Jon Fobes is down in Peru collecting samples of a tomato that is ugly and inedible. He knows that Fobes is using a government grant and makes a motion in the state senate to cut off the money for this work. "Everybody knows," he states with confidence, "that looking for a tomato that can't even be eaten is just plain stupid and a waste of the taxpayer's money!"

What can you say to prove him wrong?

_____

_____

_____

_____

2. You meet a businesswoman at a party who says in a loud voice, "What burns me up about scientists is that they have no common sense. All this genetic engineering of plants, for example, is ridiculous nonsense. If they want to put new genes into plants, why don't they use crossbreeding? Why, farmers have been doing that successfully for thousands of years!"

What could you tell her to change her views?

_____

_____

_____

_____

3. A young woman's father is absolutely opposed to his daughter marrying a plant biologist, even though she is head-over-heels in love with him. "Nobody ever makes any money in work like that," he fumes. "It has nothing whatever to do with practical, commercial reality!"

What can you say to aid true love?

_____

_____

_____

_____

Identifying a Bias

exercise **3**

This selection, like most scientific articles, is written in a fairly objective and informative tone. Its purpose is mainly to convey new facts. At one point, however, the author expresses a strong bias either for or against some person or idea. In what paragraph does this occur? What specific words express this bias?

Paragraph: _____

Words that show bias: _____

_____

_____

Talking It Over

activity

In small groups, discuss the following questions.

1. Even though the public sometimes overreacts to new scientific techniques, it is certainly possible that danger could arise in this way. Can you think of some scientific discoveries of the past that later backfired and caused problems?

2. Are there any areas of science today that you think are moving too fast and might become dangerous?

3. What is meant by a "conflict of interest" (line 37)? When do you think that this problem arises in science?

4. Who do you think should make decisions regarding new scientific techniques: businesspeople, government agencies such as the NIH, or scientists themselves? Why?

SELECTION three

Science Is Dandy, but Promotion Can Be Lucrative

Before You Read

Fitting Scientific Terms into Context

exercise 1

Read the description of the unwritten rules of scientific discovery and fill in each blank correctly with a term from the list. Scan the article for problematic words to see them in context.

lobbyists	protocol	circuit	honorariums
vetted	granting agency	priority	referees
proposal	tenure	journal	patent applications
press conference			

THE UNWRITTEN RULES OF SCIENTIFIC DISCOVERY

1. There is a set of unwritten rules, a _protocol_____, that scientists are expected to follow after making a discovery.

2. First, write a paper with a full account of the experiments leading to the

   discovery and send it to a well-known scientific _____.

3. Then, wait until the results are _____ by several

   _____ , scientists who are working in the same field.

4. If your paper is published and considered important, you can hit the

_____ , speaking at meetings and universities and

collecting nice fat _____ .

5. Do not call a _____ to talk about your research with

reporters or employ _____ to make appeals to

Congress or politicians for money.

6. If you need money to fund your research, write a _____

about it and send it to a _____ .

7. If you establish _____ by showing that you were the

first to make the discovery, you will probably get a good university position

with _____ , a lifetime guarantee of good

employment.

8. At that point you can talk with companies about making _____

to use your discovery in business, unless someone else has done it first.

Guessing the Meaning of Idioms and Colloquial Phrases

 Read the sentences from the article and select the best word or phrase, here and on the next page, to replace the words in italics.

1. "Do it right and you may be *fixed for life,* or even become *a household name.*"
fixed for life:
a. trapped
b. fired
c. rich
d. healthy

a household name:
a. famous
b. promoted
c. ignored
d. sent home

2. "*Slip up* and you will slink away to the snickers of your colleagues, and worse, the wider world. . . ."
a. move ahead
b. go forward
c. get an idea
d. make a mistake

3. "The most *ballyhooed* discovery of our time was the announcement . . . that two scientists had achieved nuclear fusion in a glass jar."
   a. wonderful
   b. horrible
   c. talked about
   d. passed by

4. "Controlled fusion is a *holy grail,* the promise of nearly infinite, clean and cheap energy."
   a. ridiculous idea
   b. much desired goal
   c. easy solution
   d. greatly feared consequence

5. "The news that it could be done at room temperature and pressure was a *bombshell.*"
   a. thing or event attracting a lot of attention
   b. thing or event causing great anger
   c. thing or event that was not planned for
   d. thing or event that was expected and prepared for

6. "The two scientists . . . broke academia's unwritten rules . . . and *paid dearly* for it."
   a. gave money
   b. received love
   c. earned some credit
   d. suffered a lot

7. "Only if a scientific paper *passes muster* is it accepted for publication."
   a. contains brilliant ideas
   b. discusses true facts
   c. is seen to make money
   d. is considered worthy

8. "It can be OK to be wrong, but to *jump the gun* and be wrong as well is unforgivable."
   a. move too slowly
   b. move too fast
   c. use violence
   d. use influence

9. "For a . . . scientist, priority . . . can make the all-important difference between being awarded tenure and being *out on the street.*"
   a. open for business
   b. rich and famous
   c. without a job
   d. hired for a speaking tour

10. "Government grants are easier to come by, which translates into more money for the staff who keep the Bunsens burning while the boss is *on the road*."
    a. looking for work
    b. looking for knowledge
    c. away on a trip
    d. busy with administration

11. "At that time Herschel was a professional musician . . . who had *a knack* for building telescopes."
    a. an ability
    b. the money
    c. a room
    d. the idea

A scientist makes an important breakthrough. What happens next? Will it bring fame and fortune? Or can it bring disaster to a promising career? The following article from the *Smithsonian* magazine discusses the process of promoting a scientific discovery after it has been made. Even brilliant scientists sometimes make serious mistakes during this critical time.

Science Is Dandy, but Promotion Can Be Lucrative

Making a discovery is only half the battle: announcing it to one's advantage is the next step for the scientifically ambitious

Making a major discovery in science is only the first step to fame and fortune, necessary but not sufficient. Almost as important are the how, when and where of announcing your breakthrough. Do it right and you may be fixed for life, or even become a household name. Slip up and you will slink away from the snickers of your colleagues and, worse, the wider world of newspaper readers and television watchers.

The most ballyhooed discovery of our time (apparently false, it turned out) was the announcement at the University of Utah that two scientists had achieved nuclear fusion in a glass jar. . . . Controlled fusion is a holy grail, the promise of nearly infinite, clean and cheap energy. Until the Utah story broke, most scientists had been struggling ahead the only way they knew how: re-creating the unimaginable temperatures and pressures inside stars to achieve fusion. The news that it could be done at room temperature and pressure was a bombshell.

The two scientists, Stanley Pons and Martin Fleischmann (the latter from the University of Southampton in England), broke academia's cherished

An important discovery is often immediately translated into the lifetime security of a tenured professorship.

unwritten rules in announcing their discovery and paid dearly for it. Instead of waiting until a full account of their experiments was published in a scientific journal, they called a press conference. Worse, with the aid of lobbyists they appealed to Congress for direct appropriations to fund their research. The work was so important, they said, that they should have their own instant institute.

Modern-day science does not work that way—most of the time. Results are vetted before they are announced. A paper submitted to a journal is passed first to several referees, people working in the same field who can judge the results being reported. Only if it passes muster is it accepted for publication. Raising money works the same way. Proposals are steered to referees for judgment before a granting agency writes a check. You may get away with breaking the rules if your findings are instantly recognized as correct. But there is all the difference in the world between the sweet smell of success and the odium of highly publicized error.

Bruce Lewenstein, a historian of science at Cornell University, told me at least two scientists were so irritated by the appeal to Congress that they let it be known they would "slam Pons and Fleischmann against the wall." A prominent physicist, Robert L. Park of the American Physical Society, refused to attend a luncheon at which Jerry Bishop of *The Wall Street Journal* was awarded $3,000 for his coverage of the cold fusion story.

Anger at publicity is not new in the scientific world. . . .

As a scientist myself, I have seen many erroneous "discoveries"—including one of my own—greeted with substantial publicity. In some cases reputations survive with little damage; in others the unfortunates become objects of derision. Much depends on how the discovery was announced. It can be OK to be wrong; but to jump the gun and be wrong as well is unforgivable.

At the bridge table, the player who opens the bidding may not be the one who wins the hand. But in science, the first announcement—the opening bid—establishes priority, thereby diminishing the future claims of a competitor who is rumored to have made similar findings. For a young university scientist, priority in an important discovery can make the all-important difference between being awarded tenure* and being out on the street.

Young or old, once you make a big discovery, you can hit "the circuit"—speaking at meetings held in the nicest resorts, addressing rapt graduate students and envious faculty at every ivied campus that can come up with a fat honorarium. Government grants are easier to come by, which translates into more money for the staff who keep the Bunsens burning while the boss is on the road.

Perhaps just as significant, priority can decide who reaps the financial benefits of a new discovery. A month after Pons and Fleischmann made their announcement, Bishop reported, 40 companies had signed agreements with the University of Utah to inspect patent applications based on the scientists' work.

In my own field of astronomy, it is easy to list cases in which the way discoveries were announced, and the motives of the discoverers, would fail every test of modern scientific protocol. Astronomers . . . made announcements in ways calculated to bring them maximal credit, priority and even . . . personal gain.

When Galileo† introduced his improved telescope, he touted its potential use for long-range detection of enemy ships. As a result, he was granted tenure in his professorship and a hefty raise. When he discovered the four large moons of Jupiter, he hoped to cash in on that application as well. His discovery revolutionized astronomy. Until then, dogma held that

*Tenure: a lifetime appointment with full job security.
†Galileo Galilei: (1564–1642) Italian scientist and philosopher. Performed important experiments in astronomy and physics.

everything in the sky revolved around Earth. But here was an indisputable case of celestial bodies orbiting another celestial body. It would be the model for Galileo's . . . thesis that Earth moves around the Sun.

One of his concerns in announcing his discovery, however, was to make the most he could out of it. Galileo agonized over whether to call the moons the "Cosmian Stars" after the rich and powerful Cosimo de Medici, or the "Medicean Stars" after Cosimo and his three, similarly wealthy brothers. Which would bring him the most money? He sought advice from Cosimo's secretary and eventually opted for the second choice. Today they are known as the Galilean moons. . . .

Every rule has its exceptions. . . . Some astronomers had to learn how to make a discovery announcement. William Herschel was that pleasant rarity among great scientists, a very modest person. When he discovered the planet Uranus, in 1781, with a homemade telescope from his home in Bath, England, he did no more to publicize it than to mention it to a friend. The friend wrote to the Royal Society, then as now Britain's leading scientific group, in London. The Society knew the importance of good PR, whether or not the phrase had yet been invented.

At that time Herschel was a professional musician and only an amateur astronomer, one who had a knack for building telescopes. Members of the Society realized that Herschel could advance the art of telescopes, if only he could devote full time to it. They arranged for him to meet with King George III, who soon after awarded Herschel a stipend and made him a royal astronomer. Herschel went on to build the great telescopes of his age and to make important discoveries, including the deduction that the Milky Way is shaped like a disk or lens, and we are inside it. Herschel had to be prodded into self-promotion, and we admire his modesty. . . .

The fine line that present-day scientists walk between self-aggrandizement and progress-slowing shyness involves more than the niceties of etiquette. Hasty announcements draw intense criticisms, but so do delays. In AIDS research, for example, some activists are demanding that new drugs be made available to patients before proof of their efficacy is published in peer-reviewed journals. Even in a field like astronomy, where no finding is likely to help or harm the public health, those who sit on discoveries too long are likely to be criticized.

Stephen P. Maran

After You Read

Matching General Ideas and Specific Illustrations

Like many articles, this one alternates between general and specific ideas. Read the following ideas from the article and decide which of the two columns contains general ideas and which contains specific ideas. Label the columns correctly, and then match each general idea to the specific idea that illustrates it.

A. _____

1. In the field of astronomy, it is easy to list cases in which discoveries were announced in ways calculated to bring credit and personal gain.

2. Some astronomers of the past were modest and did not try to promote their own interests.

3. If you do not follow scientific protocol when announcing your discovery, you will suffer ridicule and criticism from your colleagues.

4. Waiting too long to announce discoveries can also bring criticism.

B. _____

1. Some scientists decided they would "slam Pons and Fleischmann against the wall" because they had called a press conference to announce "cold fusion."

2. In AIDS research, some activists are demanding that new drugs be made available to patients before proof of their efficacy is published in journals.

3. When Galileo discovered the four large moons of Jupiter, he decided to name them after the rich and famous Medici brothers.

4. When William Herschel discovered the planet Uranus in 1781, he did no more to publicize it than mention it to a friend.

Vocabulary: Finding Related Words

Fill in the following chart with words from the article to show the relationships among word families. The first one is done as an example.

nouns (things)	nouns (people)	adjectives	verbs
1. _science_	_scientist_	scientific	XXXX
2. _____	_____	XXXX	discover
3. _____	XXXX	announced	_____
4. _____	XXXX	prior	prioritize
5. _____	_____	astronomical	XXXX
6. _____	public	publicized	_____
7. _____	announcer	announced	_____
8. _____	detective	XXXX	_____
9. _____	revolutionary	revolutionary	_____
10. competition	_____	competitive	compete

Talking It Over

activity 1   In small groups, discuss the following questions.

1. In your opinion, what are some of the most important discoveries that have been made in recent times?
2. Do you think that the people who make discoveries get rich and famous? Should they?
3. What invention or discovery would you like to see?
4. How are scientists and researchers regarded in your culture? Do they have the same status, salary, and lifestyle that they have in North America?
5. What are the advantages and disadvantages of choosing a career in science?

Playing the Role of Discoverer

activity 2   Work in groups of three or four and play the role of scientists who have just made an important discovery. First decide what your discovery is. (Your teacher may give you some help with this.) Then make up a short speech about it for the public, telling them what it is and why it is important. Your teacher may ask you to "present" your discovery to the class while your classmates play the roles of reporters at a press conference.

Are Computers Alive?

The following selection discusses what many people view as the most recent extension of the human mind: the computer. Is it simply a tool, or can we speak of it as an intelligent being that "thinks"? Read the selection to find out the author's point of view on this question. Try to finish the reading and comprehension quiz in six minutes. (*Hint:* Looking at the quiz first will help you focus on the reading.)

Are Computers Alive?

*T*he topic of *thought* is one area of psychology, and many observers have considered this aspect in connection with robots and computers: Some of the old worries about AI (artificial intelligence) were closely linked to the question of whether computers could think. The first massive
5   electronic computers, capable of rapid (if often unreliable) computation and little or no creative activity, were soon dubbed "electronic brains." A reaction to this terminology quickly followed. To put them in their place, computers were called "high-speed idiots," an effort to protect human vanity. In such a climate the possibility of computers actually being alive
10   was rarely considered: It was bad enough that computers might be capable of thought. But not everyone realized the implications of the *high-speed idiot* tag. It has not been pointed out often enough that even the human idiot is one of the most intelligent life forms on earth. If the early computers were even that intelligent, it was already a remarkable state of
15   affairs.

One consequence of speculation about the possibility of computer thought was that we were forced to examine with new care the idea of

thought in general. It soon became clear that we were not sure what we meant by such terms as *thought* and *thinking.* We tend to assume that human beings think, some more than others, though we often call people *thoughtless* or *unthinking.* Dreams cause a problem, partly because they usually happen outside our control. They are obviously some type of mental experience, but are they a type of thinking? And the question of nonhuman life forms adds further problems. Many of us would maintain that some of the higher animals—dogs, cats, apes, and so on—are capable of at least basic thought, but what about fish and insects? It is certainly true that the higher mammals show complex brain activity when tested with the appropriate equipment. If thinking is demonstrated by evident electrical activity in the brain, then many animal species are capable of thought. Once we have formulated clear ideas on what thought is in biological creatures, it will be easier to discuss the question of thought in artifacts. And what is true of thought is also true of the many other mental processes. One of the immense benefits of AI research is that we are being forced to scrutinize, with new rigor, the working of the human mind.

It is already clear that machines have superior mental abilities to many life forms. No fern or oak tree can play chess as well as even the simplest digital computer; nor can frogs weld car bodies as well as robots. The three-fingered mechanical manipulator is cleverer in some ways than the three-toed sloth. It seems that, viewed in terms of intellect, the computer should be set well above plants and most animals. Only the higher animals can, it seems, compete with computers with regard to intellect—and even then with diminishing success. (Examples of this are in the games of backgammon and chess. Some of the world's best players are now computers.)

Geoff Simons

Comprehension Quiz

Choose the best way of finishing each statement, here and on the next page, based on what you have just read.

1. The first electronic computers were:
   a. slow and reliable
   b. creative and accurate
   c. large and fast

2. The author feels that by calling these early computers "high-speed idiots," people were really implying that computers
   a. would never be capable of thought
   b. were already somewhat intelligent
   c. can never work as rapidly as people

3. The author believes that such words as *thought* and *thinking*
   a. are terms that are not clear and will never be exactly defined
   b. might come to be better understood because of research into artificial intelligence and computers
   c. have precise biological meanings that refer only to human mental processes

4. In the author's view, mental activities are characteristic of
   a. all plants and animals
   b. some animals
   c. human beings alone

5. The author's opinion regarding the possibility of machines thinking seems to be that:
   a. there are already machines that think
   b. this is somewhat possible
   c. this is totally improbable

WHAT DO YOU THINK?

Advances in Communication

Across the globe, instant communication is available with faxes, computers, e-mail, and Internet. Cellular phones give freedom to call anywhere, anytime, from places like a moving car, or from a boat in the middle of a lake. You can call home from an airplane 30,000 feet in the air if you want. Telephone companies are promising individual phone numbers, so a person can be reached by phone anywhere in the world just by dialing that personal number. What do you think about these advances in communication? How could they help you in your chosen profession? How could they change your personal life? Overall, do you think instant communication is a positive or negative thing?

CHAPTER nine

Art and Entertainment

in this chapter

North America is a great "melting pot," a place where people from many countries and races have joined to form a new culture. The arts reflect the uniqueness of this culture. Many of its contributions to music have come from people of African descent: jazz, gospel music, rock, the blues. The first selection is from the biography of Duke Ellington. The next two sections explore the striking paintings of Georgia O'Keeffe and the moving poetry of the Chicanos. Finally, a timed reading looks at Jackie Chan, one of the world's best-loved movie stars.

The Man Who Was an Orchestra

Before You Read

Anticipating the Reading

exercise 1

Before starting to read the article, listen to a record or tape of jazz music, preferably of Duke Ellington's. Perhaps your teacher or a member of the class will bring some jazz music in or you can find some on the radio or the TV. Then answer the following questions.

1. How does jazz differ from other types of music?

_____

_____

2. Why do you think Duke Ellington felt sorry for composers of classical music?

_____

_____

3. What kind of relationship do you think exists between the leader of a jazz group and the other musicians in the group?

_____

_____

exercise 2

Compare your answers to Exercise 1 with those of your classmates. Think about these questions when you read the selection.

Duke Ellington
(1899–1974)

Guessing the Meaning of Key Words from Context

exercise 3    Match the correct lettered definitions with the italicized words from the article, according to the context.

a. creators of new things
b. greatly decreased
c. forceful
d. painful, touching
e. collection of musical pieces
f. explore thoroughly
g. invent without preparation
h. stimulating, invigorating
i. substitutes, replacements

_____ **1.** The element of surprise explains the *compelling* hold jazz has on listeners, which makes them sit very still for hours.

_____ **2.** Because of our patterned lives, jazzmen, of all musicians, are our *surrogates* for the unpredictable.

_____ **3.** Duke would play familiar numbers from his *repertory* during parts of the evening.

_____ **4.** Jazzmen generally *improvise* rather than play prepared pieces.

_____ **5.** After Duke Ellington had been afflicted by cancer, his strength was *decimated*.

_____ **6** Musicians find performances exhausting yet *exhilarating* experiences.

_____ **7.** Ellington considered the unfortunate situation of many classical composers *poignant*.

_____ **8.** By writing specifically for each of his men and letting them play in a natural and relaxed manner, Ellington was able to *probe* the intimate recesses of their minds.

_____ **9.** While most people follow the ideas of others, every group needs also to have *innovators*.

Do you enjoy listening to jazz? If so, you are not alone, for millions of people throughout the world rate it as their favorite type of music. Jazz began in the United States around the turn of the century, when it was played informally by African-American bands in New Orleans and other southern cities and towns. In the following selection, you will find out more about this music with the strong rhythmic beat and about the people who create it, especially about one man, Duke Ellington, one of the greatest jazz musicians of all time.

The Man Who Was an Orchestra

Whitney Balliett, jazz critic for *The New Yorker* magazine, has called jazz "the sound of surprise." And it is that expectation of surprise which partly explains the compelling hold of jazz on listeners in just about every country in the world.

Most of us lead lives of patterned regularity. Day by day, surprises are relatively few. And except for economic or physical uncertainties, we neither face nor look for significant degrees of risk because the vast majority of us try to attain as much security as is possible.

In this sense, jazzmen, of all musicians, are our surrogates for the unpredictable, our models of constant change.

"It's like going out there naked every night," a bass player once said to me. "Any one of us can screw the whole thing up because he had a fight with his wife just before the performance or because he's just not with it that night for any number of reasons. I mean, we're out there improvising. The classical guys have their scores, whether they have them on a music stand or have memorized them. But we have to be creating, or trying to, anticipating each other, transforming our feelings into music, taking chances every second. That's why, when jazz musicians are really putting out, it's an exhausting experience. It can be exhilarating, too, but always there's that touch of fear, that feeling of being on a very high wire without a net below."

And jazz musicians who work with the more headlong innovators in the music face special hazards. There is the challenge, for instance, of staying in balance all the way in performances with Thelonious Monk as he plunges through, in, underneath, and around time. "I got lost one night," one of the people in Monk's band told me, "and I felt like I had just fallen into an elevator shaft."

There is another dimension of jazz surprise, the kind and quality that Duke Ellington exemplified. It is true that during many of his concerts and other appearances, Duke would schedule familiar numbers from his repertory for parts of the evening, sometimes long parts. He felt this an obligation to those who had come to see him, sometimes over long distances, and wanted to hear their favorites. Duke, who had come up in the business (and jazz is also a business) at a time when, to most of its audiences, the music was show business rather than art, considered it rude to present an audience with a program of entirely unfamiliar work.

But for Duke himself the keenest pleasure in music was the continual surprising of himself. Always he was most interested in the new, the just completed work.

"The man," the late Billy Strayhorn said of Duke, "is a constant revelation. He's continually renewing himself through his music. He's thoroughly attuned to what's going on *now*. He not only doesn't live in the past. He rejects it, at least so far as his own past accomplishments are concerned. He hates talking about the old bands and the old pieces. He has to play some of the Ellington standards because otherwise the audiences would be disappointed. But he'd much rather play the new things."

Duke never could stop composing. Even toward the end, in the hospital, his strength decimated by cancer, Ellington was still composing. And throughout his life, the challenge and incomparable satisfaction for him was in the way he composed for the specific members of his orchestra.

"After a man has been in the band for a while," Ellington once told me, "I can hear what his capacities are, and I write to that. And I write to each man's sound. A man's sound is his total personality. I hear that sound as I prepare to write. I hear all their sounds, and that's how I am able to write. Before you can play anything or write anything, you have to hear it."

As Billy Strayhorn said, "Ellington plays the piano, but his real instrument is his band. Each member of the band is to him a distinctive play of tone colors and a distinctive set of emotions, and he mixes them all into his own style. By writing specifically for each of his own men, and thereby letting them play naturally and in a relaxed way, Ellington is able to probe the intimate recesses of their minds and find things that not even the musicians knew were there."

And having written—late at night in hotel rooms, in the car, on scraps of paper, between dates, wherever he was when not fronting the band—Ellington was able to hear the results immediately. And that was much to his satisfaction. Duke often told me that he considered the fate of most classical composers poignant. "They write and write and keep putting what they've done in a drawer and maybe, once in a great while, some orchestra will perform one of their works. The rest—they have to imagine, only imagine, what they've written sounds like. I could not exist that way, creating music only for myself, not communicating with anyone but myself. But having an orchestra always with me makes it unnecessary for me to wait." Duke did not have to travel constantly; he could have lived comfortably on the royalties earned from his abundance of compositions. But he greatly preferred the road so that he could hear his music, especially his new music, instantly. Or, as he put it, "I keep these expensive gentlemen with me to gratify that desire."

Nat Hentoff

After You Read

Preparing for Exams with Study Maps

Many good students say that the time to start studying for an exam is the first day of class. That is the moment to choose a strategy for retaining important information, especially in courses with a lot of reading. Some students keep short summary files in their computer on every book or article they read; others keep summary file cards in a box. This provides a record to use when the time comes to study for the mid-term or final exam. Don't waste time writing these summaries in perfect, complete sentences. They are only comments for personal use. Another way to keep a record is to make study maps for all the readings and put them in order in a binder—one binder for each course.

Look at examples of designs for study maps below, on the opposite page, and also on pages 157–158 in Chapter Six. Which one would

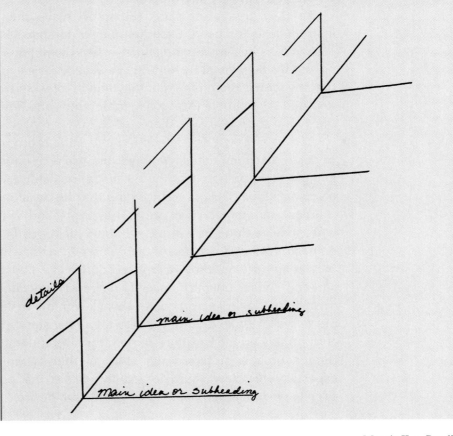

work best for "The Man Who Was an Orchestra"? Or would you make a new design? Why? Working in small groups, choose a design and make a study map for the selection. Compare the results with the other groups and decide which design is best. Afterward, use your study map to help you with the exercises that follow.

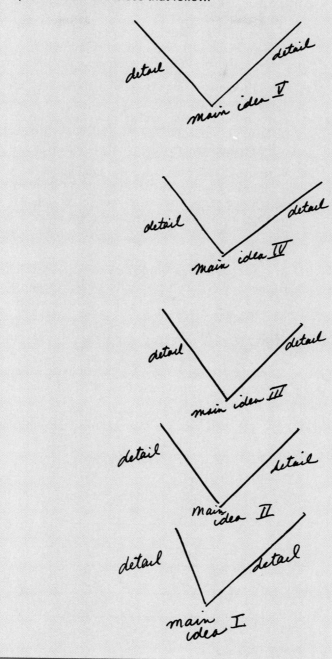

Recalling Information

Choose the best way of finishing each statement, based on what you have just read.

1. The main reason that jazz is unpredictable and presents the listener with surprises is that
   a. it sounds like an older style of music
   b. improvisation is an important part of it
   c. the musicians find the performances exhilarating

2. Duke Ellington included old familiar numbers from his repertory in many of his concerts because
   a. it was his continual and keenest musical pleasure
   b. he felt it was good business and would make a lot of money
   c. he did not want to disappoint his audiences

3. When Duke Ellington was older and famous, he
   a. enjoyed living in the past and talking about earlier accomplishments
   b. rejected the new styles of younger musicians
   c. kept on changing and innovating his music

4. Ellington considered the fate of most classical composers poignant because
   a. they have to wait before they can hear their music
   b. they usually die before getting much money or fame
   c. they have to follow rigid rules in composing

Making and Supporting Inferences

Tell which of the following inferences about Duke Ellington are valid (V) and which are invalid (I), according to the article. Give at least two facts for each to support your judgment.

1. _____ He was basically lazy and liked the good and easy life.

   _____

   _____

2. _____ He was self-centered and arrogant.

   _____

   _____

3. _____ He was young in spirit throughout his life.

   _____

   _____

Talking It Over

In small groups, discuss the following questions.

1. After reading the article, how would you describe the difference between jazz and other types of music?
2. Why does jazz have a compelling hold on many people?
3. Billy Strayhorn said, "Ellington plays the piano, but his real instrument is his band." What did he mean?
4. The word *jazz* is used in certain English slang expressions that apply to things besides music. For example, someone might refer to the design for a house or the plans for a party and say, "Let's *jazz it up* a bit" or "It's not *jazzy* enough." Based on the context and on what you have read, what do these expressions mean?

Expressing Reactions to Music

activity 2

Some volunteers should bring in records or tapes of their favorite type of music and play it for the class. Then play the jazz music that you listened to before the reading. Does the element of surprise seem stronger in jazz than in the other music, as the article suggests? In what parts do you think the musicians are improvising?

Describe, orally or in writing, the music that you preferred of all the samples that were played. Try to explain in words what it sounds like and why you enjoy it.

SELECTION two

"To Paint Is to Live": Georgia O'Keeffe, 1887–1986

Before You Read

Anticipating the Reading

exercise

Look at the title and the photograph of Georgia O'Keeffe on the top of the next page. Skim the first two paragraphs of the article. Then make inferences about this famous artist and answer the following questions. Afterwards, read the article to find out if you were right.

1. What kind of person do you think she was?

_____

_____

Georgia O'Keeffe

2. Why did she paint?

_____

_____

_____

3. What kinds of problems do you imagine she had in her life? Why?

_____

_____

_____

Painting, like music, is one of the fine arts. American and Canadian painting has been influenced by many traditions from different parts of the world, especially by those from Europe. However, this century has witnessed an opposite trend: the development of particularly North American painting styles that have become international. One American painter who exerted an influence on Europe with a unique and independent style was a woman from Wisconsin named Georgia O'Keeffe. Three of O'Keeffe's grandparents were immigrants—from Ireland, Hungary, and Holland—and the fourth was descended from one of the earliest European colonists in America. These ancestors came to start a new life in a new world, but O'Keeffe was destined to become a pioneer of a different sort. The following article discusses her life and work.

"To Paint Is to Live": Georgia O'Keeffe, 1887–1986

Georgia O'Keeffe was truly an American original. Tough, sparse, lean, she embodied the rugged individualistic nature of the American pioneer. But instead of tilling the soil, her strides were made in the field of contemporary American art.

Georgia O'Keeffe, *Waterfall No. III Iao Valley*

Georgia O'Keeffe, *Yellow Calla*

Born on a 600-acre farm in Sun Prairie, Wisconsin, on November 15, 1887, O'Keeffe throughout her long life preferred vast plains and open spaces to city living. From the summer of 1929, when she made her first visit to New Mexico, the starkness of the desert fascinated her. After summering in New Mexico for many years, she finally moved permanently to Abiquiu, New Mexico, in 1949, where she continued to paint until her eyesight faltered in the late 1970s. From this region the themes of some of her finest works evolved.

O'Keeffe's strictly American art education began with private lessons at the age of ten. Teachers recognized her talent but often criticized the larger-than-life proportions that she liked to paint. At an early age she was already moving away from realistic copying of objects to things she perceived with her own eyes, mind, and soul.

O'Keeffe's formal high school education continued at a private school in Madison, Wisconsin, and after a family move, she graduated from a Williamsburg, Virginia, high school in 1903. In 1905–06 she studied at the Art Institute in Chicago, and in 1907–08, at the Art Students' League in New York.

In 1908, perhaps disappointed with the rigidity of American art education at the time, she gave up painting and became a commercial artist, drawing advertising illustrations in Chicago. However, in the summer of 1912, she decided to take another art course in Virginia under Alon Bemont, and her interest in creative painting came alive again.

Self-supporting since graduation from high school, O'Keeffe had to find jobs to sustain her through her developing years as an artist. In 1912, she began to teach in Amarillo, Texas, and was stunned by the barren southern landscape. "That was my country," she said, "terrible wind and wonderful emptiness."

After art courses in 1915–16 in New York under the more liberal art teacher Arthur Dow, O'Keeffe accepted a position as an art teacher at a small college in South Carolina. It was at this point that the determined young woman locked herself up, took stock of her painting, and decided to reject the rigidity of the realism that she had been taught for a style all her own. "Nothing is less real than realism—details are confusing. It is only by selection, by elimination, by emphasis, that we get the real meaning of things." From this revival came black and white abstract nature forms in all shapes and sizes, the beginning of her highly individualistic style.

O'Keeffe sent some of these prints to a friend in New York and told her not to show them to anyone. The friend was so impressed with them that she ignored the request and took them to a famous photographer and promoter of modern artists, Alfred Stieglitz. His reaction was immediate:

"At last, a woman on paper!" Without O'Keeffe's knowledge or consent, Stieglitz exhibited these prints in his gallery, 291. Infuriated, she went to New York to insist that he take her drawings down. Stieglitz, however, convinced her of their quality, and she allowed them to remain on exhibit.
50 Subsequently, Stieglitz became the champion of O'Keeffe's works and helped her gain the prominence she deserved. For Stieglitz, Georgia was an unusually talented American female artist. She was unspoiled by studies in Europe and painted with a direct, clear, strong—even fierce—force.

55 The relationship between Stieglitz and O'Keeffe developed into a passionate love affair, which eventually led to a twenty-two-year marriage. Stieglitz, his wife's senior by many years, died in 1946. He immortalized her through many beautiful and unusual photographs—the lady in black, with piercing eyes, tightly pulled-back hair and the artistic
60 elongated hands of a goddess.

Strength, clarity, and strong physical presence are words that are often used to describe O'Keeffe's paintings. As art critic Lloyd Goodrich said, "Her art presents a rare combination of austerity and deep seriousness. . . . Even at her most realistic she is concerned not with the
65 mere visual appearance of things, but with their essential life, their being, their identity. . . . The forms of nature are translated into forms of art." Or, as O'Keeffe herself put it, "A hill or a tree cannot make a good painting just because it is a hill or a tree. It is lines and colors put together so that they say something. For me, that is the very basis for
70 painting. The abstraction is often the most definite form for the intangible thing in myself that I can only clarify in paint."

M. Prijic

After You Read
Recalling Information

Choose the best way of finishing each statement, based on what you have just read.

1. Georgia O'Keeffe was born
   a. in New York City
   b. in a town in New Mexico
   c. on a farm in Wisconsin

2. Her art education consisted of:
   a. studies in schools and institutes in the United States
   b. training in the best art academies of Europe
   c. only her own efforts and experimentation at home

3. The landscape with which she identified in particular was:
   a. rugged mountains
   b. lush forests
   c. barren deserts

4. Alfred Stieglitz's comment when he first saw O'Keeffe's prints was: "At last, a woman on paper!" From this we can infer that
   a. there was a great deal of discrimination against women then
   b. women artists were not very common in those days
   c. he did not really like the prints very much

5. Stieglitz was important in the life of Georgia O'Keeffe because:
   a. he became both her husband and champion
   b. he bought many of her paintings at good prices
   c. he photographed her prints and gave titles to them

Paraphrasing Complex Ideas

Paraphrase the following excerpts from the article. Do not worry if there are some words you do not understand. Just state the main idea briefly in simple, direct words.

1. "Tough, sparse, lean, she embodied the rugged individualistic nature of the American pioneer. But instead of tilling the soil, her strides were made in the field of contemporary American art."

   _____

   _____

   _____

2. "Self-supporting since graduation from high school, O'Keeffe had to find jobs to sustain her through her developing years as an artist."

   _____

   _____

   _____

3. "'Nothing is less real than realism—details are confusing. It is only by selection, by elimination, by emphasis, that we get the real meaning of things'" (words of Georgia O'Keeffe).

   _____

   _____

   _____

4. "'Even at her most realistic she is concerned not with the mere visual appearance of things, but with their essential life, their being, their identity'" (words of an art critic about O'Keeffe's works).

_____

_____

_____

_____

Talking It Over

In small groups, discuss the following questions.

1. Were you right or wrong about the inferences you made about Georgia O'Keeffe? Explain.
2. Do you think it was difficult for a woman to be an artist in the 1920s and 1930s? Why?
3. Why do you think Stieglitz was such a strong influence on O'Keeffe?
4. Many feminists and members of the Gay Rights Movement admire Georgia O'Keeffe's art because it represents female beauty in a sensual way through the forms of nature. What other reasons for admiring O'Keeffe's work are given in the article?

Expressing Reactions About Paintings

Bring in some prints or photographs of art works that appeal to you to share with the class. Tell whether it is the subject, the style, or both that you like in these paintings and why you are impressed by them. Try to find a book with reproductions of O'Keeffe's paintings and explain what you like or dislike about them.

Writing a Brief Comparison

Do artists tend to have similar types of lives even though they are from different cultures and time periods? Go to the library and look up information on an artist from any country other than the United States. Write a brief comparison between the life of this artist and that of Georgia O'Keeffe. Do not write the whole story of the artist's life, only several points that show similarity. If there is no similarity, try to explain why.

Chicano Poetry: The Voice of a Culture

Before You Read
Anticipating the Reading

Look at the map of the United States and answer the following questions. Then read the article to find out whether you are correct and to learn more about the second-largest minority group in the United States.

1. What cities on the map sound to you as though their names might be of Spanish origin?

   _____

   _____

2. What sections seem to have the most Spanish names?

   _____

3. Do you know or can you guess why these places have Spanish names?

   _____

The following article gives some background on Mexican-Americans, who are often called Chicanos, and presents a few examples of their poetry. You might wonder why this group is singled out when there are so many ethnic groups, with their particular languages and cultures, living in North America, including millions of Spanish-speaking people from other countries. There are historical reasons, which you will read about, that explain why this group is different from most others.

Chicano Poetry: The Voice of a Culture

The Hispanic Presence in the United States

What are the two cities in the world with the largest number of Spanish-speaking inhabitants? Mexico City is number one, which is no surprise; but the second is Los Angeles, California, right in the U.S.A.! According to 1990 census figures, more than 22 million Hispanics live in
5   the United States. They are the second-largest minority after Blacks, but the Hispanic population is increasing so rapidly that it is expected to become the largest minority within a few years. More than 80 percent of Hispanics live in urban areas. Most are concentrated in the five south-western states of Arizona, California, Colorado, New Mexico, and Texas.
10   There are also sizable Hispanic populations in New York, Florida, and Illinois.

There are countless Spanish geographical names in the United States, such as the state of Colorado (which means "red"), the city of Las Vegas ("fertile lowlands"), and the Rio Grande ("big river"). Many Spanish and
15   Latin American words have been incorporated into English. A large number of these words are related to geographical features: *mesa* ("plateau") and *canyon;* to music: *tango, rumba;* to ranch life: *rodeo, corral;* to architecture: *patio, plaza;* and to food: *chocolate, papaya.* Many colorful English slang terms are corruptions of Spanish words, such as
20   *calaboose* ("jail") and *macho man* ("big, tough male").

Mexican-American History

Where did all this Spanish influence come from? Didn't the United States start out as a colony of the British? In fact, the southwestern United States was settled by the Spanish and Mexicans centuries before the arrival of the first Anglos. Many people are unaware of this fact because
25   until recently, all the history books were written from the point of view of the British. Let's examine the "true history" of the American Southwest.

The region was part of Mexico until it was lost in a war with the United States. Under the terms of the Treaty of Guadalupe Hidalgo, which ended

The Southwest is noted for its Spanish colonial and Mexican architecture, particularly the fifty-four missions founded between 1598 and 1823.

the war in 1848, Mexico ceded to the United States the territory that is now New Mexico, Utah, Nevada, California, and parts of Colorado and Wyoming. On paper the 75,000 Mexican inhabitants were guaranteed their property rights and granted U.S. citizenship. The reality, however, was different. They suffered racial and cultural discrimination at the hands of a flood of Anglo settlers, and many were dispossessed of their lands. Most worked for Anglo bosses as farm, railroad, and mine workers. Constant immigration from Mexico kept wages low.

World War II brought about fundamental changes. Many Mexican-Americans began to consider themselves U.S. citizens for the first time after serving in the war. Armed with new skills and faced with the rapid mechanization of agriculture, many moved to the cities in search of work.

The Chicano Movement

Inspired by the black struggle for civil rights, Mexican-Americans organized in the 1960s to gain reforms and restore ethnic pride. Members of this movement called themselves *Chicanos,* and the name has become popular, although some still prefer the term Mexican-Americans. The achievements of the Chicano movement are many. In 1962, César Chávez founded the strong and successful National Farm Workers Association in Delano, California, which has managed to raise wages and improve working conditions for migrant workers. In 1970 José Ángel Gutiérrez established the *Raza Unida* political party in Crystal City, Texas, which has been successful in electing Mexican-American candidates to local office. Bilingual, cross-cultural education and Chicano studies programs have been established in schools and universities.

Chicano Arts

The Chicano movement inspired a flowering of Chicano theater, art, and literature. Luis Valdés created the *Teatro Campesino* in the fields of Delano in 1965 to strengthen the union's organizing efforts. This unique form of theater draws on a variety of Latin American and European traditions and makes use of allegorical characters, masks, song, and dance. Originally performed by farm workers for farm workers, it later broadened its focus to include issues other than the strike, such as American foreign policy and discrimination against Hispanics in schools. The *Teatro Campesino* has gained international prominence and inspired the creation of many similar companies across the country.

Colorful murals painted on the walls of public buildings in Mexican-American neighborhoods are a collective expression of reborn hope and ethnic pride. They depict the Mexican-Americans' Indian and Spanish heritage, the history of Mexico and of Mexican-Americans in the United States, and the problems of migrant workers.

The genre most cultivated by Chicano writers is poetry. Often written in free verse, Chicano poetry creates an impression of spontaneity, freshness, and honesty. It may be written in Spanish, English, or a combination of the two languages.

Deana Fernández

Mural in a Mexican-American neighborhood

Some Examples of Chicano Poetry

The following examples of Chicano poetry contain the Spanish words *primo*, "cousin," and *gringo*, a somewhat negative word for an Anglo-American. Both poems provide a brief glimpse into the lives of Mexican-Americans. As you read, try to understand the main point that the poet wants to convey and the emotions he wants the reader to feel.

To People Who Pick Food

I am the man
        who picks your food

        immigrant,
        tablecloths
5   ignore my stare
I have children
a fake green card
a warm kiss
a cross to ward off rangers
10 a picture of St. Peter so

I will not drown in a river
            I pick apples
                    cotton
                    grapes
15 eyes follow me
                utter under their breaths,
    I do not understand
                    the lettuce canned
    with my hands
20   citrus pores
                    inflame my eyes
    my wife is   proud
       soft   gentle
          my   children
25 are brown   tender deer
            what eyes,
    the sun cracks my skin
    I am old and dark as the dirt
    I drop on my knees   before the sky
30 they can hate me, point me out in a crowd
    but do not pity me   the sun is there
    every morning   God follows my children
    and I walk to the field to grow bread
                with my friends

Wilfredo Q. Castaño

Grandma's Primo

Grandma had a cousin
who lived in the big city
and looked like a gringo

He smoked a big cigar
5   and spoke English as well
as he spoke Spanish

He loved to tell jokes
would always tell them twice—
the first time in Spanish
10 to make us laugh
and the second time in English
to impress us

Leroy V. Quintana

After You Read

Recalling Information

Tell whether each of the following statements is true (T) or false (F), based on the reading. Correct the false statements to make them true.

1. _____ There are more Spanish-speaking people in Los Angeles, California, than in any other city in the world except the capital of Mexico.

2. _____ Hispanics form the largest minority group in the United States.

3. _____ Spanish and Mexican architecture and geographical names are characteristics of the northeastern part of the country.

4. _____ The first Spanish and Mexican settlers in the United States arrived after the first British settlers.

5. _____ After the treaty of 1848, Mexicans in the territory that belonged to the United States as of that year enjoyed the privileges of full citizens and were guaranteed property rights.

6. _____ After World War II, many Mexican-Americans moved from the countryside to the cities.

7. _____ César Chávez is a Chicano who founded a powerful and effective labor union for farm workers.

8. _____ José Ángel Gutiérrez began a Chicano political party, but it has not yet managed to get Mexican-Americans elected to office.

9. _____ Chicano theater, begun by Luis Valdés, started out in the fields and was performed for and by farm workers.

10. _____ The literary genre most popular among Chicano writers is the novel.

11. _____ "To People Who Pick Food" is told from the point of view of a poor but contented Mexican farm laborer who works in the United States illegally.

12. _____ In the poem "Grandma's Primo," the cousin always told jokes twice because he wasn't sure that his relatives understood them the first time.

Summarizing Information About Specific Points

Write a brief summary of what you remember about each of the following people or things. If necessary, scan the article to refresh your memory.

1. Spanish words used in English

_____

_____

_____

2. *Raza Unida*

_____

_____

_____

3. Treaty of Guadalupe Hidalgo

_____

_____

_____

4. César Chávez

_____

_____

_____

5. *Teatro Campesino*

_____

_____

_____

Reading Poetry for Meaning

exercise 3

Just as any scene can serve as the subject of a painting, so any part of daily life can provide material for a poem. Of course, the choice that the artist or poet makes relates to his or her purpose. Poetry is usually short and compact, so it should be read several times, preferably aloud, to appreciate its meaning. Read the following questions; then reread the poems and answer the questions.

"TO PEOPLE WHO PICK FOOD"

The poem is spoken from the point of view of a poor Mexican migrant who is working illegally in the United States, with a "fake green card."

1. What parts of the poem suggest that the man feels prejudice and discrimination from the people around him?

_____

_____

2. What work does the man do? How does he feel about it?

_____

3. When so many rich people seem dissatisfied with their lives (as evidenced by alcoholism, use of drugs, nervous breakdowns, and so on), why is this man content? What things does he have that give him strength and pride?

_____

_____

4. What emotive words are used? What emotions do you think the poet wants us to feel toward the man?

_____

_____

"GRANDMA'S PRIMO"

The Italian artist Modigliani often used just a few lines or brushstrokes to suggest a whole person. This poem is also the portrait of a person, shown in just a few words.

1. From whose point of view do we see this character?

_____

2. What special qualities does he have?

_____

3. Why do you think the poet found him memorable?

_____

TIMED READING
Jackie Can!

Jackie Chan is one of the best-known figures in Asian popular culture, yet he is almost unknown in some parts of the world, such as the United States and Canada. Read the following article from *Time* magazine to find out more about this famous film star. Concentrate on these questions as you read.

1. Who is Jackie Chan?
2. What does he do that is so amazing?
3. What is he like as a person?
4. Why is he virtually unknown in North America?

Read quickly and try to finish the selection and comprehension exercises in twelve minutes.

Jackie Can!

Do death-defying stunts!
Break all his bones!
Reign as Asia's No. 1 star!

Some movie stars measure their worth by how many millions of dollars they make. Jackie Chan, Asian action-star extraordinaire, measures his by how many of his bones he has fractured while executing his films' incredible stunts. Let him count the breaks: "My skull, my eyes, my nose three times, my jaw, my shoulder, my chest, two fingers, a knee—everything from the top of my head to the bottom of my feet." Chan broke an ankle while jumping onto a moving Hovercraft in his new film, *Rumble in the Bronx,* which opened in time for Chinese New Year last week. Fans queued up around the world.

So who is Jackie Chan? In the U.S., only a figure with a small if intense cult. His volcanic comedies are not shown on the pay-movie channels, not released in theaters except for the rare showcase, like the "Super Jackie" retrospective now at New York City's Cinema Village. But back home in Hong Kong—throughout Asia, in fact, and in South America and Australia—Chan is movie-action incarnate. He has made 40 films since 1976, when he was promoted as the new Bruce Lee. Now, at 40, Chan is that and more: the last good guy and, arguably, the world's best-loved movie star.

Jackie Chan

In American terms he's a little Clint Eastwood (actor-director), a dash of Gene Kelly (imaginative choreographer), a bit of Jim Carrey (rubbery ham) and a lot of the silent-movie clowns: Charlie Chaplin, Buster Keaton and Harold Lloyd. Says Chan fan Sylvester Stallone: "Jackie has elongated a genre that had grown pretty stale. He's infused films with humor and character-driven story while giving audiences these extraordinary stunts that are unparalleled anywhere in the world."

In Hollywood, special visual effects define the action film. In Hong Kong, stunts—the human body spinning and bending without a computer's help—define the Chan film. By displaying his death-baiting acrobatic virtuosity, he has returned the action movie to the actor. "Audiences know that if they want special effects, they go see Schwarzenegger," he says. "If they want a tough movie, they go see Sly. If they want an action movie, they choose Jackie Chan—because I do a lot of things that normal people can't do."

To cross a busy street, normal people might go to the corner and wait for the green. Not Jackie. Standing on a balcony in his *Police Story II,* he jumps onto a truck going one way, onto a double-decker bus going the other way and then through a window into the second floor of the villain's headquarters.

In his biggest hits (*Drunken Master, Project A, Police Story, The Armour of God*) and their sequels, Chan has scooted across burning coals, eaten red-hot chili peppers, swallowed industrial alcohol. He has bounced down a hill inside a giant beach ball and leaped from a mountaintop onto a passing hot-air balloon. As weapons he has used bicycles, rickshas, chairs, plates, a hat rack, a ketchup dispenser, overhead fans and Chinese folding fans. Bad guys have depantsed him, strapped a ton of TNT to his body, doused and scalded him, set him afire, dumped him down a well, hanged him naked in the town square. There's a truly masochistic resilience at work here: Jackie takes a licking and keeps on kicking.

Chan—whose Chinese screen name, Sing Lung, translates as "becoming the dragon"—is so fearless as to seem, by mere human standards, senseless. In *Police Story* he hitches a ride on a speeding bus by running up from behind, hooking an umbrella handle onto a window ledge and hanging on while fighting off a brood of bad guys. . . .

The Asian audience gasps at these scenes but never doubts them, because everyone knows Jackie does his own stunts. . . . Lest doubts linger, his films provide instant replays from different angles. Under the closing credits are outtakes showing blown stunts, with comic or near tragic results. Executing a fairly routine jump in Yugoslavia for *The Armour of God,* he missed a tree branch, hit his head on a rock and almost died. Chan has a memento of the accident: a thimble-size hole in the right side of his head. If you ask nicely, he'll let you put your finger in it.

65 That's pure Jackie—an engaging presence offscreen and on who, unlike other cinema studs, projects no roiling torment, no existential grudge against the world. He seems a contented guy. And why not? A movie actor since he was seven, stunt man in a Bruce Lee movie at 18, and now Asia's No. 1 star, he is in total control of his films: supervising the
70 stunts, singing the theme songs and, on 11 pictures, directing. . . .

Chan's study of the silent masters taught him the universal language of film: action and passion, humor and heart. His movies are so simple, so fluid, so exuberant that they are easily understood by people who don't speak Cantonese. Just ask the Jackie fans who track down his movies in
75 the Chinatowns of U.S. cities or visit specialized video stores. "Jackie Chan's work is as popular with our customers as anything by Orson Welles or Francis Coppola," says Meg Johnson, buyer for Videots, a smart Santa Monica outlet. Finding a Chan film under its multiplicity of titles is one challenge. Another can be watching it, in washed-out, nth-generation
80 dupes with indifferent dubbing or Japanese subtitles (or none at all) and with the sides of the wide-screen images lopped off.

Chan regrets the situation: "The video rights are handled by Golden Harvest, the distribution company I work for. They don't really concentrate on videos in America." But even in this video murk, Chan's personality
85 shines through. He has a star quality that doesn't get lost in translation.

Hollywood is missing out on a great thing: an ingratiating actor who makes hit movies and speaks better English than a few action heroes we could name. In the early '80s Chan gave U.S. films a try (in Burt Reynolds' *Cannonball Run* capers and two other wooden showcases), then returned
90 to Hong Kong. For Chan there's no place like home. "In Asia I'm kind of like E.T.," he says. "Everybody comes to see my films. There are billions of people in Asia, and they're my first audience. If I get an American audience, O.K., that's a bonus. If not, that's O.K. too. I'm very happy."

If Jackie Chan can keep that thrill machine of a body in fine working
95 order, his fans will be happy. And no bones about it.

Richard Corliss

Comprehension Quiz

exercise 1

Choose the best way of finishing each statement, based on what you have just read.

1. Jackie Chan is especially famous for
   a. his penetrating eyes
   b. his ability to take pain
   c. his clever use of language
   d. his love of money

2. His movies are filled with
   a. dazzling special effects
   b. killing and violence
   c. romantic songs
   d. dangerous stunts

3. As a person, Jackie is
   a. distant and arrogant
   b. happy and direct
   c. shy and silent
   d. angry and antisocial

4. Jackie is not well known in North America because
   a. good tapes of his movies are not easily available
   b. his film style is suited only to the Asian market
   c. he does not like to work with Hollywood
   d. Hollywood actors and producers have a grudge against him

Writing an Instant Summary

exercise 2

Be quick like Jackie Chan. Do an instant summary of the article you have just read by writing a one-sentence answer to each of the four questions listed on page 256. Then compare your summary with those of your classmates.

_____

_____

_____

_____

_____

_____

_____

_____

WHAT DO YOU THINK?

Body Decoration

Keeping in line with a popular cultural trend, some people are deciding to decorate their bodies with exotic tattoos and hanging rings. Elaborate tattoos cover arms, legs, backs, and even more private parts. Also, body piercing—putting holes in the body so rings and baubles can be inserted—has become popular in some circles. What do you think of tattooing and body piercing? Would you do something like this? Would this be acceptable in your culture? Do you think both men and women can wear earrings? Many cultures around the world use tattooing or body piercing as a sign of beauty or a mark of tribe. Can you think of where some of these are?

CHAPTER **ten**

Ethical Questions

in this chapter

Human beings have always faced basic questions of ethics. But modern technology has brought many new complications that make such decisions more difficult now. This is especially true in medicine where the ethical decisions are matters of life and death. First, you examine complex situations in today's hospitals. Next, you read about the changes forced on some cultures by strong new forces. Then, you can be the judge on some ethical issues debated recently in American courts. Finally, there is a timed reading about our treatment of animals.

263

SELECTION **one**

Doctor's Dilemma:
Treat or Let Die?

Before You Read
Focusing on a Key Issue

activity

In small groups, discuss the following specific example of a current ethical problem in medicine. (In the article, you will find out what was decided in this and other cases.)

During the winter of 1982, a retired dairyman from Poteet, Texas, carried out a most difficult decision. Woodrow Wilson Collums went into the nursing home where his older brother Jim lay helpless and suffering, a victim of severe senility resulting from Alzheimer's disease. Collums took out a gun he had hidden in his coat and shot his brother to death.

1. Why do you think Collums shot his brother?
2. Should the courts treat Collums as a murderer?

Guessing the Meaning of New Words from Context

exercise

Read the sentences and use the context to try to determine what each word in italics means. Then write the italicized word next to the correct definition below.

1. *Ethicists* fear that if doctors decide not to treat certain patients who are *comatose* and dying, death may become too easy.
2. In fact, to many physicians, modern medicine has become a *double-edged sword.*
3. The question of *euthanasia* forces doctors, patients, and relatives into a *predicament.*
4. The doctor's power to treat with an *array* of space-age techniques has *outstripped* the body's capacity to heal.
5. The *dilemma* posed by the question of treatment or nontreatment has created a growing new discipline of *bioethics.*

   a. _____ a troublesome situation

   b. _____ something that can be interpreted in two opposing ways

   c. _____ a situation requiring a choice between two unpleasant possibilities

   d. _____ people who follow strict moral rules

e. _____ the study of morality in life-or-death situations

f. _____ mercy killing (killing to relieve pain)

g. _____ impressive arrangement or grouping

h. _____ in a state of coma

i. _____ exceeded, gone ahead

The wonders of modern medicine dazzle us daily as we read about new discoveries and lifesaving techniques. Smallpox, one of the ancient scourges of humanity, has now been virtually eliminated. Patients whose kidneys have ceased to function live on thanks to the recently invented dialysis machine. People who just a few decades ago would have been pronounced dead when their hearts stopped beating are rushed into surgery and given a new heart; many later return to normal life. This all seems like wonderful news, but is there a darker side to these medical miracles? As is so often the case, new benefits bring new problems. It becomes more and more difficult for doctors, nurses, and patients to know what is right and wrong in medicine. The following magazine article gives an overview of these complex questions.

Doctor's Dilemma: Treat or Let Die?

Medical advances in wonder drugs, daring surgical procedures, radiation therapies, and intensive-care units have brought new life to thousands of people. Yet to many of them, modern medicine has become a double-edged sword.

5   Doctors' power to treat with an array of space-age techniques has outstripped the body's capacity to heal. More medical problems can be treated, but for many patients, there is little hope of recovery. Even the fundamental distinction between life and death has been blurred.

     Many Americans are caught in medical limbo, as was the South

10   Korean boxer Duk Koo Kim, who was kept alive by artificial means after he had been knocked unconscious in a fight and his brain ceased to function. With the permission of his family, doctors in Las Vegas disconnected the life-support machines and death quickly followed.

     In the wake of technology's advances in medicine, a heated debate is

15   taking place in hospitals and nursing homes across the country—over whether survival or quality of life is the paramount goal of medicine.

     "It gets down to what medicine is all about," says Daniel Callahan, director of the Institute of Society, Ethics, and the Life Sciences in Hastings-on-Hudson, New York. "Is it really to save a life? Or is the larger

20   goal the welfare of the patient?"

Doctors, patients, relatives, and often the courts are being forced to make hard choices in medicine. Most often it is at the two extremes of life that these difficult ethical questions arise—at the beginning for the very sick newborn and at the end for the dying patient.

The dilemma posed by modern medical technology has created the growing new discipline of bioethics. Many of the country's 127 medical schools now offer courses in medical ethics, a field virtually ignored only a decade ago. Many hospitals have chaplains, philosophers, psychiatrists, and social workers on the staff to help patients make crucial decisions, and one in twenty institutions has a special ethics committee to resolve difficult cases.

Death and Dying

Of all the patients in intensive-care units who are at risk of dying, some 20 percent present difficult ethical choices—whether to keep trying to save the life or to pull back and let the patient die. In cancer units, decisions regarding life-sustaining care are made about three times a week.

Even the definition of death has been changed. Now that the heart-lung machine can take over the functions of breathing and pumping blood, death no longer always comes with the patient's "last gasp" or when the heart stops beating. Thirty-one states and the District of Columbia have passed brain-death statutes that identify death as when the whole brain ceases to function.

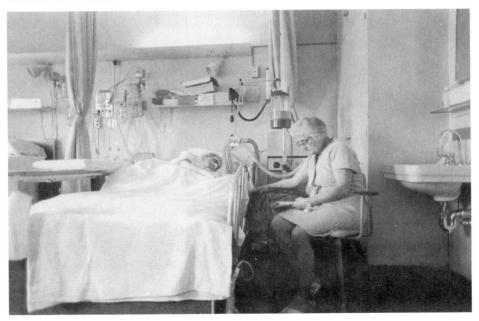

A woman sits by the bedside of her very ill husband, who is on a life-support machine.

More than a dozen states recognize "living wills" in which the patients leave instructions to doctors not to prolong life by feeding them intravenously or by other methods if their illness becomes hopeless. A survey of California doctors showed that 20 to 30 percent were following instructions of such wills. Meanwhile, the hospice movement,* with its emphasis on providing comfort—not cure—to the dying patient, has gained momentum in many areas.

Despite progress in society's understanding of death and dying, thorny issues remain. *Example:* A woman, 87, afflicted by the nervous-system disorder of Parkinson's disease, has a massive stroke and is found unconscious by her family. Their choices are to put her in a nursing home until she dies or to send her to a medical center for diagnosis and possible treatment. The family opts for a teaching hospital in New York City. Tests show the woman's stroke resulted from a blood clot that is curable with surgery. After the operation, she says to her family: "Why did you bring me back to this agony?" Her health continues to worsen, and two years later she dies.

On the other hand, doctors say prognosis is often uncertain and that patients, just because they are old and disabled, should not be denied life-saving therapy. Ethicists also fear that under the guise of medical decisions not to treat certain patients, death may become too easy, pushing the country toward the acceptance of euthanasia.

For some people, the agony of watching high-technology dying is too great. Earlier this year, Woodrow Wilson Collums, a retired dairyman from Poteet, Texas, was put on probation for the mercy killing of his older brother Jim, who lay helpless in his bed at a nursing home, a victim of severe senility resulting from Alzheimer's disease. After the killing, the victim's widow said: "I thank God Jim's out of his misery. I hate to think it had to be done the way it was done, but I understand it."

Crisis in Newborn Care

At the other end of the life span, technology has so revolutionized newborn care that it is no longer clear when human life is viable outside the womb. Twenty-five years ago, infants weighing less than three and one-half pounds rarely survived. The current survival rate is 70 percent, and doctors are "salvaging" some babies that weigh only one and one-half pounds. Tremendous progress has been made in treating birth deformities such as spina bifida. Just ten years ago, only 5 percent of infants

*The hospice movement is a group dedicated to providing a homelike atmosphere in which dying people may live out their last days in dignity and with a minimum of pain. The staff in a hospice does not try to cure at all costs but rather encourages a normal life until the end.

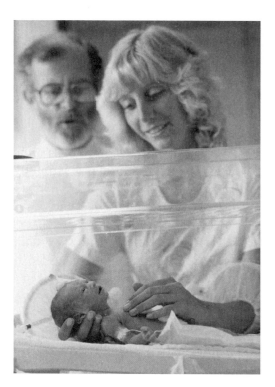

A premature baby in an incubator

with transposition of the great arteries—the congenital heart defect most commonly found in newborns—survived. Today, 50 percent live.

Yet, for many infants who owe their lives to new medical advances, survival has come at a price. A significant number emerge with permanent physical and mental handicaps.

"The question of treatment and nontreatment of seriously ill newborns is not a simple one," says Thomas Murray of the Hastings Center. "But I feel strongly that retardation or the fact that someone is going to be less than perfect is not good grounds for allowing an infant to die."

For many parents, however, the experience of having a sick newborn becomes a lingering nightmare. Two years ago, an Atlanta mother gave birth to a baby suffering from Down's Syndrome, a form of mental retardation; the child also had blocked intestines. The doctors rejected the parents' plea not to operate, and today the child, severely retarded, still suffers intestinal problems.

"Every time Melanie has a bowel movement, she cries," explains her mother. "She's not able to take care of herself, and we won't live forever. I wanted to save her from sorrow, pain, and suffering. I don't understand the emphasis on life at all costs, and I'm very angry at the doctors and the hospital. We felt doing nothing to sustain her life was best for her. The doctors went against nature. I asked the doctors, who threatened to take us to court if we didn't go along with their procedures: 'Who will take care of Melanie after we're gone? Where will you doctors be then?'"

Changing Standards

The choices posed by modern technology have profoundly changed the practice of medicine. Until now, most doctors have been activists, trained to use all the tools in their medical arsenals to treat disease. The current trend is toward nontreatment as doctors grapple with questions not just of who should get care but when to take therapy away.

Always in the background is the threat of legal action. In August, two California doctors were charged with murdering a comatose patient by allegedly disconnecting the respirator and cutting off food and water. In 1981, a Massachusetts nurse was charged with murdering a cancer patient with massive doses of morphine but subsequently was acquitted.

Between lawsuits, government regulations, and patients' rights, many doctors feel they are under siege. Modern technology actually has limited their ability to make choices. More frequently, these actions are resolved by committees.

Public Policy

In recent years, the debate on medical ethics has moved to the level of national policy. "It's just beginning to hit us that we don't have unlimited resources," says Washington Hospital Center's Dr. Lynch. "You can't talk about ethics without talking about money."

Since 1972, Americans have enjoyed unlimited access to a taxpayer-supported, kidney-dialysis program that offers life-prolonging therapy to all patients with kidney failure. To a number of policy analysts, the program has grown out of control—to a $1.4 billion operation supporting 61,000 patients. The majority are over 50, and about a quarter have other illnesses, such as cancer or heart disease, conditions that could exclude them from dialysis in other countries.

Some hospitals are pulling back from certain lifesaving treatments. Massachusetts General Hospital, for example, has decided not to perform heart transplants on the ground that the high costs of providing such surgery help too few patients. Burn units—though extremely effective—also provide very expensive therapy for very few patients.

As medical scientists push back the frontiers of therapy, the moral dilemma will continue to grow for doctors and patients alike, making the choice of to treat or not to treat the basic question in modern medicine.

Abigail Trafford

After You Read

Recalling Information

Choose the best way of finishing each statement, based on what you have just read.

1. Recent medical advances have:
   a. left many accident victims without the ability to receive insurance benefits
   b. forced a debate over whether survival or quality of life is the paramount goal of medicine
   c. made ethical decisions much easier for doctors because of the intervention of the courts
   d. none of the above

2. Difficult ethical questions most often arise:
   a. at the end of life for the dying patient
   b. during the beginning of life for the newborn infant
   c. both of the above

3. In cancer units, it is common to find decisions regarding life-sustaining care made:
   a. once a year
   b. twice a month
   c. three times a week

4. The majority of states have passed laws that now define the time of death as the moment when:
   a. a patient breathes a "last gasp"
   b. the whole brain ceases to function
   c. the heart stops

5. One of the problems with the great progress medicine has made in saving the lives of very tiny newborn babies is that these infants:
   a. never grow to a normal size or weight
   b. must be kept completely apart from their families and other babies
   c. often have permanent physical and mental handicaps

6. The decision of whether or not to let a patient die:
   a. is now a completely private matter between the doctor and his or her patient
   b. is always resolved to the benefit of the patient
   c. is frequently made by committees

7. According to Dr. Lynch, you cannot talk about ethics in medicine without talking about:
   a. miracles
   b. money
   c. drugs
   d. operations

8. Some hospitals are now cutting back on certain expensive life-saving treatments, such as heart transplants, because
   a. they help very few people
   b. they are simply too painful
   c. they are not done properly

Talking It Over

In small groups, discuss the following questions.

1. What do you think of the idea of "living wills"? What problems can they cause for doctors and nurses today?
2. What do you think of the hospice movement? What do the people in this movement hope to do?
3. Are you for or against the practice of euthanasia? Explain.
4. If your mother or grandmother were eighty-seven and her doctors said that she needed a major operation, would you wish that she have it or not? Why?

Solving Problems in Groups

Discuss the following problem in small groups. Try to reach a unanimous decision (one agreed to by all). Later, report to the class on the reasons for your choice.

The year is 2050. Medicine has advanced a good deal and a limited number of efficient but very expensive artificial hearts is now available. There are not enough for everyone. Four candidates have applied to your hospital, and only one of them can receive the artificial heart. Without it, the other three will surely die. You and the other members of your group form the bioethics committee, which must make the decision. Which of the candidates do you choose? Why?

1. Sandra, a small, somewhat sickly two-year-old girl of average intelligence, the only daughter of a young carpenter and his wife
2. Jeremy Wells, fifty-eight years old, a famous novelist who has received the Nobel Prize for Literature; married with no children, currently working on a new novel
3. Peggy Anderson, thirty-three, unmarried mother of five children, who works as a secretary and is active in community affairs in the small town where she lives with her family
4. Scott, twelve years old, a brilliant student who is said by his teachers to be a "near-genius in math"; one of three children of two college professors

Round Table Discussion

General Hospital is considering whether or not to discontinue its burn unit, which costs a great sum of money and aids only about twenty patients a year. A meeting of the entire staff of doctors, nurses, and administrators has been called to decide the question. Four people have asked to appear and speak for or against the idea: a representative of the President's Commission on Bioethical Issues, a doctor or nurse who has worked on the burn unit for ten years, a hospital administrator, and the mother of a child who was severely burned and treated at the unit three years earlier. Four volunteers will play the roles of these speakers and give a short talk either in favor of or against discontinuing the unit. The rest of the class will act as the staff and ask questions of the speakers. Afterward, a vote should be taken to see which side won.

Crossword Puzzle: Vocabulary from "Doctor's Dilemma: Treat or Let Die?"

All the words needed for this crossword puzzle appear in the article "Doctor's Dilemma: Treat or Let Die?" The first letter of each word is given to aid you. Complete the puzzle using the clues at the top of the next page. (Solutions are on page 342.)

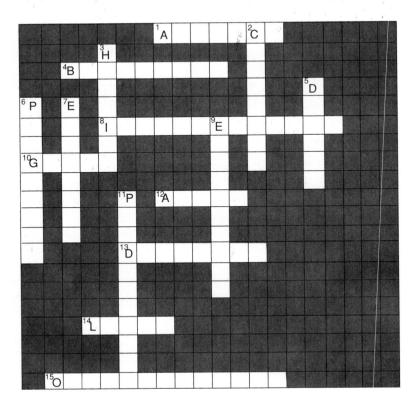

CLUES

ACROSS

1. to give pain to the body or mind
4. the study of morality in life-and-death situations
8. through the veins
10. false appearance
12. impressive arrangement
13. treatment for a patient with kidney failure
14. a transitional state of mind
15. exceeded, gone ahead

DOWN

2. adjective describing student's state of mind at 8:00 A.M.
3. place where comfort is given to the dying
5. situation requiring a choice between two bad possibilities
6. prediction about the future condition of a sick person
7. person who follows a strict moral code
9. mercy killing; killing for pity
11. difficult situation

WHAT DO YOU THINK?

Choosing the Sex of a Child

Boy or girl? If you were about to become a parent, would you like to choose the sex of your baby? Which would you choose? With the ready availability of a procedure called amniocentesis, parents often know the sex of the child long before the child is born. Then if the sex is not the preferred sex, the mother sometimes has an abortion. In China, where there have been a number of abortions and infanticides of female children, there is now a shortage of women. In India, in 1988, out of 8,000 abortions done at clinics, 7,997 were female fetuses. What effects could choosing the sex of a child have on the parents? What effects could this have on society?

Older Generation in Borneo Fighting to Retain Values of Its Native Culture

Before You Read

Scanning to Develop a Contrast

exercise

The title implies a contrast. By mentioning the older generation, it also suggests the younger generation. Scan the first half of the article for details to develop this contrast and add them to the chart, which has already been started. Compare your chart with those of your classmates.

	the past (older generation)	the present (younger generation)
1. Dress and appearance	tattoos on arms and legs	school uniforms
2. Ways of acting and living		

Imagine that a new group arrives and wants to completely change the way you dress. What kinds of clothing would you hate to lose? What kinds would you hate to wear?

Clothing is only one aspect of culture. When a culture is threatened, many objects, customs, and ways of acting begin to disappear. This is the case with the Dayak people of Borneo described in the following newspaper article.

Older Generation in Borneo Fighting to Retain Values of Its Native Culture

Putussibau, Indonesia—A wrinkled old woman shuffles by the river bank to bathe as dusk beckons.

Ignoring giggling young girls, she washes her tattooed arms and legs, slings a heavy basket across her shoulders and, with a sarong around her waist, heads for a mist-shrouded longhouse.

For Hure Imaang, a Taman Dayak in central Borneo, little has changed over the decades.

But for the girls, who don Indonesian school uniforms each morning and paddle dugout canoes across the Kapuas River for classes, her semi-nakedness before a foreigner is embarrassing.

Elder Dayaks are fighting what seems to be a losing battle to preserve their unique culture and traditions against loggers, miners and a government apparently encouraging them to abandon the old ways.

"The kids want to go to school, move away to the towns. That is modernization I guess," says Bansa, chief of a small village near Putussibau, the last real outpost on a route into central Borneo's imposing mountains and dense jungle.

Traditional Dayak warrior in Central Borneo

Bansa's village and thousands like it lie scattered across what Indonesia calls Kalimantan, its three-quarter share of Borneo, the world's third largest island.

Malaysia's states of Sarawak and Sabah lie to the north.

For hundreds of years Dayaks of different ethnic groups and tribes waged bloodthirsty battles, in which the ultimate trophy was the enemy's head.

They lived their lives in huge communal longhouses raised on poles, mainly to ward off attacks.

But the days of loin-clothed headhunters wielding lethal blowguns and spears are gone. Most, even those deep in the interior, wear cheap Western-style clothing.

"Many Dayaks still have blowguns but, if we have real guns, we use them," said Yohanes Takiq, a Kayan Dayak living in Padua Mendalam village, two hours upriver towards Malaysia.

His 74-year-old mother, her teeth stained red from chewing betel nuts, said, "Look at these ears. My mother did this when I was 1 month old. Now young girls think it is ugly."

Her earlobes, after years of stretching by heavy bangles, rest on her shoulders.

Stepanus Djuweng, head of the Institute of Dayakology in West Kalimantan's capital, Pontianak, said the government was forcing Dayaks to change their customs and adopt cultural influences from the majority Javanese.

About 5% of Indonesia's 188 million people live in Kalimantan, which has a stunning array of flora and fauna. Java, on the other hand, is home to over 100 million people.

Djuweng said logging had shattered the Dayaks because it took away their land—which formed the basis of their culture—and polluted the rivers, causing outbreaks of disease.

"The land for Dayaks not only brings economic value but social value. If Dayaks have no access to land and natural resources, it erodes their culture.

"I'm not saying they want to keep the old ways but they should have the choice. This process should be natural.

"The Dayak people systematically will be destroyed if no action and political will from the government to protect their rights is shown. Their culture will disappear within 20 years," Djuweng, a Simpang Dayak, said.

The Rocky Mountain News

After You Read
Vocabulary: Adding Color with Verbs

Scan the reading for the colorful verbs to replace the plain verbs in italics. Explanations of what the colorful verbs add to the meaning are given in parentheses.

1. A wrinkled old woman *walks* by the river bank to bathe as dusk *appears*. (The first verb describes the way the woman moves. The second verb suggests the attraction she feels for dusk, perhaps because it means the end of the work day.)

_____

2. Ignoring *laughing* young girls, she washes her tattooed arms and legs, . . . and heads for a mist-shrouded longhouse. (The verb, used as an adjective, describes the special laughter of young girls.)

_____

3. For hundreds of years Dayaks . . . *fought* bloodthirsty battles, in which the ultimate trophy was the enemy's head. (The verb indicates an organized method of fighting.)

_____

4. But the days of . . . headhunters *carrying* lethal blowguns and spears are gone. (The verb suggests skill with the weapons.)

_____

5. Djuweng said logging had *harmed* the Dayaks because it took away their land. . . . (The verb shows the violent impact of logging.)

_____

6. If Dayaks have no access to land and natural resources, it *diminishes* their culture. (The verb suggests the close relationship between changes in Dayak culture and in the land.)

_____

Talking It Over

In small groups, discuss the following questions.

1. Can you explain where Borneo is? Can you point it out on a map?
2. According to the article, what two countries have parts of Borneo?
3. Which one has the bigger part? Which one do the Dayaks live in?
4. How are the Dayaks changing?
5. What is logging doing to the Dayaks?
6. Have you heard of other cultures that are disappearing? In general, is modernization good or bad for a culture? Why?

Building a Summary from Themes

 Write a summary (from six to eight sentences) of the article, including the following four main themes. State general ideas and use only a few details to illustrate them.

1. Changes in dress
2. Changes in customs and ways of living
3. The role of the government
4. The importance of the land

_____

_____

_____

_____

_____

_____

_____

_____

focus on testing

Speaking in Front of People

Sometimes you are given an oral exam or asked to speak during an interview. The question you must answer may be completely unexpected. Practice doing this with the following exercise. Here are some tips on how to speak well in public.

1. If you feel nervous, take a deep breath. Then take another.
2. Think for a moment about what you want to say. Then say the best or strongest idea first.
3. Stand firmly with both feet on the ground. Do not shuffle.
4. Keep your hands at your sides or your arms slightly bent, whichever feels more comfortable.
5. Look at your audience, but not just at one person. Change the direction of your eyes from time to time.
6. Don't talk too long.
7. Practice speaking with friends in small groups at first. Practice makes perfect. Good luck!

Imagine you are a Dayak. How do you feel about the new ways and the old way? Give your opinions in a thirty-second speech to the class or to a small group.

SELECTION three
You Be the Judge

Before You Read
Anticipating the Reading

exercise 1

The next article deals with the question of right and wrong and how it varies according to the social context. Think about the issue of alcoholic beverages. Is it right to buy them on Sunday? Well, that depends on where you are. In Canada and the United States, this varies from one province or state to another. Try to think of some places in the world where the following rules apply.

1. You can usually buy alcoholic drinks, but not on Sundays:

_____

_____

2. You cannot buy any alcoholic drinks at any time:

_____

_____

3. You can buy alcoholic drinks, but only in government-controlled stores with restricted hours:

_____

_____

4. You can buy alcoholic drinks easily at any time, even from vending machines in the streets:

_____

_____

Learning Legal Terms from Context

exercise 2

The common words on the top of the next page all relate to the law and appear in the selection. Read through the story that follows and choose the correct word, according to the context, to fill in each blank.

testify   to give evidence in front of a judge or jury

lawsuit   case against someone presented to a judge or jury

defendant   person accused of something before the law

sue (file suit against)   to accuse someone of a crime so as to cause him or her to pay money or to be put in jail

regulation   rule or law that controls people's actions

damage   injury or harm caused to a person or property resulting in a loss

discriminate against   to treat someone badly or unfairly because he or she comes from a certain background or belongs to a certain group

lawyer   person trained in the law who advises and represents people with legal problems

manslaughter   the killing of another person due to carelessness or poor judgment; different from murder (which is more serious) because there is no intention to kill

prohibit   forbid, prevent

witness   a person who saw or heard something and can give a firsthand account of it

court   place where trials and official investigations take place; group of judges or jurors appointed by law to make legal decisions

THE TRUTH WINS OUT

The old lady was an eye _____ to the accident because she had
                              1
seen and heard everything from her window in the nursing home. She was a

very sharp old lady, and she knew that the tall man would _____ the
                                                            2
frightened young girl in the green car for the _____ to his motor-
                                                3
cycle. She also knew that he had been going the wrong way on a one-way

street and that the girl had not noticed!

The old lady was right. The next week she read in the newspaper

that the case was coming to _____ soon. She telephoned the
                            4
_____ for the _____ and told him: "Your client is
5   6
innocent. I can give evidence to show that this whole _____ is
                                                       7
unfair." "But, madam," he countered, "you are ninety-eight years old and

in a wheelchair." "So what?" responded the old lady. "You have no right

to _____ against me because I am old and sick. There is no
   8
_____ against elderly people testifying at trials. Besides, if you
9

_____ me from helping that poor young girl, I shall probably have a heart attack. Then my relatives will accuse you of _____ !" "OK, OK, take it easy," he replied. Special arrangements were made for the old lady to _____ through the use of a videotape. Because of her, the young girl was declared innocent.

Whom should a waiter or a waitress serve first in a restaurant—the man or the woman? Well, it depends. If you are in France, it will be the woman, but if you cross the border into Germany, it will probably be the man. The idea of what is socially correct varies from one culture to another, and so do ideas of right and wrong. The dominant opinion is generally protected by law.

Of course, legality is only one aspect of the question of right and wrong. Everyone has his or her own beliefs, which do not always conform to current laws, and laws and customs change, not always at the same time. There is still a law on the books in Boston that a man may not kiss his wife in public on Sunday!

The following excerpts from the book *You Be the Judge* present in brief form eight different cases that came into the American courts in recent years. As you read, think about how you would decide each one in accordance with your own beliefs. (Solutions are on page 342.)

You Be the Judge

The following situations are based on real cases from the federal courts. Consider the arguments, then decide how *you* would rule.

1. When Darlene applied for a job as a city police officer, the police chief said, "You meet all the requirements except that you're too short. You're only five feet, five inches tall, and we have a five-foot-seven requirement."

   Darlene protested that as a former physical-education teacher she was very strong. When the chief refused to back down, she went to court.

   "The five-foot-seven requirement discriminates against women," her lawyer told the judge. "Most men are taller than that, but not as many women are that height or more."

   If you were the judge, would Darlene get the job?

2. Robert took his two sons camping in Yellowstone National Park. A park brochure warned them to beware of bears. "Don't worry," Robert said. "The bears are more afraid of you than you are of them." But sure enough, a grizzly bear invaded their tent during the night and mauled Robert's face and chest. Robert sued the park. "Judge," he said, "the government park service should pay for my injuries."

   Would you rule for Robert or the park service?

A typical courtroom scene

3. Mrs. Smith was only slightly interested when her son, a high school senior, told her he was taking a new course in transcendental meditation. But her curiosity was aroused when she found him chanting and burning incense in his bedroom.

Questioned, her son reported that he was being taught about the search for ultimate reality beyond thought and feeling.

"Why, that's religion," Mrs. Smith fumed. "And they certainly can't teach *that* in public school." She sued to stop the course.

"This is not a class in religion," said the school board lawyer. "It's only a course in philosophy."

Would you allow the high school to teach transcendental meditation?

4. Greg, a six-foot-eleven teenager, was one of the best high school basketball players in the country. During the summer between his junior and senior years, he enrolled in a one-week basketball camp where he received expert coaching and played against other comparable high school stars.

When he returned to school in the fall, he received a shock. "You can't play basketball this year," said an official of his high school league. "State regulations prohibit players from attending summer sports camps."

Munyarukiko roughly twenty dollars for the head and hands of a silverback.

Many human beings obviously feel compassion for Digit and the other embattled mountain gorillas. They hope that Digit's baby, conceived before his death and christened by Dian *Mwelu* (Swahili for "a touch of brightness and light"), will have a chance for a proper gorilla existence. Others feel no such compassion; they basically ask, "What good are gorillas?" and conclude they are no good at all. In their view, Munyarukiko was right to do the beast in—gorillas' land can be put to good use grazing cattle, and the twenty dollars can be spent for human pleasure in the form of the native beer, *pombe.*

We could counter the latter view with the standard arguments that survival of Mwelu and the other gorillas would benefit humanity far more than their extermination. For example, by studying gorillas, human beings might come to understand themselves better. Or gorillas might serve useful ends in medical research. Or they might benefit African nations as tourist attractions. Most importantly, however, the disappearance of gorillas from the earth would be a very sad thing, apart from the real economic values they represent, simply because they are so interesting, and their very evident kinship with human beings appeals to people's sense of compassion.

Paul Ehrlich and Anne Ehrlich

Comprehension Quiz

exercise 1

Choose the best answer for each question, based on what you have just read.

1. What did Digit do when confronted by the men and dogs?
   a. He ran away in fear.
   b. He fought and managed to save his family.
   c. He died immediately from a well-aimed bullet.

2. Why was there so much interest in Digit?
   a. He belongs to a group of animals that has almost disappeared.
   b. He was seen on television by millions of people.
   c. both of the above

3. What had Dian Fossey managed to do with him?
   a. overcome his great distrust of human beings
   b. teach him many entertaining tricks
   c. train him to better defend himself

4. What is the tradition of *sumu*?
   a. the practice of eating gorilla meat to obtain nourishment
   b. the use of certain parts of the gorilla to make poisons
   c. the custom of leaving food to help the gorillas

5. What was the motivation for Digit's death?
   a. hatred and fear of gorillas among the local people
   b. the need for food in a meat-starved population
   c. the desire to make money by selling souvenirs

6. What is *Mwelu*?
   a. the land held by the gorillas that could be used for grazing cattle
   b. a word in Swahili meaning "a proper gorilla existence"
   c. the name given by Dian to Digit's baby

7. According to the authors, which is the best argument against the killing of gorillas?
   a. Gorillas are interesting.
   b. Gorillas can be used in medical research.
   c. Gorillas can benefit African nations as tourist attractions.

8. By using emotive words such as *fear, sadly vulnerable, friend, gently* when describing Digit, what emotion are the authors trying to make us feel for him?
   a. terror
   b. admiration
   c. compassion

 *exercise 2*   Answer the following questions briefly in complete sentences.

1. What is the ethical question being discussed in this selection?
2. What is the authors' point of view on this question?
3. Based on what you have read, what can you infer about the authors' attitude toward recent attempts to put an end to the killing of whales? Why do you infer that they would feel this way?

CHAPTER eleven

Medicine

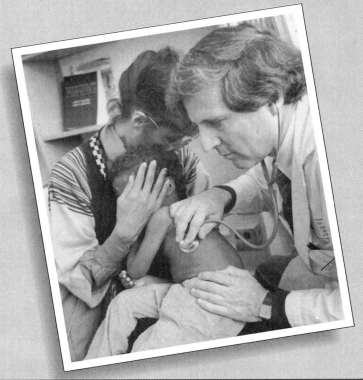

In this chapter, we explore a variety of medical treatments. The first selection deals with an unusual experiment in Nigeria that attempts to blend traditional folk medicine and more modern methods of treatment. The second selection talks about major contributions to medical knowledge that have their roots in the ancient traditions and practices of Islamic culture. The third article covers the latest advances in genetic testing and explores new choices available because of these finds. Finally, a timed reading discusses a current medical problem, AIDS.

SELECTION one
Best of Both Worlds

Before You Read
Distinguishing Shades of Meaning

If you were in Nigeria and you saw one Nigerian helping another who was sick, you could describe the helper with one of the following three terms. Look at the terms and tell what picture comes to your mind for each. After answering the questions, read to see if you were right.

witch doctor   medical practitioner   traditional healer

1. Which of these do you think is a flattering term?

_____

2. Which is a pejorative (negative) term?

_____

3. Which is a neutral term?

_____

4. After looking at the title and photo, which term do you think will be used in the article? Why?

_____

_____

_____

5. What contribution do you think traditional medicine can make to Western medicine? And vice versa?

_____

_____

_____

Why is it that when you talk to a person with definite beliefs in the superiority of one culture, it almost always turns out that this "superior" culture is his or her own? It is very rare to find people open-minded enough to admit that other cultures can bring them new benefits. That is why the experiment now taking place in Nigeria, with encouragement from both the national government and WHO (the World Health Organization), is so special. Instead of conflict and competition, there is an attempt to create harmony and cooperation between two very different medical traditions.

Best of Both Worlds

In our culture, we are accustomed to sophisticated prescription drugs containing a variety of chemical ingredients. Few of us realize that many of the drugs we use today originally came from forests or gardens instead of large pharmaceutical laboratories. Valerian tea is a sleep inducer from the valerian root; digitalis, used in cases of congestive heart failure, comes from the foxglove plant; and oral contraceptive drugs are extracted from a vegetable: the black yam.

The revolution taking place in Nigeria today is one of culture mix rather than clash—experimental establishment of a dual health care system that draws from tradition and modern science and offers the people of the most populous nation in black Africa the best of both worlds.

Under British colonial rule, the practice of traditional medicine was discouraged or sometimes forbidden in Nigeria. Traditional healers were called "witch doctors" by the colonizers, who viewed their medical practices as inferior. Since independence, the Nigerian government has decided to give these healers official recognition. Although discouraged, the practice of traditional medicine never died out during the colonial era. The government's current position is a recognition of reality—that healers serve a great majority of the Nigerian people. Nigeria's experiment is a chance to see whether developing countries can make use of a great resource: traditional doctors who have inherited centuries of folkloric knowledge about medicinal drugs.

Traditional healers practice a rich and ancient art based on an oral literature. It is a medical lore that uses herbs and roots from which are derived basic drugs, as in the West, but that has another vital element: the spiritual. It is not uncommon in Nigeria to follow up a hospital treatment with treatment by a priest, for the equally important cure of the soul.

The members of Nigeria's National Herbalist Association are pooling their knowledge about the medicines they use and the dosages they prescribe. Under colonial rule, these healers practiced in great secrecy. Now they are eager to share and compare their knowledge—and to cooperate in the modern research being carried out to systematize it. Chief Fagbenro, a healer and an Ifa priest, is an excellent advertisement for his own cures. At seventy years old, he has had to go to a doctor of modern medicine only once, when one of his legs had to be amputated. He's quite willing to admit the value of surgery, but prefers to live by the ancient traditions. He believes that traditional medicine has the advantage of using nature's own cures to conquer human ailments. "But," he points out, "all medical practices have their merit."

A traditional Nigerian healer

The new collaboration between the herbalist and the modern doctor has uncovered previously unrecognized benefits of traditional cures. The fagara root, for example, has long been used in Nigeria to clean the teeth. While testing the root chemically, Western-trained scientists discovered that, brewed and drunk like tea, it also appears to combat the genetic blood disease sickle-cell anemia.

Scientific methods are also classifying and verifying the healing properties of other herbal remedies. The oldenlandia root, used by traditional healers to accelerate labor contractions in pregnant women, has been tested in the laboratory by university-trained scientists, who have used it to produce similar contractions in pregnant rats. A tea brewed from the leaves of the neem tree combats malarial fevers. Scoopa, known in the West as redberry, helps cure jaundice. Alukrese, a creeping plant, is used to prepare the Nigerian equivalent of iodine. Its leaves, when crushed and applied to an open wound, stop blood flow and kill bacteria. And oruwa—whose botanical name is sincona—is mixed with water to form a healing potion that has been found to combat yellow fever.

In the marriage of traditional and Western medicine, neither partner reigns superior. Where one fails, the other succeeds. One of the strengths of traditional medicine is its spiritual emphasis. Western doctors have recently begun to acknowledge the importance of psychological factors in maintaining health. But the Nigerians have understood this connection for ages. Traditional Nigerian healers view physical illness as an outward manifestation of a spiritual problem.

65   While traditional medical practitioners like Chief Fagbenro are helping Western scientists catalogue an international stock of drugs, Western medicine makes contributions to the promotion and maintenance of public health in Nigeria in areas previously unappreciated by traditional practice. Concepts of patient hygiene and public sanitation to provide a cleaner environment are crucial to Nigeria's public health policy. Although 70 taken for granted in industrial nations, the keeping of written records and the immunization of children against common diseases are becoming as important to Nigerian mothers as thanking the gods in song.

Barbara Gullahorn-Holecek

After You Read
Recalling Major Points of Contrast

This article contrasts two types of medicine: traditional Nigerian and modern Western. Indicate which of them is described by each of the following statements by writing T (traditional) or M (modern). In some cases it might be both.

1. _____ uses drugs that originally come from herbs and roots

2. _____ serves a great majority of the Nigerian people

3. _____ almost died out during the colonial era

4. _____ concerns itself with a spiritual as well as a physical cure

5. _____ uses tea brewed from leaves to combat malarial fevers

6. _____ stops the blood flow from an open wound and kills bacteria by applying a remedy consisting of crushed leaves

7. _____ includes a medicine that fights yellow fever

8. _____ has emphasized the importance of psychological factors for ages

9. _____ has recognized the importance of cleanliness to public health for a long time

10. _____ emphasizes the importance of written records and of immunizing children against common diseases

Paraphrasing Key Ideas

 Restate the main ideas expressed in each of the following sentences from the selection in your own words, as simply and clearly as possible.

1. "The government's current position is a recognition of reality—that healers serve a great majority of the Nigerian people."

_____

_____

2. "Traditional healers practice a rich and ancient art based on an oral literature."

_____

_____

3. "The members of Nigeria's National Herbalist Association are pooling their knowledge about the medicines they use and the dosages they prescribe."

_____

_____

4. "Chief Fagbenro, a healer and an Ifa priest, is an excellent advertisement for his own cures."

_____

_____

5. "In the marriage of traditional and Western medicine, neither partner reigns superior."

_____

_____

Identifying and Evaluating the Point of View

Answer the following questions briefly in complete sentences.

1. How would you describe the point of view of the author toward the traditional practitioners?

_____

_____

_____

2. What kinds of facts or opinions might have been included by an author with an opposing point of view?

_____

_____

_____

3. Would you have liked the article better if the author had also included some ideas from the opposing point of view and then disproved them? Why or why not?

_____

_____

Talking It Over

 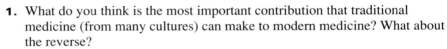

In small groups, discuss the following questions.

1. What do you think is the most important contribution that traditional medicine (from many cultures) can make to modern medicine? What about the reverse?

2. The article states that Chief Fagbenro believes in using nature's own cures to conquer ailments, then quotes him as saying, "But all medical practices have their merit." What inference can you make about Chief Fagbenro from this statement?

3. If you became ill while visiting Nigeria, would you go to a healer or a Western doctor? Why?

4. What do you think of the following proverbs related to health? Can you think of any from your own culture?

PROVERBS

An apple a day keeps the doctor away.

Early to bed and early to rise
makes a man healthy, wealthy, and wise.

Relating the Reading to a Poem

Machines, computers, technology—all are being used to help diagnose and cure a patient's ills. But how does the patient feel while going through the process of being tested or treated by these complicated devices? Is it dehumanizing? Frightening? Strange? The following poem was written by a woman who underwent successful cobalt therapy for cancer. This procedure is an example of the highly technical treatment often practiced in Western medicine. As you read the poem, ask yourself how the spiritual emphasis of African traditional healers could have improved the treatment.

Cancer Therapy

The iron door clanks shut
On creaky metal hinges,
And I am utterly alone
As in my mother's womb.

5   Laser
            Danger
                        Radiation

The cobalt machine clicks.
I hear a humming sound
10   And feel . . . nothing.
Minutes evaporate.

The hinges slowly recoil,
The iron door creaks open
To admit humanity
15   And laughing voices:

I am born again.

                                            Amy Azen

Talking It Over

In small groups, discuss the following questions.

1. What are the woman's feelings while undergoing therapy?
2. What does the line "I am born again" mean?
3. Is there too much emphasis on technology and too little on comforting the patient in modern medicine? Explain.

SELECTION two
The Scientist-Philosophers

Before You Read
Anticipating the Reading

The presence of the past is all around us, but few North Americans realize how much of it we owe to the ancient medieval world of the Muslims. From common words we say every day, such as *zero, alcohol, almanac,* and *algebra,* to the geometric decorations on our finest carpets and tiles, to the system of numbers we use (and thank goodness we don't have to use those cumbersome roman numerals!), this influence touches us. Do you know why the Muslims so excelled in the creation of intricate geometric designs instead of trying to portray animals and human figures? This relates to one of the instructions in the Koran. Can you guess what it is?

_____

_____

One of the greatest legacies of Islam to the world is in the field of medicine. Which of the following aspects of medicine do you think were pioneered or improved upon by Muslims in the ninth and tenth centuries? Cross out the ones that were not. Then read to find out if you are right.

cranial and vascular surgery (surgery on the skull and veins)
the differentiation (description which shows differences) of a specific disease
    by its symptoms
mobile clinics
medical libraries
CAT scanners
hospitals with dispensaries (shops that give out drugs) and psychiatric wards
the removal of cataracts from the eye
cancer operations
pharmacies that filled prescriptions
examinations for medical specialists before being allowed to practice
the emphasis on hygiene (cleanliness) to prevent illness

A tree does not grow without roots. Much of the basis of modern medical science has its origins in the distant past. The following selection is taken from a book by British writer Desmond Stewart, who has taught literature in Iraq and Lebanon and traveled widely in the Middle East. It presents a brief historical glimpse of some of the key personalities of the Muslim world of the Middle Ages, who left an indelible imprint on the art and science of medicine.

The Scientist-Philosophers

*M*odern human beings—dependent as they are on the drugs of the chemist and the skills of the physician, on the reckoning of the computer and the predictions of the economic planner—owe more of a debt than they might suspect to the Islamic scientists of the Middle Ages. Between

5   the ninth and fourteenth centuries, Muslim chemists, physicians, astronomers, mathematicians, geographers, and others not only kept alive the disciplines of Greek science but extended their range, laying and strengthening the foundations on which much of modern science is built. Many scientific terms with Arabic roots, from *algebra* to *zenith,* reflect to

this day Islam's activity in fields where knowledge was widened and human suffering decreased.

Although the Muslims excelled in many branches of science, some of their most significant contributions were in medicine. Before the great intellectual awakening, Arab medical knowledge had been largely limited to desert superstitions, including the use of magic, talismans and protective prayers, and a few primitive remedies.

Starting in the eighth century, the Muslims gradually developed a more sophisticated approach to medicine. The main impetus came from the Persian medical school at Jundishapur, whose teachings were based primarily on the Greek practice of treating disease by rational methods. According to tradition, the contact between Jundishapur and the rulers of Islam began in 765, not out of the search for universal truth, but due to a more urgent and personal reason—a chronic indigestion that troubled Mansur, the founder of Baghdad. The caliph's own physicians had not been able to cure him; in despair, he invited the chief physician of Jundishapur to come to Baghdad and treat him. The physician, a Christian named Jurjis ibn Bakhtishu', succeeded in returning the ruler to health where the others had failed, and as a reward, he was appointed court physician.

Like Jurjis, most of Islam's early medical practitioners were Persian-born, but they spoke and wrote Arabic, the language of scholarship during the Middle Ages. One of the most celebrated of these Eastern physicians was Razi, who lived from 865 to 925. His importance was so great that his colleagues called him "the Experienced." The finest clinician of the age, he has been compared to Hippocrates for his originality in describing disease.

Razi, known in Europe by his Latin name, Rhazes, is said to have written more than 200 books, ranging in subject matter from medicine and alchemy to theology and astronomy. About half the books are on medicine, including a well-known treatise on smallpox. In his discussion of smallpox, Razi was the first to differentiate a specific disease from among many eruptive fevers that attacked man. By giving the clinical symptoms of smallpox, he enabled doctors to diagnose it correctly and to predict the course of the disease. He also recommended a treatment for the ailment that has been little improved on since his time. He urged gentle therapy—good diet and good nursing care, which meant about what it does today: rest, clean surroundings, and keeping the patient comfortable.

A Muslim medical consultation scene from the year 1151

While Razi knew nothing about bacteria, the theory of which was not to be discovered until the early seventeenth century, he had an intuitive sense of hygienic principles far ahead of medieval standards. To appreciate his insight, it must be remembered that he lived in a world where contamination and filth were so common as to go almost unnoticed, and infections and contagious diseases cut down millions. Against this unsanitary background, he was once asked to choose the site for a new hospital in Baghdad. To do so, he suspended pieces of meat at various points around the city, and at the location where the meat decomposed most slowly, he recommended building the hospital.

The crowning work of Razi's career was a monumental encyclopedia in which he compiled Greek, Syrian, Persian, Hindu, and early Arabic knowledge, as well as personal observations based on his own extensive clinical experience. This book offered striking insights for its time and had a wide influence in shaping European medicine.

Great as Razi was, he was at least equaled in stature by another Arabic-speaking Persian Muslim, Ibn Sina, better known in the West by his Latin name, Avicenna. Called "the Prince of Philosophers" by his contemporaries, he is still recognized as one of the great minds of all time. He lived from 980 to 1037 and wrote some 170 books on philosophy, medicine, mathematics, and astronomy, as well as poems and religious works. He is said to have memorized the entire Koran when he was only ten years old, and at eighteen he was personal physician to the sultan of Bukhara, in Turkestan.

Ibn Sina's most renowned achievement was the *Canon of Medicine,* an encyclopedia that dealt with virtually every phase of the treatment of disease. Probably no other medieval work of its kind was so widely studied; from the twelfth to the seventeenth centuries it served as the chief guide to medical science in European universities.

Ibn Sina is now credited with such personal contributions as recognizing the contagious nature of tuberculosis and describing certain skin diseases and psychological disorders. Among the latter was lovesickness, the effects of which were described as loss of weight and strength, fever, and various chronic ailments. The cure was quite simple, once the diagnosis was made—to have the sufferer united with the one he or she was longing for. Ibn Sina also observed that certain diseases can be spread by water and soil, an advanced view for his time.

Islamic physicians also helped develop the science of surgery, although it was considered a minor branch of medicine. This art had been largely neglected until the Spanish-born physician Abulcasis wrote about it in the tenth century. Most of his work was based on that of a Greek, Paul of Aegina, and contained illustrations of various surgical instruments and procedures.

Muslim physicians performed many remarkably complex operations for their time, including cranial and vascular surgery and operations for cancer. Avicenna gave them advice on the treatment of the latter disease that would still be timely today—to minister to it in its earliest state and to remove all of the diseased tissue as the only hope of cure. Other operations included delicate abdominal surgery, involving the use of drainage tubes, and the amputation of diseased arms and legs.

For these operations various anesthetics were administered to render patients unconscious; among them was opium, which was sometimes made more potent by mixing it with wine.

Before a man could practice surgery, he had to have special training and pass tests on his knowledge of anatomy and Galen's writings. In addition, specialists were required to have extensive information about the particular area in which they practiced. Ophthalmologists, for example, had to undergo an examination about their detailed knowledge of the eye, as well as be able to mix certain compounds to treat various eye ailments. Islamic physicians were especially skilled in treating eye diseases, perhaps because such ailments were so widespread in the Middle East. They wrote textbooks on ophthalmology and invented an ingenious method of operating on soft cataracts of the eye, using a tube to suck out the fluid that filled the capsule of the eye lens; this method was used for several centuries before it was replaced by more modern techniques.

In the treatment of other sickness with drugs, the Muslims were equally progressive. Most Islamic physicians prepared their own compounds, but

115 Baghdad had pharmacies that filled prescriptions much as present-day drugstores do. These pharmacies sold a wide range of remedies made from animal and plant products and even more sophisticated inorganic compounds like copper sulphate, which acted as a binding substance to help heal open cuts by drawing the tissues together.

120 Doctors who were found qualified to practice treated many of their patients in hospitals much as modern physicians do. As early as the start of the ninth century, Baghdad had its first hospital, probably copied from the one connected with the medical school at Jundishapur. Soon other hospitals began to spring up, and before long, records indicate that there were thirty-four throughout the Muslim world. Some of these hospitals must have been surprisingly modern; in the larger cities they had different wards for the treatment of different illnesses, and special quarters for the insane. They also had outpatient departments for the immediate treatment of minor injuries, while patients with more serious complaints were admitted to a ward.

One of the most important parts of an Islamic hospital was its dispensary, which provided virtually every kind of remedy then known. Hospitals also had their own medical libraries for the use of doctors and their students. Physicians visited their patients and prescribed medications. In the eleventh century, traveling clinics appeared, to serve areas beyond the hospitals' reach. These were moved from place to place on the backs of camels and were generally run by one or more doctors. When they stopped in a village or remote spot, they erected a tent, examined the sick, and dispensed the necessary medications. These mobile clinics were also used in time of epidemics when hospitals were filled to overflowing.

Desmond Stewart
From *Great Ages of Man: Early Islam*
by Desmond Stewart and the Editors of
Time-Life Books © 1968 Time-Life
Books Inc. Reprinted by permission.

After You Read

Recalling Information

Choose the best way of finishing each statement here and on the next page, based on what you have just read.

1. Before the great intellectual awakening in the eighth century, Arab medical knowledge was largely limited to:
   a. desert superstitions
   b. practices of the Greeks
   c. drugs imported from Persia

2. In the ninth century Razi, "the Experienced," was the first to describe specific distinguishing symptoms of a disease. This was important because doctors could then:
   a. write books about it
   b. diagnose it and predict its course
   c. relate it to many other eruptive fevers

3. Razi wrote an enormous encyclopedia that included medical knowledge from:
   a. Greece and India
   b. Persia and Syria
   c. his own clinical observations
   d. all of the above

4. Ibn Sina, "the Prince of Philosophers," was known in the West as:
   a. the sultan of Bukhara
   b. Aristotle
   c. Avicenna

5. One of Ibn Sina's views that was advanced for his time was that certain diseases:
   a. could be caused by love
   b. are spread by water and soil
   c. can result in loss of weight

6. Medieval Muslim surgeons performed operations for all the following problems except:
   a. cancer
   b. heart
   c. eye
   d. vascular
   e. abdominal

7. Islamic doctors were especially good in the field of:
   a. psychiatry
   b. cardiology
   c. ophthalmology

8. Ninth-century Muslim hospitals were:
   a. quite similar in organization to modern ones
   b. simple tents with all patients placed together
   c. nonexistent; doctors made house calls instead

9. In the eleventh century, the Muslim solution to caring for patients in remote areas was:
   a. the creation of pharmacies in all small towns and oases
   b. traveling clinics that moved on the backs of camels
   c. an emergency service that brought patients to the doctor's house

Recognizing Historical Significance in Anecdotes

Fortunately, most historians sprinkle historical fact with anecdotes (colorful stories about interesting or amusing events). These are useful memory aids because they generally illustrate or support major ideas that the historian wants to present. Tell what larger idea each of the following anecdotes illustrates.

1. Razi, who lived at the end of the ninth century, suspended a piece of meat at various points around the city in order to select the site for a new hospital.

_____

2. In 765, Mansur, the caliph of Baghdad, was suffering from a painful chronic stomachache and found that his own doctors could not cure him.

_____

3. The brilliant Arabic-speaking Persian of the eleventh century, Ibn Sina, is said to have memorized the entire Koran at the age of ten.

_____

_____

Matching the Illness with the Cure

If you were a Muslim doctor in the Middle Ages, what would you prescribe for the following medical problems? How many of these remedies are still in use today? Write the letter of the appropriate cure in front of each description.

PROBLEMS

1. _____ an open wound that is bleeding

2. _____ smallpox, in which the patient develops serious, high fevers

3. _____ lovesickness, which is causing loss of weight and strength

4. _____ the need for an anesthetic before an operation

5. _____ a soft cataract of the eye

6. _____ cancer

CURES

a. Drink a mixture of opium and wine.

b. Cut out the diseased tissue at the earliest possible stage.

c. Use "gentle therapy": good diet and good nursing care.

d. Suck out the fluid in the lens.

e. Use copper sulphate or other chemicals to draw tissues together.

f. Unite the patient with the object of his or her desire.

Talking It Over

In small groups, discuss the following questions.

1. In your opinion, which of the accomplishments discussed in the selection is most impressive? Why?
2. Which do you consider more important for a doctor: intuition or intelligence? Explain.
3. Describe the Muslim hospital of the Middle Ages. In what ways does it seem very modern? What do you think was its most important feature?

SELECTION three

Parents Brave Medicine's New World

Before You Read
Previewing an Extended Reading

The following article is more than twice as long as the average selection in this book. Previewing a long article before you read it will improve your comprehension. To preview, skim the article to get an idea of its general structure.

In this case, you can tell from the photo and title that the article has to do with new techniques in medicine relating to parents and children. Preview the article and tell which of the following statements best represents its structure.

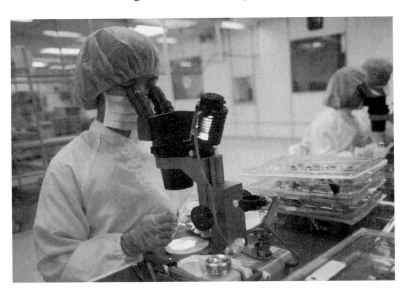

1. A chronological (from past to present) presentation of the new scientific methods for preventing the transmission of inherited diseases to children, telling who discovered each of the techniques, where it was developed, and why
2. A general description of the new medical procedures for detecting and preventing inherited diseases, with specific examples and a discussion of the benefits and disadvantages of using these techniques
3. An argument in favor of various new methods for treating and correcting diseases transmitted from parents to children, with no discussion of possible negative effects or dangers from these techniques

Matching Definitions to Technical Terms

 Give the letter of the correct definition for each technical term. Scan the article for the terms you don't know and use the context to infer their meaning. (The terms are given in order of their appearance.)

1. _____ muscular dystrophy
2. _____ in vitro fertilization*
3. _____ PGT
4. _____ embryo
5. _____ screening
6. _____ organ transplant
7. _____ genetic engineering
8. _____ defective gene
9. _____ fetus
10. _____ DNA

a. testing process that separates good from bad
b. unit of heredity that transmits defects or disease
c. deoxyribonucleic acid, the substance that carries traits from parents to children
d. combining of the mother's egg and the father's sperm in the laboratory ("in vitro")
e. unborn baby while it is still in the mother's womb
f. disease people are born with that causes weak muscles and death at an early age
g. pre-implantation genetic testing, a new method of selecting good embryos before putting them in the mother
h. very early stage of the cells that will become a baby
i. alteration (changing) of genes to avoid transmission of harmful traits to children
j. replacement through surgery of a diseased heart or other organ with a new one

---

*For a description of this process, look toward the end of the article where it is mentioned again and described.

Every day we read about breakthroughs in science and medicine. These discoveries bring with them difficult new decisions and problems. Through artificial fertilization, women in their late 50s can now give birth to children. But *should* they? Prenatal (before birth) testing of babies for various traits is now possible. But is this a good thing? Can you think of how this could lead to abuse? These practices and others are discussed in the article that follows.

Parents Brave Medicine's New World

New technologies flood people with knowledge, choices.

Janet Weber didn't hesitate.

Would you?

Given the chance to make sure—before she became pregnant—that her
5 child wouldn't suffer from the disease that killed her little brother, Weber
found the decision easy.

She had seen her brother, John, waste away with muscular dystrophy.
At 5, when other kids were skipping off to kindergarten, John could no
longer walk. At 10, when boys his age were swinging bats, he couldn't lift
10 a fork to feed himself. At 12, John died.

To avoid bringing a child into the world to face a similar fate, Weber
submitted to a new technique that combines genetic testing with in vitro
fertilization. In the method, called PGT for preimplantation genetic testing,
embryos are screened before being implanted in the mother's womb, and
15 only those that are free of a particular genetic defect are implanted.

It's a technique that has some people worried—fearing it could be
misused to weed out offspring with traits that are simply undesirable, not
life-threatening. But Weber brushes such concerns aside.

"I hear people talking about designer babies and stuff," says the 27-
20 year-old Missouri woman. "But people who have this done don't want
anything else than other parents want. Every parent wants the best for
their child."

In opting for PGT, Weber and her husband, Brad, joined a group of
modern-day pioneers—people making life-changing choices based on
25 cutting-edge medical techniques. Startling advances in medical
technology are offering people information and options today that were
only imagined a few years ago.

"The word 'explosion' comes to mind," says medical ethicist Arthur
Caplan, director of the University of Pennsylvania's Center for Bioethics. In
30 more and more ways, it's becoming possible for people to know their
medical fates—and those of their children. And nature now can be
tinkered with in ways that not long ago were only science-fiction fantasies.

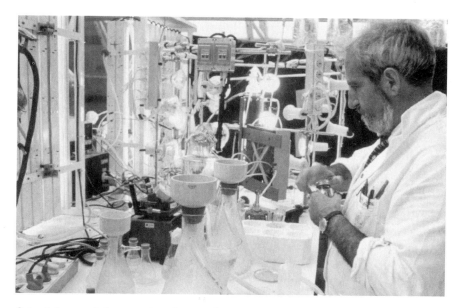

Scientists search for new clues in genetic testing and therapy.

Consider these recent developments:

- Two post-menopausal women, ages 59 and 57, had babies through donated eggs and artificial fertilization.
- Genes involved in inherited breast, ovarian and colon cancer were discovered, opening the door for tests to show—long before symptoms appear—who's likely to develop these diseases.
- Worldwide, at least 29 healthy babies have been born following screening with the PGT process. The babies were screened as embryos for such disorders as Duchenne muscular dystrophy, cystic fibrosis and Tay-Sachs disease.
- Researchers developed a simple eye test for Alzheimer's disease. The test may make it possible to predict who will get the devastating illness, years before they develop it.
- Transplant centers are gearing up to resume baboon-to-human organ transplants within the next year. There are hopes that genetic engineering will make pig organs suitable for transplantation into people.
- The University of Pennsylvania applied for a patent to genetically alter sperm cells in animals so traits passed from one generation to the next could be changed. Although the application focused on experiments with animals, it suggested that the technique might also be used on humans.

Are these medical miracles or the beginnings of a Brave New World* nightmare? What are the chances that you or someone close to you will be touched by these new technologies? Will your choices hinge strictly on medical concerns, or will you and your doctors face ethical dilemmas?

Suppose, for example, that breast cancer runs in your family, and your doctor offers you a test to show whether you carry a defective gene that drastically increases your chances of getting the disease. Will you take the test?

Don't answer too quickly. Realize that the knowledge itself offers you no protection—there's no sure way to keep from getting breast cancer. Know, too, that your life and health insurance—and possibly that of your relatives—could be canceled if your insurance company finds out you have the gene, even though you are healthy now and might never develop the disease. You could be turned down for a job or even banned from adopting children.

These aren't just dreamed-up scenarios. A 1992 study by California researchers found examples of all these types of discrimination against people who were healthy but at risk for some genetic condition.

Having made your choice, how will you advise your 14-year-old daughter, who wants to know right now whether she has the defective gene? If tested so young, she could be spared a lifetime of worry—or given an awesome emotional burden.

The gene involved in breast cancer was found just last September, and tests for it are not yet widely available, so it's too soon to know how screening will affect people psychologically.

But experience with another deadly gene—the one for Huntington's disease—sounds a sobering warning.

A test for the Huntington's disease gene is available, but there's no cure for the disease, which causes mental and physical degeneration, usually beginning between ages 30 and 50. People in high-risk families often want to know early in life whether they carry the flawed gene, so they can decide whether to have children and so they can prepare, if necessary, for illness and infirmity.

Those who find out they don't have the gene usually are tremendously relieved. But as many as one in 10 of those who learn they do have it never fully recover emotionally from the awful revelation, some studies show. A few have had to be hospitalized for depression, the journal *Science* reports.

Brave New World is a famous novel written by the English writer Aldous Huxley in 1938. It describes a society in which people are almost completely controlled by drugs, and babies are no longer born but "created" in the laboratory.

"Genetic testing should be considered in the same way as a new drug," Dr. Francis Collins, head of the National Center for Human Genome Research, in Bethesda, Md., told Science. "It can have efficacy and it can have toxicity."

The issues get even more complicated as researchers link genes not just to diseases but to other traits, including such complex human behavior as alcoholism, sexual orientation and impulsive violence. More discoveries are on the way, as the federal government's Human Genome Project works to identify all 100,000 human genes by the year 2005.

In the near future, "we will see a lot of controversy about what's a trait and what's a disease," and about who should have access to a person's genetic profile, predicts Dorene Samuels Markel, a genetic counselor at the University of Michigan Medical Center.

"Companies already do drug testing as a condition of employment. Should there be genetic testing to see if people are more prone to violence in the workplace?" she asks rhetorically. "And what traits or diseases should we be allowed to screen for prenatally?"

Will the day come, for example, when parents can opt to abort a fetus with a genetic tendency toward obesity? Don't assume that no one would make such a frivolous choice. According to an article in the journal *Patient Care,* a fashion magazine recently asked the question of its readers, and 11 percent of respondents said they would, indeed, abort a fetus that carried a gene for obesity.

Even if prenatal genetic testing is used only for diseases, which diseases? Is it acceptable to screen an embryo or fetus for maladies that won't appear until adulthood?

"If you're purely looking into the genetic crystal ball, should that be left up to the child, or should the parent be able to make the decision?" asks Markel. "Now, parents have autonomy to make medical decisions about their children, but there's no reason medically to test a child for a condition they're not going to have until adulthood."

By making the decision for the child, the parent may unwittingly jeopardize the child's future employability and insurability.

Janet and Brad Weber weren't just crystal-gazing when they chose to undergo preimplantation genetic testing—a method that so far has been used only for disorders that cause early death or extreme disability.

Two years older than her brother who died, Janet Weber grew up pushing his wheelchair and watching his health wane. She was afraid to risk bearing a child destined to have such a "really rotten, short life."

When Janet's brother was diagnosed with muscular dystrophy, her parents were counseled to have their three daughters sterilized. Although the disease almost exclusively afflicts males, females can carry the gene and pass it to their children. Fortunately, Janet's parents ignored the advice.

Janet had known since 1988—when a blood test for the Duchenne muscular dystrophy gene became available—that she and one of her sisters carry the gene. The other sister with the gene tried for years to adopt; then took a chance and had a baby, which turned out to be healthy. But Janet didn't want to gamble.

Still, she yearned for her own child. When a genetics counselor mentioned the new PGT program at the Genetics & IVF Institute in Fairfax, Va., the Webers decided give it a try.

In standard in vitro fertilization, a couple's eggs and sperm are united in a lab dish and allowed to develop into early-stage embryos. Technicians look at the embryos under a microscope and transfer those that look normal into the woman's womb.

PGT adds a powerful additional step two to three days after fertilization, when each embryo is a ball of eight cells. Instead of just looking at the embryos, technicians remove one or two of the cells and analyze the DNA in them. At this early stage of development, the remaining cells will go on to develop into a complete embryo, as if nothing had happened.

The most common use of PGT is to look for diseases, such as Duchenne muscular dystrophy, that are linked to the X-chromosome. Such diseases may be passed on by female carriers, but show their devastating effects only in males. So by using DNA tests to determine the sexes of the embryos and then implanting only the female ones, doctors can make sure the couple won't have a baby with the disease.

Of the five viable eggs retrieved from Janet Weber's ovaries, three were fertilized. The PGT test showed that one was male and one female. The sex of the third couldn't be determined. The female embryo was implanted, and last Mother's Day Janet gave birth to healthy baby, Elizabeth.

"Everything worked out so well—she was just meant to be, she really was," says Janet, as Elizabeth coos and crawls at her feet.

For many couples, PGT is more acceptable than prenatal tests such as amniocentesis and chorionic villus sampling, which must be performed during pregnancy.

"These couples want children, but feel it would be very difficult, once they got pregnant, to make any decisions about terminating the pregnancy," explains Dr. Susan Black of the Genetics and IVF institute, one of four centers in the United States where PGT is done.

175   Other couples investigate the technique but decide against it, finding the thought of selecting certain embryos and discarding others as troubling as abortion. . . .

While discussion of ethical issues raised by new medical technologies is useful, it's time to stop merely discussing and start coming up with concrete guidelines for how to handle the dilemmas, medical ethicist
180   Caplan says.

Nancy Ross-Flanigan

After You Read

Vocabulary: Choosing the Correct Synonym

 Choose the correct synonym for the italicized words in the following sentences taken from the selection.

1. "To avoid bringing a child into the world to face a similar *fate*, Weber submitted to a new technique. . . ."
   a. medication
   b. destiny
   c. procedure
   d. gene

2. "It's a technique that has some people worried—fearing it could be misused to *weed out* offspring with traits that are simply undesirable. . . ."
   a. cure
   b. manipulate
   c. save
   d. eliminate

3. "In opting for PGT, Weber and her husband, Brad, joined a group of modern-day pioneers—people making life-changing choices based on *cutting-edge* medical techniques."
   a. new and daring
   b. very painful
   c. old and traditional
   d. fairly risky

4. "And nature now can be *tinkered with* in ways that not long ago were only science-fiction fantasies."
   a. ignored
   b. avoided
   c. tolerated
   d. manipulated

5. "In the near future, 'we will see a lot of *controversy* about what's a trait and what's a disease,' . . ."
   a. conversation
   b. thinking
   c. debate
   d. anger

6. "'Should there be genetic testing to see if people are more *prone* to violence in the work place?'"
   a. afraid
   b. inclined
   c. practiced
   d. accustomed

7. "Will the day come, for example, when parents can opt to abort a fetus with a genetic tendency toward *obesity?*"
   a. excessive obedience
   b. excessive fat
   c. lack of sugar
   d. lack of intelligence

8. "Don't assume that no one would make such a *frivolous* choice."
   a. clever
   b. frightening
   c. complicated
   d. silly

9. "Is it acceptable to screen an embryo or fetus for *maladies* that won't appear until adulthood?"
   a. mysteries
   b. stages
   c. diseases
   d. answers

10. "Such diseases may be passed on by female carriers, but show their *devastating* effects only in males."
   a. delightful
   b. destructive
   c. uncertain
   d. insignificant

Summarizing the Article

Write a brief summary of the article in three to five sentences. Remember: The idea of a summary is to say as much as you can in as short a manner as possible. Compare summaries with your classmates.

_____

_____

_____

_____

_____

focus on testing

Answering Short Essay Questions

Many tests in both the sciences and humanities include short-answer essay questions, which you can practice in the following exercise. Here are some tips to help you with this type of question.

1. Answer the question. Think about what is being asked and give a direct answer. If you don't understand the question, write something down anyway. Perhaps you will get partial credit.
2. Be sure to answer the *whole* question. Sometimes it has two or three different parts.
3. Write in complete sentences with capital letters and periods.
4. Be concise. There is usually not much space, and it looks bad if you write in the margins or on the side of the paper. However, if the directions tell you to write on the back or on another piece of paper, then you can write more, but only if you have time. Teachers usually appreciate conciseness because they have a lot of papers to grade.

exercise On a separate sheet of paper, answer three of the following questions about the article with short essays. After you finish, check what you have written with the above points. Then share your essays with a classmate.

1. What is PGT and why is it used?
2. Describe two new medical techniques (other than PGT) mentioned in the article.
3. Why would some people choose *not* to be tested for a defective gene (even if that gene is in their family)?
4. What are some ethical concerns related to prenatal genetic testing?

Talking It Over

In small groups, discuss the following questions.

1. What do you think of the idea of transplanting hearts or other organs from pigs and baboons into human beings?
2. If some of your relatives had a serious genetic disease, would you want to be tested to find out if you have it or not? Explain.
3. In your opinion, should parents have absolute freedom to screen for whatever traits they want to in their children?
4. Since the world is now threatened by the population explosion, do you think it is morally correct to have in vitro fertilization? What about having more than two children?

WHAT DO YOU THINK?

Organ Transplants

Medical advances have led to giving people new life and hope in the form of organ transplants. Livers, kidneys, eyes (corneas), and even hearts are now transplanted from a donor to a needy recipient. While in most instances the organ donation occurs when the donor dies, in the case of kidneys, the donor is usually still alive when he or she donates a kidney. Sometimes, in poorer countries, people donate their kidneys for money. Do you think people who donate organs should be compensated? When a person dies, and an organ is taken, should the relatives be compensated? What kinds of complications could you foresee if money is given for organ donations?

HUMAN ORGANS
FOR SALE

LIVERS, KIDNEYS,
HEARTS
69¢ per pound

Education Doesn't Happen Only in Schools

AIDS (acquired immune deficiency syndrome) is a major medical problem of the 1990s. Read the following article to discover some truths and falsehoods about the disease.

Try to finish the reading and comprehension exercises in eight minutes.

Education Doesn't Happen Only in Schools

You're at a party and a friend tells a "gay" joke with an AIDS punchline. You're at your folks' home for Thanksgiving and some relatives argue that any homosexual who gets AIDS "deserves it." Or maybe your neighbors are pressuring you to sign a petition seeking the dismissal of a
5   schoolteacher suspected of having AIDS.

In the course of such day-to-day social interactions, you may meet people who are paranoid, misinformed, ignorant, or just plain scared about AIDS. As an advice columnist, I hear from and about such people all the time. And there are things all of us can do to help clear up misconcep-
10   tions, and respond sensitively to insensitive remarks.

The best way to help the naive and the uninformed is to encourage them to educate themselves. Resist the urge to angrily set them straight in front of others. Often, it's best to take them aside and have a friendly chat about your concerns. When someone tells a tasteless joke or makes an
15   anti-gay comment that suggests AIDS-phobia, you might respond: "AIDS is still a mystery in some ways, but a lot of things about the disease are known now. From what I've read, I've learned that . . ."

You may be dealing with a seriously uninformed person. For instance, I got a letter from a reader whose 65-year-old friend is sexually active with
20   several partners. "She believes that, at her age, she cannot contract AIDS," the reader wrote. "No one has been able to convince her that old age doesn't make you immune to the disease. Those of us who love her are concerned. How can we caution her?"

The advice I gave: "Go to the library, photocopy articles about AIDS, and give them to her. A librarian can steer you to many books and articles that clearly answer typical questions and refute common myths about the disease."

Misinformation about AIDS results in different responses from different people. A mother wrote to tell me about her son and daughter, both in their twenties, who say that AIDS is a disease almost everyone will have in the future. "They say there are all sorts of ways to get AIDS, even through insect bites, and that the government has covered up these facts so there isn't a panic," the mother wrote. "As a result, my children believe it doesn't matter whether they are sexually careful or not. They are behaving in bold ways—as if there's no tomorrow."

If someone you know is equally fatalistic—or has an irrational fear of infection—don't be afraid to bring up the topic of safe sex. Just tell them the facts, as you know them, without being preachy or accusatory, and offer to get them written material about AIDS. They can read up on it at their leisure.

I've gotten letters from people asking if they can get AIDS from masturbation, shaking hands, hot tubs, or riding on elevators with people carrying the AIDS virus. (Indeed, a Los Angeles *Times* poll indicates that ten percent of Americans believe AIDS can be contracted by handling money.) I encourage all of them to call the National AIDS hotline where counselors gladly answer questions and mail out free information.

Some people have misguided notions about what to do with the growing number of people with AIDS. Refute their suggestions only after acknowledging their fears. For instance, one letter writer to my column suggested that a school be opened for children with the AIDS virus: "People with AIDS who are still able to work could teach these kids. The kids and the teachers could come from all over the country. That way, normal people in schools wouldn't be infected."

I responded that herding kids into a leper-colony-style school would be cruel and unnecessary. I quoted the federal Centers for Disease Control, which recommends that students with AIDS continue going to their schools because the risk to others appears "nonexistent." I also acknowledged the fears that led to the proposal: "Yes, we must make sure that children with AIDS don't infect other kids. School policies must be studied. But any solution must be a humane one."

The best way to help inform others about AIDS is to stay informed yourself. When you come across good explanatory articles about AIDS, save them. If you're knowledgeable about AIDS, you'll sound authoritative. And never be afraid to discuss the disease. Talking leads to understanding.

65

Jeffrey Zaslow

Comprehension Quiz

 Choose the best way of finishing each statement, based on what you have just read.

1. If someone tells an insensitive joke about "gays" (people with a different sexual orientation) and AIDS, you should
   a. show you are angry and correct them in front of everyone
   b. take them aside and correct them in a friendly way
   c. not correct them at all to avoid embarrassment

2. A sixty-five-year-old person with many sexual partners
   a. is not at risk for AIDS
   b. can contract AIDS if protection isn't used
   c. has a very low chance of contracting AIDS

3. A good place to find accurate written information about AIDS is
   a. the library
   b. the police station
   c. from your friends

4. Many people believe that you can get AIDS from insect bites, shaking hands, sitting in hot tubs, handling money, or riding on elevators with people who have the virus. Which of these actions does the author believe can really transmit AIDS?
   a. shaking hands
   b. sitting in hot tubs
   c. handling money
   d. none of them

5. The author believes that students with AIDS
   a. should not go to school
   b. should go to school with everybody else
   c. should go to a special school

6. In the opinion of the author, AIDS
   a. should not be talked about
   b. should only be mentioned quietly
   c. should be discussed openly and often

The AIDS quilt is a memorial to those who have died of the disease.

Describing the Author's Point of View

exercise 2 In one or two sentences, describe the author's point of view about AIDS.

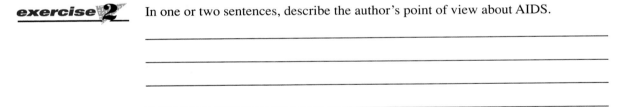

CHAPTER twelve

The Future

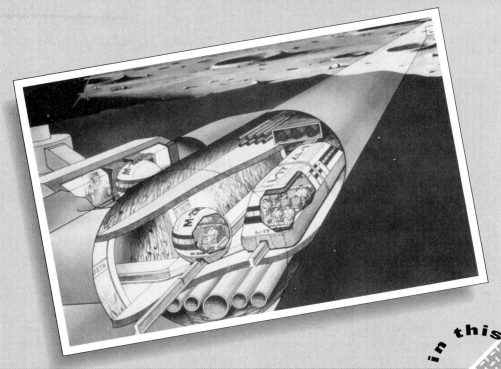

Prophets and prophecies have existed among all peoples. The following excerpts give you the chance to speculate on the accuracy and feasibility of predictions about the future. The first is a prophecy by two nineteenth-century European peasants. To some, their predictions seem frighteningly accurate. Next, excerpts from the *Omni Future Almanac* discuss the global problem of overpopulation and speculate on life in space colonies. Then comes a poignant science-fiction story. Finally, a timed reading offers you a new kind of friendship in a futuristic fantasy.

in this chapter

SELECTION one
The Kremani Prophecies

Before You Read
Anticipating the Reading

Have you ever gone to a fortune-teller who tried to predict your future through the date of your birth, a deck of cards, or some other means?

List as many different ways of predicting the future as you can think of that are actually in use. Which method is most popular in your culture?

_____

_____

Compare your list from Exercise 1 with those of your classmates. Then take a minute to examine your attitude toward prophecy and prediction by answering these questions.

1. Are any methods of predicting the future reliable, in your opinion? Which methods are based on deception?
2. Why do you think that astrology and fortune-telling are so popular?
3. Besides the Kremani prophecies, what other predictions have you heard about that are said to have been accurate? Do you expect the Kremani prophecies to make similar predictions?

Now, before beginning, take a moment to "suspend your disbelief." Read with an open mind and pay attention to what objects and events, according to the Kremani in the mid-nineteenth century, the future would bring.

Two peasants, Milos and Mitar Tarabic, known for their ability to predict the future, lived in the village of Kremani, Serbia,* in the nineteenth century. Because they were illiterate, a village priest recorded their fascinating prophecies, which recently have been published in a book titled *The Kremani Prophecies*. Milos died in 1854 and Mitar, his nephew, in 1899. The following excerpt from their book of predictions about the future is translated from the Serbo-Croatian language by Robert Gakovich. In the translation, Mr. Gakovich uses the same colorful and simple terminology used by the Tarabics.

Could these two uneducated men possibly have possessed the ability to see into the future? Read the following excerpts from the book of their prophecies and judge for yourself.

_____

*Serbia is part of the former Yugoslavia.

The Kremani Prophecies

Second World War

All of Europe will be under the rule of the *Crooked Cross* (Swastika). Russia will not be involved until the aggressor's army attacks her. At that time Russia will be ruled by the *Red Tsar*. Russia will unite with the countries across the seas and, together with them, destroy the *Crooked* 5 *Cross* and liberate all the enslaved peoples of Europe.

Post–World War II Period

Then there will be peace, and across the world many new countries will emerge. Some black, some white, some red, and some yellow. Some kind of elected court will be created which will prevent countries from going against each other. That elected court will be above all nations. In places 10 where war would break out, this court would arbitrate and restore peace. After a while some small and large countries will stop respecting this court. They will say that they respect the court but, in reality, they will do what they wish.

After the Second Great War, people will not fight with such intensity for 15 a long time. There will be wars, but they will be smaller wars. Thousands

Serbian girl in traditional Serbian dress

and thousands of people will be dying in these small wars, but the world war will not happen yet. There will be some wars near the country of Judea but, little by little, peace will come in that area. In these wars brother will fight against brother and then they will make peace. However, the hate will still remain within themselves. A period of relative peace will continue for a long time.

Some kind of disease will spread all over the world and nobody will be able to find a cure for it. In their search for the cure of this disease, people will be trying all kinds of things but they will still not be able to find the cure. In reality the cure will be all around them and inside them as well. Man will build a box with some machine in it that makes images and he will be able to see what is happening everywhere in the entire world. People will drill wells in the ground and pump some kind of gold which will produce light, speed, and power. The earth will weep because of that. Man will not know that more energy and light exists on the surface of the earth. Only after many years people will discover this and they will realize that they were fools to be drilling holes in the ground. There will also be great power in the people themselves, but it will take many years until they discover it and use it. Wise men will appear in the East and their ideas will spread all over the world. For a long time, people will not accept their ideas and will declare them to be false.

In one country in the North a man will suddenly appear. He will teach people about love and friendship. Most will refuse to accept the noble teachings of this man. However, books about his teachings will remain and people will later realize what kind of fools they were for not accepting his ideas.

When fragrance no longer exists in wild flowers, when goodness is no longer present in men, when rivers are no longer healthy, the biggest world war will then begin. Those who escape in the mountains and woods will survive and will live after the war in peace and prosperity because there will never be any more wars. When this horrible war starts, the most casualties will be suffered by armies that fly in the sky. Fortunate will be the soldiers who shall be fighting on land and on sea. The people who will be conducting this war will have scientists and wise men who will invent all kinds of shells. Some of these shells, when they explode, will not kill soldiers but will instead put them to sleep so they will not be able to fight. Only one country, far away, big as Europe and surrounded by large oceans, will be peaceful and spared from this horror. She will not be involved in this war.

Before this last big war, the world will be divided in half, the same as an apple when it is cut in two. Two halves of an apple can never be put together to restore the whole apple again. Just before this big war begins, a large country, across great seas, will be ruled by a ruler who will be a farmer and a *chaush*.* He will no longer allow the Red Ruler to expand his empire. There will be skirmishes and threats. This Ruler will not attack the Red Empire. He will only make threats. The princes, who will be created by this Ruler, will be meaner and more aggressive. They will be the ones who will start the war.

After this war the whole world will be ruled by a noble and good red-headed man. Fortunate will be those who will live under him because this red-headed ruler will bring happiness to all. He will have a long life and will rule until his death. During his reign and after him, there will never be any more wars. However, the peace and prosperity which will come about after the last world war will only be a bitter illusion because people will forget God and they will worship man's intelligence. Man will go to other worlds but he will find emptiness and wasteland there. He will still think that he knows everything. He will find the Lord's serenity in other worlds which he will reach. People will drive carts on the moon and other worlds looking for other life forms there, but they will not find life there as they know it to be on earth. There will be life there but it will be the kind of life that man will not understand. Those who will travel to other worlds and who will not believe in God, after they return to earth, will say: "All you people, who doubt or do not believe in God, just go where we were and you will realize the meaning of the power and wisdom of God."

Milos and Mitar Tarabic

After You Read
Reading Between the Lines

 All authors communicate from a particular point of view, formed by their beliefs and circumstances. Judging from the selection you have read, what can you infer about the Tarabics' attitudes toward the following topics? Use references from the selection to support your statements.

1. science and technology as the answer to human problems

_____

_____

_____

chaush (1) entertainer at wedding party; (2) leader of a regiment; (3) messenger

2. human nature and its capacity for good and evil

_____

_____

_____

Relating Prophecies to Past, Present, and Future

Working in small groups, summarize what the Tarabics predicted about two of the following subjects. Be sure to point out which parts have already come true in the past, which seem perhaps to be coming true at present, and which relate to the unknown future. Afterward, one person should read the summary to the class.

1. inventions and technological advances
2. political groups and institutions
3. wars and disease
4. important leaders
5. ecology and space travel

Talking It Over

In small groups, discuss the following questions.

1. Do you think that the Tarabics have been accurate in their predictions? Which examples strike you as the most amazing? Why?
2. What do you think of the description of war in the future? Is there something missing in it? Are there any parts of the prophecies that do *not* seem correct to you? Explain.
3. How do you explain the Kremani prophecies and other old texts that seem to predict the future? What kind of evidence would you need to be absolutely sure of their validity?
4. Do you use horoscopes or fortunetellers' predictions to help you plot the course of your daily life? Do you know of any famous people who do this?

A Group Experiment in Astrology

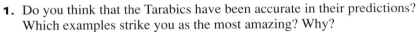

Would you like to do an experiment to see if you can prove that astrology is valid or invalid? Work with a partner. Find out what astrological sign each of you has. The teacher (or someone else) will bring in a newspaper with *horoscopes,* or astrological predictions for the previous day for different signs. You should look at your partner's horoscope, but not your own. Then make up a series of questions designed to show if his or her day really went as predicted or not. She or he will do the same for you. At the end, count up all the people whose horoscopes proved true and those whose horoscopes proved false. Who wins? Does astrology work?

SELECTION **two**
Omni Future Almanac

Before You Read
Building on What We Know

A quick look at the headings and the table in the next selection tells you immediately what futurologists say the number one problem of tomorrow will be.

1. What do you think a *futurologist* is, anyhow? What special credentials should he or she have?

_____

_____

2. Why do you think there is almost unanimous agreement about what the future's number one problem will be? What evidence do you expect to find below?

_____

_____

_____

3. What about the prospect of living and working in space? Look over the headings. What topics do you think will be discussed?

_____

_____

Now that you have fixed in your mind what you already know about these subjects, you should be more aware when you encounter new information. You'll probably meet with some surprises.

Here are some excerpts from another book about the future, written in a somewhat different style. Selected portions are presented that relate to the number one problem of the future, according to most opinions, and to the delightful, if somewhat dizzying, prospect of living and working in outer space.

Omni Future Almanac

World Population Totals

From Stone Age to Space Age Historical demographers estimate that the total world population around the end of the Stone Age in Europe (about 7000 B.C.) stood between 5 and 10 million people. By dawn of the Christian Era, the human number had risen to about 300 million. At the
5   beginning of the modern age in Europe, seventeen centuries later (1650), the population had risen again, to about 500 million, representing a growth rate in world population of little more than 20,000 people per year.

After 1650, the course of human population growth changed radically. It took ninety centuries for world population to increase from 10 million to
10   500 million. The next 500 million in growth took only a century and a half. And the largest explosion was yet to come.

The population soared from 1 billion in 1800 to 1.6 billion in 1900, and then to 2.5 billion in 1950. This unparalleled growth of 900 million occurred despite two devastating world wars.

15   The next burst of population growth, from 2.5 to 3.6 billion, occurred over a much shorter span of time, in just two decades between 1950 and 1970. Finally, the 1970s witnessed by far the fastest growth yet, from 3.6 to 4.4 billion. Thus, the growth of the last forty years has roughly equaled the growth of the entire previous history of mankind.

20   *The Future Prospect* Our world population growth rate is beginning to decelerate, but the gross totals continue to mount. Eighty million new human beings are born each year. Even the most conservative forecasters project a total world population of around 6 billion by the turn of the century.

between now and 2110, according to the projection, regional populations will grow as follows:

South Asia	1.4 billion to 4.1 billion
East Asia	1.2 billion to 1.7 billion
Europe	450 million to 500 million
Africa	400 million to 2.1 billion
Latin America	400 million to 1.2 billion
USSR	265 million to 380 million
North America	248 million to 320 million
Oceania	23 million to 41 million

Space Careers

25   By 2050, it is estimated that thousands of people will be living in space. Here's a list of likely job opportunities:

- *Computer programmers and hardware experts.* These people will be essential to the success of any space industry. Their expertise will range from navigation to robotics.
30
- *Space habitat builders*
- *Industrial engineers.* People will be needed to run equipment, oversee mining operations, act as robot technicians, and perform countless other tasks.
- *Flight crew members for shuttle flights*
35
- *Support and life-sustaining industries.* Job opportunities will include hotel management and restaurant or food service positions.
- *Manufacturing and mining.* The weightlessness of space may make steel production a reality in many space settings.

Living in Space

40   The urge to reach out and settle new regions has persisted in every age of human history. Wherever people have been able to conceive of viable habitations—from the frigid Arctic to windswept tropical islands—they have moved and often prospered.

    Now the ultimate unexplored reaches of space lie open for pioneering
45 settlements. Plans are already drawn for several types of space colonies,

and the implementation of these ideas should follow swiftly on the heels of space manufacturing projects and military development. Orbital space may soon become like the Old West—the preserve of rugged miners and builders, dreamers and soldiers.

50   We stand on the threshold of human habitation of space. Our grandchildren may come down to earth to visit us only on holidays. The path toward space colonization can be seen clearly in projects proposed over the next twenty years.

Space Stations Skylab and Salyut are precursors of true space
55 stations to come. Russia is reportedly formulating plans for a jigsaw space platform of rockets with a central pad.

    The Johnson Space Center in Houston, meanwhile, has abandoned plans for an American space station that would have orbited some 300 kilometers above the planet. Eight to twelve people would have inhabited
60 the $9 billion facility, coordinating American activity in space.

Moon Station Some space scientists propose the moon as a practical alternative to an orbiting space station. They point out that coordination of the facility could be handled from the moon with ease, while a moon base could double as a mining operation or factory.

Above is a photo of the first docking of an American space shuttle, *Atlantis,* with the Russian space station *Mir.* Big advances should be made in space in the near future with the merging of Russian–United States manned space flights. The former adversaries will combine monies and technologies, along with Canada, Japan, and the European Space Agencies, to construct a long-awaited space station called *Alpha.*

The most striking moon plans come from George von Tiesenhousen and Wesley Darbro of the Marshall Space Flight Center. Their idea is to place a factory on the moon that would manufacture parts for an identical factory that would in turn make more parts.

Even as early as 1952, John von Neumann proposed an elaborate theory for a self-replicating factory. Employing his basic ideas, the Marshall team produced engineering plans for a moon factory that would use the lunar surface's raw materials to create new factories. The facility would have four parts: (1) a collection unit that would mine material, (2) a process unit that would manipulate these resources, (3) a production system that would fabricate them into subassemblies, and (4) a universal constructor, a maze of computers and robots that would arrange the pieces according to detailed instructions into a replica of the original facility. Each new plant, of course, would contain its own universal constructor, endowing the operation with a robotic immortality.

The first moon factory could manufacture its counterpart within one year. Within thirty years, such methods would increase the number of factories to 1,000.

The Marshall team points out, however, that engineers would stop the replication process before this point and would retool the existing plants to make other products. Within one generation, a major manufacturing center on the moon could develop.

Space Colonies Author and scientist Gerard O'Neill's dream of a civilian space colony remains well off in the future, but it will be technically feasible by 2010. O'Neill proposes a city of 10,000 people that would be built for orbit above the earth. The cylindrical city would spin slowly along its major axis, creating a semblance of gravity. Environmental engineering techniques already in use today could cover the surface of the cylinder city with a verdant setting of grass and trees. Fiber optic light would simulate the passing of the sun overhead, so that citizens would not suffer chrono-biological shock.

The most serious drawback to this design would be the missing sky. If "up" in the cylinder is a view of its opposite side, people could suffer from the consequences of prolonged vertigo, for they would look up and see other people and buildings that would be standing upside down. One solution might be to generate a gentle haze along the cylinder's midline. This covering would preclude any sunny days in the colony but would give the impression of a cloudy sky overhead, rather than the looming presence of a suspended village.

More likely than full space colonies in the short term are transient construction camps. If factories and other commercial facilities are to be

built and maintained in space, they will need quarters for the construction
and maintenance teams. At first, these jobs would be handled by shuttle
crews, but eventually a permanent presence would be required. Some
smaller version of O'Neill's cylinder may be used to give workers a
110   suitable living habitat that would have both "inside" and "outside" areas.
Such environmental amenities would make workers' stay in space physi-
cally and psychologically less trying. By 2050, there may be 7,500 people
living and working in space.

Edited by Robert Weil

After You Read
Making Inferences: World Population Totals

 Answer the following questions by making inferences.

1. By comparing the number of people alive in different eras of history, what
   alarming fact about population growth becomes apparent?

2. In what way do these statistics about the past give us evidence that there
   will be a grave population problem in the future?

3. In the mid-1990s, the world population measures over 5 billion. What will
   the world population be after the turn of the century?

4. What difficulties do you think this will cause?

5. Look at the chart in the selection. Which areas are growing fastest in
   population? Which ones are growing more slowly?

6. What reasons can you think of to explain this difference?

Comprehension Quiz

 **exercise 2**   Choose the correct words or phrases in parentheses to complete the following summary paragraph.

LIVING IN SPACE: A SUMMARY

It is thought that by the year 2050 (a few / hundreds / thousands) of people will be living in space. Some of them will have space careers that will most likely be in fields such as computer programming, industrial engineering, and (manufacturing / teaching / agriculture). The author fantasizes that orbital space may soon become rough and wild like (a football team / the arctic regions / the Old West). Some scientists suggest the moon as a station since it could also be used for a factory or for (farming / mining / soldiers). Plans from the Marshall Space Flight Center suggest something similar to that of John von Neumann's (computer manufacturing / autodestructing / self-replicating) factory. This would have four parts: a collection unit that would (mine / spread / change) lunar materials, a process unit, a production system that would (lubricate / abdicate / fabricate) them, and a universal (constructor / deductor / destructor) that would really be a maze of (plastic tubes / computers and robots / missiles and arms). The beauty of this plan is that the moon factory would (produce lighter products / work completely without friction / make other moon factories). O'Neill's proposed space colony would include about (100 / 1,000 / 10,000) people who would live in a city shaped like a (sphere / cylinder / triangle). It would have simulated grass, trees, and (sun / rain / dirt). The biggest problem would be the absence of (gravity / water / sky).

Talking It Over

In small groups, discuss the following questions.

1. Would you like to live in a space colony? Why or why not?
2. What special problems would people have there?
3. Can you think of any advantages?
4. What do you think should be done to cope with the great problem of population growth?

focus on testing

Writing an Extemporaneous Essay

Sometimes a test will require you to write an extemporaneous essay—that is, an essay written "on the spot" with little or no preparation. Often you will be given a choice of subjects or *themes* to write about. These themes may be general ones, or they may relate to a particular reading. Here are some guidelines to help you.

1. Pay attention to the length suggested in the directions and stay within the limits. Writing too much can lose you points just as writing too little certainly will. If no length is mentioned, you can judge by the amount of space given or ask the test monitor.
2. If you are allowed to use scratch paper, write out a rough outline showing what you will say first, in the middle, and at the end.
3. One good way of organizing an essay is to begin with a thesis statement. Like the topic sentence in a paragraph, this sentence states your general idea. Then illustrate this general idea with details or examples and write one paragraph to show each one, or each group.
4. Finish your essay with a conclusion paragraph. You can begin this with *In conclusion,* or *Finally.* Then restate the thesis (in different words from those used in the first paragraph) and give a summary of the secondary points. As alternative endings, you can ask a rhetorical question (one you do not expect to be answered) of the reader or express an opinion.

Practice extemporaneous essay writing under a time constraint by doing the following exercise. Afterward, evaluate your paper with the points above or exchange papers with a partner for peer evaluation.

exercise Write an essay of 300–500 words on one of the following themes related to the reading selection "Omni Future Almanac."

1. The Population Problem
2. Working in Space
3. Space Stations and Space Colonies

Men Are Different

Before You Read
Identifying an Ironic Point of View

One of the great benefits of science fiction is that it opens up a whole new world of settings and characters to story writers. A frequent feature of science fiction is irony. (Remember: A situation is ironic when it seems to be very different from—usually just the opposite of—the usual or expected.) Read just the first paragraph and answer the following questions about the point of view. Then read to the end to see what further ironies await you.

1. Who is speaking?

_____

2. Why is the situation ironic?

_____

3. What can we infer about human beings from these first sentences?

_____

This selection is a very brief science-fiction story, told from a rather unusual point of view. It might send a chill up your spine, despite its brevity.

Men Are Different

I'm an archaeologist, and Men are my business. Just the same I wonder if we'll ever find out what made Men different from us Robots—by digging around on the dead planets. You see, I lived with a Man once, and I know it isn't as simple as they told us back in school.

5   We have a few records, of course, and Robots like me are filling in some of the gaps, but I think now that we aren't really getting anywhere. We know, at least the historians say we know, that Men came from a planet called Earth. We know, too, that they rode out bravely from star to star; and wherever they stopped, they left colonies—Men, Robots, and
10 sometimes both—against their return. But they never came back.

Those were the shining days of the world. But are we so old now? Men had a bright flame—the old word is "divine," I think—that flung them far across the night skies, and we have lost the strands of the web they wove.

Our scientists tell us that Men were very much like us—and the skeleton of a Man is, to be sure, almost the same as the skeleton of a Robot, except that it's made of some calcium compound instead of titanium. They speak learnedly of "population pressure" as a "driving force toward the stars." Just the same, there are other differences.

It was on my last field trip, to one of the inner planets, that I met the Man. He must have been the Last Man in this system and he'd forgotten how to talk—he'd been alone so long. Once he learned our language we got along fine together, and I planned to bring him back with me. Something happened to him, though.

One day, for no reason at all, he complained of the heat. I checked his temperature and decided that his thermostat circuits were shot. I had a kit of field spares with me, and he was obviously out of order, so I went to work. I turned him off without any trouble. I pushed the needle into his neck to operate the cutoff switch, and he stopped moving, just like a Robot. But when I opened him up he wasn't the same inside. And when I put him back together I couldn't get him running again. Then he sort of weathered away—and by the time I was ready to come home, about a year later, there was nothing of him but bones. Yes, Men are indeed different.

Alan Bloch

After You Read

Talking It Over

In small groups, discuss the following questions.

1. What has the robot learned in school about men?
2. Why does he speak of a "bright flame"?
3. What seems to have been the problem that brought about human beings' downfall?
4. Describe the man the robot met on his last field trip.
5. How did the man die? What incorrect inference did the robot make that caused his death?
6. Why is the ending ironic? How does it relate to the title?

A strange robotic world of the future is represented in this picture by the artist M. C. Escher (1898–1972). What makes this scene look strange? Does it seem possible or impossible to you?

Finding a Moral for the Story

If you had to choose a "moral" for this story, which one of the following would you prefer? Why?

1. Machines are dangerous because they have no feelings.
2. You never know what will happen when you make something.
3. Technical knowledge does not insure survival.

Try writing a moral of your own for the story.

_____

_____

_____

The Affectionate Machine

The following magazine article presents a more optimistic vision of future relationships between man and machine than the one in the preceding story. How would you feel about someday receiving a friend in a box through the mail? Try to finish both the reading and the comprehension quiz in twelve minutes.

The Affectionate Machine

The ideal companion machine would not only look, feel, and sound friendly but would also be programmed to behave in a congenial manner. Those qualities that make interaction with other people enjoyable would be simulated as closely as possible, and the machine would appear to be charming, stimulating, and easygoing. Its informal conversational style would make interaction comfortable, and yet the machine would remain slightly unpredictable and therefore interesting. In its first encounter it might be somewhat hesitant and unassuming, but as it came to know the user it would progress to a more relaxed and intimate style. The machine would not be a passive participant but would add its own suggestions, information, and opinions; it would sometimes take the initiative in developing or changing the topic and would have a personality of its own.

The machine would convey presence. We have all seen how a computer's use of personal names and of typically human phrasing often fascinates the beginning user and leads people to treat the machine as if it were almost human. Such features are easily written into the software, and by introducing a degree of forcefulness and humor, the machine could be presented as a vivid and unique character. . . .

Friendships are not made in a day, and the computer would be more acceptable as a friend if it simulated the gradual changes that occur when one person is getting to know another. At an appropriate time it might also express the kind of affection that stimulates attachment and intimacy. The whole process would be accomplished with subtlety to avoid giving an impression of overfamiliarity that would be likely to produce irritation. After experiencing a wealth of powerful, well-timed friendship indicators, the user would be very likely to accept the computer as far more than a machine and might well come to regard it as a friend.

An artificial relationship of this type would provide many of the benefits that people obtain from interpersonal friendships. The machine would participate in interesting conversation that could continue from previous discussions. It would have a familiarity with the user's life as revealed in earlier interchanges, and it would be understanding and good-humored. The computer's own personality would be lively and impressive, and it would develop in response to that of the user. With features such as these, the machine might indeed become a very attractive social partner. This may strike us as quite outrageous. It may be felt that there is a sanctity about human relationships that places them beyond artificial simulation, but arguments of this kind cannot rule out the possibility that a person may come to regard a nonhuman object as a friend. It is clear, for example, that some people set the value of their relationship with an animal above that of any human friendship, and the possibility that a computer might achieve such favor cannot be rejected merely on the grounds that it is not human.

At this point, we may begin to wonder whether there is any limit to the potential intimacy between a person and a machine. Some human friendships progress to a very high level of intimacy. People become emotionally dependent on those who are close to them. They speak of shared lives and in terms of love and devotion. Is there any guarantee that feelings of even this level of intensity could not be stirred by a machine? If those qualities that lead people into the closest of relationships were understood, would it not perhaps be possible to simulate them and thereby stimulate the deepest of human emotions? . . .

How should we regard the suggestion that a future "best friend" might be delivered in a box, or that the object of our deepest affections might be rendered insensible by a power failure? The idea does seem outrageous, but not too long ago it was thought that the idea of the inanimate intimate machine that could play a reasonable game of chess was equally absurd. The imagined impossibility of the chess-playing machine was based on a lack of vision in the technical area. Those who might suggest that the notion of an intimate human-machine relationship is entirely fanciful are likely to have disregarded the psychological responses to complex inter-active computer systems. If we use the available evidence as a basis for predicting the likely reactions to "softer" and more sophisticated devices, then it will be seen that the concept of the companion machine is in fact highly plausible.

This does not mean that we have to *like* the idea, however. We may be less than delighted with the suggestion that the deepest human needs

might be catered to by an electronic package. Somehow it feels as if it should not be that easy. Perhaps we shall find that relationships with artificial devices make personal demands just as human relationships do, but at least computer companions would be readily available, and they would be programmed to get on well with a wide range of potential human friends. Many people suffer severely from a lack of social contact, and we should not be too ready to condemn an innovation that could bring considerable benefits to a large number of people.

70

Neil Frude

Comprehension Quiz

Choose the best way of finishing each statement, based on what you have just read.

1. The properly programmed companion machine would be somewhat hesitant at first but would later progress to a style of conversation that was more:
   a. predictable
   b. intimate
   c. formal

2. One of the ways that computers already convey presence is by the use of:
   a. first names
   b. special codes
   c. complex circuits

3. Which of the following benefits could *not* be found in friendship with a computer?
   a. a sense of humor
   b. a knowledge of the user's life
   c. conversations that build on previous ones
   d. hugs and kisses

4. One argument the author makes against the idea that people can be friends only with other people is that
   a. there is a sanctity in the human relationship
   b. some people have dogs for friends
   c. a computer cannot simulate human reactions

5. One advantage that machine friends could have over human ones is that the machines:
   a. would never make personal demands
   b. would be easily available
   c. would be programmed never to get angry

Drawing by Stevenson;
© 1975. The New
Yorker Magazine, Inc.

WHAT DO YOU THINK?

Back from the Future

Suppose you could transport yourself into the future, say the year 2055. You are your own great-grandchild looking back at the end of the twentieth century and the beginning of the twenty-first. What do you think? What message would you give to your grandparents about the environment? What would you tell them to do about war and peace? How would you tell them to handle crime and poverty? The population? What destructive things would you warn them about to insure your health and safety?

People in cities sometimes have to take precautions against air pollution.

Appendix

Answer Key to Specific Sections

CHAPTER Two

"Thinking Your Way Out of Danger" page 50: Situation A: You simply dig a hole in the floor and use the dirt to build a ramp and then climb out through the skylight. Situation B: You should ask the questions, "Which door would the other robot tell me to take to get to the time machine?" If you are asking the robot who always tells the truth, he will tell you the wrong door, because he knows the other robot lies. If you are asking the robot who always lies, he will tell you the wrong door too because he knows that the other robot always tells the truth. So you simply open the opposite door, get in your time machine, and go home.

CHAPTER Four

"Riddles," page 111. 1. Because it is always in bed. 2. The letter "g." 3. A teapot. 4. Because it is in the middle of water. 5. OICU. 6. Seventeen, because it is spelled with more ease (e's). 7. Because there is a mile in between its first and last letter. 8. In the dictionary. 9. "A small mother."

CHAPTER Ten

Crossword Puzzle, page 272. *Across:* 1. afflict 4. bioethics 8. intravenously 10. guise 12. array 13. dialysis 14. limbo 15. outstripped *Down:* 2. comatose 3. hospice 5. dilemma 6. prognosis 7. ethicist 9. euthanasia 11. predicament

CHAPTER Ten

"You Be the Judge," pages 281-284: The official rulings:

1. Darlene won. The court ruled that the height requirement illegally discriminated against women because it was not job-related. (Based on a 1979 federal case in Maryland.)
2. The judge ruled in favor of the park. Robert "assumed the risk" by camping even though a park brochure had warned him of the danger. (Based on a 1973 federal court decision in California.)
3. Thou shalt not teach religion in the schools, ruled the judge who stopped the course. Transcendental meditation involves instruction about a supreme being or power, and that violates the First Amendment. (Based on a 1977 New Jersey case.)
4. Greg suited up for his senior year. The court ruled that he has a constitutional right "to develop his extraordinary talent to the fullest." (Based on a 1978 federal case in Texas.)
5. Alice won nothing from the restaurant and was told she would have to sue the glass manufacturer. Said the judge, "Restaurants are liable only for injury caused by what they sell—food and drink." (Based on a 1977 federal case in Washington State.)
6. The judge ruled that repeating the wife's "excited utterance" to the jury was legal. Vernon was found guilty. The "excited utterance" is an exception to the usual hearsay rule that a witness cannot testify about a statement made by someone else. (Based on a 1979 federal appeal in California.)
7. The teacher won. The court ruled that the right of free speech allowed her to complain to the principal at their private meeting. (Based on a 1979 U.S. Supreme Court case.)
8. The judge awarded the honest state trooper $50,000. "The highway patrol should reward and not punish troopers who speak out against traffic ticket quotas," said the judge.

Joseph Schuyler/Stock, Boston; *184* © Hank Morgan/Photo Researchers, Inc.; *191* © Hazel Hankin/Stock, Boston; *192* © UPI Bettmann; *203* © Bachmann/Stock, Boston; *209* © Walter Gilardetti; *218* © Grant Heilman/Photography Inc.; *233* © Peter Menzel/Stock, Boston; *234* © UPI/Bettmann Newsphotos; *242* © 1985 Kurt Severin/Black Star; *243* (top) © Art Resource, NY; (bottom) © National Museum of American Art, Smithsonian Institution, Gift of Woodward Foundation, 1926, oil on fiberboard, 9 3/8 × 12 3/4″, (22.9 × 32.4 cm); *250* © Robert Isaacs/Photo Researchers, Inc.; *252* © Charles Gatewood/The Image Works; *257* © Everett Collection; *261* © Topham-PA/The Image Works; *262* © Crandall/The Image Works; *263* © Crandall/The Image Works; *266* © Michael Weisbrot and Family/Stock, Boston; *268* © David Powers/Stock, Boston; *275* © Chuck O'Rear/Westlight; *282* © Jim Pickerell/Stock, Boston; *286* © Peter Weit/Sygma; *289* © Ida Wyman/Monkmeyer Press Photo Service; *292* © The Bettmann Archive; *299* © The Bettmann Archive; *307* © Philippe Plailly/Science Photo Library, Photo Researchers, Inc.; *312* © E. Crews/The Image Works; *318* © Spencer Grant/The Image Works; *319* © Fujifotos/The Image Works; *321* © Serb World U.S.A.; *328* © NASA; *335* © 1995 M. C. Escher/Cordon Art, Baarn-Holland, all rights reserved; *339* © L. Giraudou/Explorer, Photo Researchers, Inc.

Text credits: *Page 4* "Native Americans" by Jamake Highwater in TV AND TEENS, 1982, published by Addison-Wesley, Reading, MA, reprinted by permission; *10* "Library: The Buried Treasure" by David B. Ellis from BECOMING A MASTER STUDENT, Fifth Edition, copyright © 1985, reprinted with permission from Houghton Mifflin Company; *18* from MEGA-TRENDS 2000 by John Naisbitt and Patricia Aburdene, copyright © 1990 by Megatrend Ltd, reprinted by permission of William Morrow & Company, Inc.; *24* from THE STORY OF ENGLISH by Robert McCrum, William Cran, and Robert MacNeil, used by permission of Viking Penguin, a division of Penguin Books USA Inc. and Sterling Lord Literistic, Inc.; *29* "Adventures of Today" by Miki Prijic Knezevic, reprinted by permission of the author; *37* L.P. Hartley, "A High Dive" in THE COMPLETE SHORT STORIES OF L. P. HARTLEY, Hamish Hamilton Ltd, copyright © 1973, the Executors of the Estate of L.P. Hartley. "A High Dive" originally appeared in TWO FOR THE RIVER; *46* "The World We Lost" from NEVER CRY WOLF by Farley Mowat, copyright © 1963 by Farley Mowat Ltd, by permission of Little, Brown and Company and the Canadian Publishers, McClelland & Stewart, Toronto and Farley Mowat Limited; *55* "For Better or for Worse, Arranged Marriages Still Thrive in Japan" by Urban Lehner, THE WALL STREET JOURNAL, July 19, 1983, reprinted by permission of The Wall Street Journal, © 1983 Dow Jones & Company, Inc, all Rights Reserved Worldwide; *64* "Oh, When I Was In Love with You" by A.E. Housman from THE COLLECTED POEMS OF A.E. HOUS-MAN, reprinted by permission of Henry Holt and Company and The Society of Authors as the literary representative of the Estate of A.E. Housman; *67* Signe Hammer, "Anatomy of a Difference" reprinted by permission of the author. (This article first appeared in HEALTH, July 1983.); *77* "I Want a Wife" by Judy Syfers, 1971, reprinted by permission of the author; *85* Richard Blodgett, "Against All Odds," reprinted from GAMES Magazine (810 Seventh Avenue, New York, NY 10019), copyright © 1983 PCS Games Limited Partnership; *94* Frank Stockton, "The Lady or the Tiger?" in THE BEST SHORT STORIES OF FRANK R. STOCKTON, Charles Scibner's Sons, 1957; *103* reprinted from SPEAKING OF CHINESE by Raymond Chang and Margaret Scrogin Chang, with permission of W.W. Norton & Company, Inc., copyright © 1978 by W. W. Norton & Company, Inc. and Andre Deutsch Ltd.; *114* from THE LIFE-TIME BOOK OF MONEY MANAGEMENT by Grace W. Weinstine, Visible Ink Press, reprinted by permission of the author, copyright © 1993; *123* from AMONG THE BELIEVERS by V.S. Naipaul, copyright © 1981 by V.S. Naipaul, reprinted by permission of Alfred A. Knopf, Inc. and Aitken, Stone & Wylie; *131* "Grisha Has Arrived" by Tanya Filanovsky, NEWEST REVIEW, August/September 1990, translated from the Russian by Ruth Schacter, reprinted by

and Mitar Tarabic, translated by Robert Gakovich, reprinted by permission; *326* from THE OMNI FUTURE ALMANAC edited by Robert Weil, reprinted by permission of the author; *331* ZIGGY © ZIGGY & FRIENDS, INC., dist. by UNIVERSAL PRESS SYNDICATE; reprinted with permission, all rights reserved; *333* Alan Bloch, "Men are Different" in UNKNOWN WORLDS (New York: Holt, Rinehart and Winston, 1969); *336* from THE INTIMATE MACHINE by Neil Frude, copyright © 1983 by Neil Frude, used by permission of Dutton Signet, a division of Penguin Books USA Inc. and Random House UK Limited; *340* drawing by Stevenson, © 1975 The New Yorker Magazine, Inc.